African American
Generals and Flag Officers

African American Generals and Flag Officers

Biographies of Over 120 Blacks in the United States Military

by
Walter L. Hawkins

McFarland & Company, Inc., Publishers
Jefferson, North Carolina, and London

British Library Cataloguing-in-Publication data are available

Library of Congress Cataloguing-in-Publication Data

Hawkins, Walter L. (Walter Lee), 1949–
    African American generals and flag officers : biographies of over
120 Blacks in the United States military / by Walter L. Hawkins.
        p.   cm.
    Includes bibliographical references and index.
    ISBN 0-89950-774-3 (lib. bdg. : 50# alk. paper) ∞
    1. Afro-American generals — Biography.   2. Afro-American admirals —
Biography.   3. United States — Armed Forces — Biography.   4. United
States — Armed Forces — Afro-Americans.   5. United States — History,
Military.   I. Title.
E181.H38   1992
355′.0089′96073 — dc20
[B]   92-50886
                                                                             CIP

Manufactured in the United States of America

McFarland & Company, Inc., Publishers
  Box 611, Jefferson, North Carolina 28640

This book is dedicated to
Ephriam "Dee" Hooks

CONTENTS

ACKNOWLEDGMENTS

I should like to express my appreciation to Sharon Crittendon for her administrative assistance, JoAnn Campbell for her technical assistance, and Clarence Green, Jr., for his assistance and technical advice regarding photographs. I am grateful to the many people who performed valuable services in the preparation of this book.

I wish to express my appreciation to the Department of Defense, the Department of the Army, the Office of the Secretary of the Army, the United States Air Force, the United States Navy, Headquarters Forces Command, Headquarters Air Force Logistics Command, United States ROTC Cadet Command, and the United States Army Military History Institute (John J. Slonaker).

INTRODUCTION

The military heritage of African Americans is as long as the history of a black presence in North America. From the first recorded visit of a black person to what is now the United States in 1528, blacks — both the enslaved and the free — have participated in military or quasimilitary actions. Such participation — certainly not undertaken without difficulty — has not received extensive coverage in general history books. White Americans have been ambivalent over the years about black participation in military organizations and in most instances have encouraged or allowed blacks in military activities only when forced by circumstances to do so.

This book does not attempt to chronicle the full range of black contributions to America's military. Rather, it presents African American military officers who changed the image of the United States military organizations, generals and naval officers. These officers have made major contributions and have set many precedents.

Included are all African American officers who have attained the rank of general or its naval equivalent. Navy flag officers are those ranking above captain.

CHRONOLOGY

5 March 1770	Crispus Attucks was among the first to die in the Boston Massacre (beginning of the Revolutionary War).
20 May 1775	Union decided to allow free blacks to participate in the Revolutionary War; slaves were rejected.
16 Jan. 1776	Continental Congress accepted Washington's proposal to enlist free blacks.
15 April 1776	John Martin enlisted in the Continental Marines (aboard the *Reprisal*) as the first black marine.
29 August 1778	All-black Connecticut Regiment distinguished itself in battle against German mercenaries fighting for the British.
15 July 1779	Pompey Lamb participated in the capture of Stony Point by Gen. Anthony Wayne.
21 Sept. 1814	Gen. Andrew Jackson called upon blacks to aid in the defense of New Orleans.
23 Dec. 1814	Blacks were a part of Gen. Andrew Jackson's defense force in the Battle of New Orleans.
13 May 1846	Blacks participated in combat during the Mexican War.
28 June 1861	Tennessee passed legislation authorizing enlistment of free blacks between the ages of 15 and 50.
16 July 1862	Congress authorized black enlistments.
1 Jan. 1863	President Lincoln issued the Emancipation Proclamation.
13 Jan. 1863	First Kansas Colored Volunteers were mustered.
22 May 1863	Bureau of Colored Troops was formed by the War Department
13 March 1865	The Confederacy passed bill to enlist blacks in the Confederate Army.
28 July 1866	Congress passed provision to form the all-black 9th and 10th cavalry regiments and 38th, 39th, 40th, and 41st infantry regiments.
3 March 1869	Black infantry regiments, 38th and 41st, were consolidated to form the 24th Infantry; the 39th and 40th Regiment consolidated into the 25th Infantry Regiment.
21 Sept. 1872	First black admitted to the Naval Academy (John H. Conyers).
15 June 1877	First black graduated from West Point (Henry O. Flipper).

25 March 1917	Washington, D.C., Guard was activated to guard nation's capital; black unit included.
12 May 1917	Army established black officers training base in Des Moines, Iowa.
24 Oct. 1917	All-black 92nd Division was formed.
27 Dec. 1917	369th Infantry Regiment was the first black unit overseas.
9 Jan. 1918	The 10th Regiment rode the last cavalry charge against Indians.
15 May 1918	Henry Johnson and Needham Roberts became first Americans to receive the French Medal of Honor (Croix de Guerre).
25 Oct. 1940	Benjamin O. Davis was promoted to brigadier general, the first black to be appointed to general rank in the history of the Regular Army.
25 March 1941	Squadron of black aviators was activated (99th Pursuit Squadron).
1 May 1941	275th Construction Company established as first black Signal Corps unit.
1 June 1941	First black tank battalion was activated (758th).
1 July 1941	Army integrated Officers Candidate School.
19 July 1941	Tuskegee Institute began black air training program.
7 Dec. 1941	Dorie Miller, a black mess steward in the Navy, said to have shot down four Japanese airplanes in the attack on Pearl Harbor (received the Navy Cross).
7 March 1942	First black pilots received commissions in the Air Corps.
7 April 1942	Navy Secretary Frank Knox advocated acceptance of blacks in general services.
15 May 1942	Army activated the all-black 93rd Division.
1 June 1942	Marine Corps opened enlistment to blacks. Blacks were allowed to enlist in the Navy in positions other than stewards.
20 July 1942	Black women were accepted into the Women's Auxiliary Corps (WAC).
24 Aug. 1942	Col. Benjamin O. Davis, Jr., became the commanding officer of the 99th Pursuit Squadron.
13 Oct. 1942	The 332nd Fighter Group was activated.
15 Oct. 1942	The 92th Fighter Group was activated.
13 Nov. 1942	Leonard Roy Harmon was awarded the Navy Cross for heroic action aboard the USS *San Francisco* in the Solomon Islands.
16 April 1943	1st Marine Depot Company sent overseas as first black unit in World War II.
24 April 1943	99th Pursuit Squadron attached to 33rd Fighter Group in North Africa.
1 June 1943	Army Air Corps formed the third black air unit (477th Bomber Group).
12 June 1943	William Pinckney received Navy Cross for heroism during the Battle of Cruz Island.

2 July 1943	Black pilots downed their first enemy aircraft over Italy (99th Pursuit Squadron).
31 Aug. 1943	The USS *Leonard Roy Harmon* became the first naval vessel commissioned and named for a black person.
3 Jan. 1944	All-black 332nd Air Unit entered the war in Europe.
23 Feb. 1944	Navy announced that two antisubmarine ships would be manned by all-black crews (USS *Mason* and PC1264).
17 March 1944	First group of black men commissioned as naval officers ("Golden Thirteen").
20 March 1944	First naval vessel with a predominantly black crew was commissioned (USS *Mason*).
14 April 1944	Ens. Joseph Jenkins commissioned as first black Coast Guard officer.
6 June 1944	All-black 320th Anti-Aircraft Barrage Balloon Battalion participated in the D-Day invasion.
8 July 1944	War Department outlawed discrimination in recreation and transportation facilities on all Army bases.
19 Oct. 1944	Black women were informed that they would be admitted into the Navy (WAVES).
26 Dec. 1944	Directive issued for black volunteers to be integrated into white units in Allied strike forces.
8 March 1945	Phyllis Mae Dailey was sworn in as the first black nurse in the Navy Nurse Corps.
24 March 1945	Black pilots participated in a raid over Berlin (332nd Fighter Squadron).
13 April 1945	Restrictions were lifted on the number of black personnel to be assigned to Navy vessels.
23 July 1945	Government made appeal for qualified black women to join the WAVES.
27 Feb. 1946	Secretary of Navy James Forrestal announced black naval personnel were eligible for all assignments.
23 June 1946	First group of black officers was integrated into the Regular Army.
2 Feb. 1948	President Truman issued a message to Congress stating that segregation in the military should end.
12 Feb. 1948	First black nurse was integrated into the Regular Nurse Corps.
1 July 1948	Black colleges established ROTC programs.
23 Oct. 1948	First black aviator was commissioned in the Navy (Ensign Jesse Brown).
1 June 1949	All-black 332nd Fighter Wing was integrated into the Regular Air Force.
3 June 1949	First black graduated from the Naval Academy (Wesley A. Brown).
23 June 1949	Secretary of the Navy Francis Matthews announced equality for all Navy and Marine personnel.

1 June 1949	Wesley A. Brown became the first black to graduate from the Naval Academy.
27 March 1950	Army abolished black enlistment quota.
20 July 1950	All-black 24th Infantry Regiment won first United States victory in Korea.
4 Dec. 1950	Ens. Jesse L. Brown became the first black to receive the Navy Distinguished Flying Cross.
21 June 1951	Sgt. Cornelius H. Charlton was awarded posthumously the Medal of Honor, the first black to receive the award since the Spanish-American War.
21 July 1951	Army announced that the 24th Infantry would be integrated into the Far East Command.
1 Oct. 1951	The 24th Infantry Regiment was deactivated.
1 April 1952	Army European Command announced integration plan.
1 Oct. 1952	First black Marine pilot was commissioned (Frank E. Peterson, Jr.).
20 Aug. 1953	Secretary of the Navy Robert Anderson ordered desegregation of facilities on naval shore installations.
12 Jan. 1954	Secretary of Defense Charles Wilson announced desegregation of schools on military bases.
16 Jan. 1954	Army announced blacks with special skills to be assigned to all units.
27 Oct. 1954	Benjamin O. Davis, Jr., was promoted to brigadier general, becoming this nation's first black general in the Air Force.
1 Feb. 1966	Thomas D. Parham, Jr., became first black chaplain to receive Navy captain's rank.
1 Sept. 1967	Navy Bureau of Personnel established the Minority Officers Recruitment Effort.
19 May 1968	Prairie View A&M College established first black Naval Reserve Officers Training Corps.
21 Aug. 1968	First black Marine posthumously awarded the Medal of Honor (PC. James Anderson, Jr.).
8 Feb. 1971	Navy announced destroyer escort to be named in honor of Ens. Jesse L. Brown, first black Navy aviator.
15 March 1971	Defense Secretary Laird announced program to end discrimination. Department of Defense established Race Relations Institute.
28 April 1971	Samuel L. Gravely became the first black admiral in the history of the United States Navy.
28 Sept. 1972	Sgt. Major Edgar R. Huff became the first black to complete thirty years of service as a Marine.
19 April 1974	Sgt. Major Gilbert H. Johnson became first Marine to have facility named in his honor.
1 July 1974	Army commissioned the first female chaplain in the armed forces (the Rev. Alice Henderson).

1 July 1974	Five black women were among the first group of female cadets at the Merchant Marine Academy.
1 May 1975	Lt. Donna P. Davis became the first black woman physician in the history of the Naval Medical Corps.
1 Sept. 1975	Daniel "Chappie" James was promoted to four-star grade and assigned as commander in chief, NORAD/ADCOM, becoming the first black American in history to be appointed to the four-star rank.
1 Sept. 1979	Hazel Winifred Johnson became the first black woman to attain the rank of a general officer.
1 Aug. 1982	Roscoe Robinson, Jr., was appointed this nation's first black four-star general in the United States Army.
1 Sept. 1987	Brig. Gen. Sherian Grace Cadoria became the first black female assigned as deputy commanding general, Total Army Personnel Command, Alexandria, Virginia.
23 April 1988	Joseph Ellis Turner was promoted to brigadier general, becoming the first black in the 81st United States Army Reserve Command to attain the rank of general.
1 Sept. 1988	Kenneth U. Jordan was promoted to brigadier general, becoming the first black to serve as the assistant adjutant general for the Tennessee Air National Guard.
1 Oct. 1989	Pres. George Bush appointed Gen. Colin L. Powell the twelfth chairman of the Joint Chiefs of Staff.
3 Aug. 1990	Russell C. Davis was promoted to and federally recognized as major general, becoming the first black in D.C. Air National Guard to achieve this grade.
1 Aug. 1990	Maj. Gen. Matthew Augustus Zimmerman was appointed the first black chief of chaplains in the United States Army.
8 Sept. 1990	Marcelite J. Harris was appointed brigadier general, becoming the first black general in the United States Air Force.
1 Aug. 1991	Brig. Gen. Clara Leach Adams-Ender became the first black female to be assigned as commanding general of United States Army's Fort Belvoir.

The
Biographies

Robert B. Adams

★★ ———————————————————— ★★

Major General

Born on August 29, 1933, in Buffalo, New York. He married the former Karen S. Nagel. Upon completion of the Reserve Officers Training Corps curriculum and the course of study at Canisius College, he was commissioned a second lieutenant and awarded a bachelor of business administration in accounting auditing. He also holds bachelor and master's degrees in automatic data processing from George Washington University. His military education includes completion of the Air Defense Artillery School, the Finance School, the United States Army Command and General Staff college, and the United States Army War College. He has held a wide variety of important command and staff positions, culminating in deputy chief of staff for resource management, United States Army Materiel Command in Alexandria, Virginia. Other key assignments include assistant comptroller for resource policy and financial planning, office of the comptroller of the Army, Washington, D.C., and deputy commanding general, finance and accounting, United States Army, Fort Benjamin Harrison, Indiana.

General Adams served in a variety of important career-building assignments preparatory to his most recent duties. In Vietnam he served initially as the finance officer, 23rd Infantry Division, later finance officer, 196th Infantry Brigade, subsequently serving as chief, finance and accounting

Maj. Gen. Robert B. Adams

division, office of the deputy chief of staff, comptroller, United States Army, Vietnam. He returned to Fort Belvoir, Virginia, as a special projects officer at the United States Army Computer Systems Command. After attending the United States Army War College at Carlisle Barracks, Pennsylvania, he became the chief, financial management and accounting division; later director, nonappropriated funds directorate; later comptroller, the Adjutant General Center, United States Army, Washington, D.C. He was named the commandant of the United States Army Institute of Administration, Fort Benjamin Harrison, Indiana, and subsequently became deputy commander for integration, United States Army Administration Center, Fort Benjamin Harrison, Indiana. Awards and decorations include the Legion of Merit (with three oak leaf clusters), the Bronze Star, the Meritorious Service Medal (with oak leaf cluster), the Army Commendation Medal (with oak leaf cluster), and the Army General Staff Identification Badge.

Clara L. Adams-Ender

★ ———————————————— ★

Brigadier General

Born July 11, 1939, the daughter of a sharecropper, in Wake County, North Carolina, the fourth of ten children, she received her baccalaureate degree in nursing from North Carolina Agricultural and Technical State University, Greensboro, North Carolina; master of science in nursing from the University of Minnesota; and master of military art and science from the United States Army Command and General Staff College at Fort Leavenworth, Kansas. Her military education includes graduation from the United States Army War College and the United States Army Medical Officer Advanced Course. While attending North Carolina A&T State University in Greensboro, she worked as a domestic and beautician to earn extra money. She joined the Army because she had an important goal in mind: She wanted to finish her education, and she needed money to do it. A veteran of over 30 years in the Army, General Adams-Ender has held such diverse assignments as chief nurse of two medical centers, assistant professor of nursing, inspector general, and chief Army nurse recruiter. During the Vietnam War, Adams-Ender served as a staff nurse with the 121st Evacuation Hospital.

Her overseas assignments include Korea and Germany, where she served as an intensive care nurse, reforger chief nurse, medical center chief nurse, and nursing consultant. For three years General Adams-Ender

Brig. Gen. Clara L. Adams-Ender

served as chief, Department of Nursing, at Walter Reed Army Medical Center, Washington, D.C., the largest health-care facility in the DOD. She is certified in advanced nursing administration and is a fellow in the American Academy of Nursing.

General Adams-Ender's career has been filled with many firsts. In 1967 she became the first female in the Army to qualify for and be awarded the expert field medical badge. In 1980 she became the first and only nurse and female to be senior marcher for 700 Army soldiers in the 100-mile four-day march in Nijmegen, Holland. In 1987 she became eighteenth chief of the Army Nurse Corps, and in 1988 she became the first Army nurse officer to be appointed as director of personnel for the surgeon general of the Army.

She was involved in the Persian Gulf War as chief of the Army Nurse Corps and director of personnel for the surgeon general of the Army. Her primary responsibilities were to make certain that policy was developed, communicated, and coordinated for members of the armed forces deployed to southwest Asia and to provide health care to the family members left in the United States. In 1991 she became the first ANC chief to be continued on active duty as a general officer after completion of her tenure as corps chief. She was reassigned as the deputy commanding general, Military District of Washington, and commanding general of Fort Belvoir, Virginia. Her awards and decorations include the Distinguished Service Medal, the Legion of Merit, the Meritorious Service Medal (with three oak leaf clusters), the Army Commendation Medal, the coveted Surgeon General's "A" professional designator for excellence in nursing administration, the Roy Wilkins Meritorious Service Award of the NAACP, and membership in the Order of Military Medical Merit.

General Adams-Ender has been awarded five honorary doctorate degrees from colleges and universities in the United States. She is a member of the Association of the United States Army, the American Nurses Association, the National League for Nursing, the American Organization of Nurse Executives, Sigma Theta Tau, International Honor Society, Delta Sigma Theta Sorority, and Chi Eta Phi Nursing Sorority. She was appointed brigadier general on September 1, 1987.

Richard C. Alexander

★★ ——————————————————— ★★

Major General

Born June 26, 1935, in Cleveland, Ohio, he and his wife, LaVera, have two sons, Jeff and Ronald, and a daughter, Gail. He is a 1954 graduate of East Technical High School in Cleveland. He attended Franklin University in Columbus. His military education includes Reserve Components National Security Course, 1987; United States Army War College; Corresponding Studies Course, 1983; Defense Race Relations Institute, 1972; Internal Review Analysis Course, 1972; Air Defense Missile Staff Officer Course, 1971; Air Defense Basic Officer Course, 1970; Missile Site Security, 1969; Air Defense Basic Officer Course, 1966; FCS Maintenance Course, 1964; Aviation Radar Repair, 1956; and Basic Electronics, 1956.

He entered the military service on October 20, 1954, when he enlisted in the United States Marine Corps. He was honorably discharged from the Marine Corps on December 18, 1958, as a sergeant but continued to serve in the Marine Corps Reserve through June 29, 1960. On June 30, 1960, he enlisted in Battery C, 1st Missile Battalion (Nike-Hercules), 137th Artillery of the Ohio Army National Guard where he began a full-time career as an Army National Guard technician. On May 6, 1965, he was appointed a second lieutenant in the Artillery Branch, Ohio Army National Guard.

He has served in a wide variety of military and civilian technician assignments in which he was required to become proficient as an engineer and personnel officer. Significant among his assignments have been commander, Battery C, 1/137th Artillery; Program Analyst, United States Property and Fiscal Office; Ohio Adjutant General Department's first National Guard Race Relations and Equal Opportunity Officer; operations and training officer for the Ohio Military Academy; labor relations specialist; topographic engineer and deputy brigade commander, 16th Engineer Brigade; director of personnel and administration for the Ohio Army National Guard and Chief of Staff of the Ohio Army National

Guard. Maj. Gen. Richard C. Alexander is Ohio's adjutant general, appointed by Gov. Richard F. Celeste on December 1, 1987, for both the Army and the Air National Guard, responsible for initiating policies and programs for the retention and betterment of the combined 21,000 member military organization. The general's decorations and awards include Meritorious Service Medal, Army Commendation Medal (with second oak leaf cluster), Army Achievement Medal, and numerous other awards and decorations. His civilian affiliations include the National Guard Association of the United States, Ohio National Guard Association, and the National Association for the Advancement of Colored People.

Wallace Cornelius Arnold

★★ ———————————————————— ★★

Major General

Born on July 27, 1938, in Washington, D.C. He received a bachelor of science degree in industrial education from Hampton Institute and a master of arts in personnel management and administration from George Washington University. He received an ROTC Commission to second lieutenant in May 1961.

From May 1961 to September 1961, he was a student in the Air Defense Artillery Officers Basic Course at the United States Army Air Defense School, Fort Bliss, Texas. From September 1961 to November 1962, he was a platoon leader in the 2nd Battalion of the 71st Air Defense Artillery in Korea. From November 1962 to August 1964, he served as assistant S-4 of the 35th Air Defense Artillery Brigade at Fort Meade, Maryland. From August 1964 to January 1966, he was the commander of H Battery of the 35th Air Defense Artillery Brigade. From 1966 to September 1966, he was a student in the Artillery Officers Advanced Course at the United States Army Air Defense School, at Fort Bliss, Texas. From October 1966 to January 1968, he served as the brigade personnel officer at headquarters of the 30th Air Defense Artillery Brigade in Okinawa. From January 1968 to March 1969, he was assigned as the S-3 of the 8th Battalion, 3rd Air Defense Artillery, in Okinawa.

He was promoted to major on February 26, 1968. From March 1969 to June 1969, he was a student at the United States Army Institute for Military Assistance, Fort Bragg, North Carolina. From July 1969 to July 1970, he served as the chief of psychological operations division, G-5, at headquarters of XXIV Corps in Vietnam. From July 1970 to June 1971, he was a student in the United States Army Command and General Staff College, Fort Leavenworth, Kansas.

Maj. Gen. Wallace Cornelius Arnold

From June 1971 to May 1972, he served as chief of the Air Defense Artillery Section at the Air Space Control Element of the 6th Battalion, 68th Air Defense Artillery, at Fort Bliss, Texas. From May 1972 to October 1974, he served as a personnel management officer for the Air Defense Artillery Branch, Officer Personnel Directorate, United States Army Military Personnel Center, in Alexandria, Virginia. From December 1974 to July 1976, he was the commander of the 3rd Battalion, 61st Air Defense Artillery, 3rd Armored Division, United States Army, in Europe.

He was promoted to lieutenant colonel on June 1, 1974. From August 1976 to July 1977, he was a student at the Naval War College at Newport, Rhode Island. From July 1977 to June 1979, he served as a computer systems software and analysis officer, Functional Systems Division, Office of the Assistant Chief of Staff for Automation and Communications, United States Army, in Washington, D.C. From June 1979 to June 1981, Arnold was a military assistant in the Office of the Under Secretary of the Army in Washington, D.C.

He was promoted to colonel on June 1, 1974. From June 1981 to April 1982, he served as the inspector general for VII Corps, United States Army, in Europe. From April 1982 to November 1984, he was the commander of the 69th Air Defense Artillery Brigade, 32nd Army Air Defense Command, United States Army, in Europe. From November 1984 to June 1987, Arnold served as director of personnel, J-1/inspector general, United States European Command.

He was promoted to brigadier general on August 1, 1985. From June 1987 to May 1990, he was the commanding general of the First Reserve Officer Training Corps Region, Fort Bragg, North Carolina. He was promoted to major general on October 18, 1989. In May 1990 he was assigned as commanding general, United States Army Reserve Officer Training Corps Cadet Command, Fort Monroe, Virginia.

He has received numerous awards and decorations: the Defense Superior Service Medal, the Legion of Merit (with oak leaf cluster), the Bronze Star (with oak leaf cluster), the Meritorious Service Medal (with four oak cluster), the Army Commendation Medal (with oak leaf cluster), and the Parachutist Badge.

Cornelius O. Baker

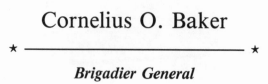

Brigadier General

Appointed to the one star rank in the Pennsylvania National Guard. The source for this fact was *Black Americans in Defense of Our Nation* (1985) published by the Department of Defense, Office of Deputy Assistant Secretary of Defense for Equal Opportunity and Safety Policy. No other information could be obtained.

Joe Nathan Ballard

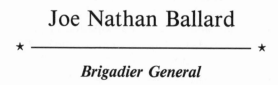

Brigadier General

Born March 27, 1942, in Meeker, Louisiana, he married the former Tessie LaRose, and they are the parents of three daughters. He received a B.S. degree in electrical engineering from Southern University A&M College in 1965. He received an M.S. in engineering management from the University of Missouri in 1972. Military schools attended include Engineer Officer Basic, 1965, and Advanced Engineer School, 1968; United States Army Command and the General Staff College, 1978; United States Army War College, 1985.

He began his career at Fort Dix as a platoon leader in the 86th Engineer Battalion. He served his first tour in Vietnam as a platoon leader in the 84th Engineer Battalion. He returned to the United States to command Company C, 2nd Battalion, 2nd Training Brigade, Fort Polk. After attending the Engineer Officer Advanced Course, General Ballard began his second tour in Vietnam where he was commander, Company C, 864th Engineer

Brig. Gen. Joe Nathan Ballard

Battalion, then chief, Lines of Communications Section Operations, 18th Engineer Brigade.

General Ballard has held a wide variety of important command and staff positions, including assistant deputy chief of staff, engineer, headquarters, United States Army, Europe; commander of the 18th Engineer Brigade in Karlsruhe, Germany; chief, Assignments Branch, Colonels' Division; and commander of the 82nd Engineer Battalion, 7th Engineering Brigade, Bamberg, Germany. From 1979 until 1982, General Ballard served as the facility energy manager, Office of the Deputy Chief of Staff for Logistics in Washington, D.C. Prior to that, he was chief, Mapping and Intelligence Section, Engineer Division, United States Forces in Korea, Eighth United States Army, then executive officer to the United States Forces, Korea, Engineer. In the seventies, General Ballard was the engineer construction planning officer, Planning and Real Estate Branch, Engineer Division, Fifth United States Army, Fort Sheridan; test and evaluation officer, Combat Developments Command Engineer Agency, Fort Belvoir; area commander, United States Army District Recruiting Command, Detroit; and operations officer, then executive officer, 326th Engineer Battalion, 101st Airborne Division.

From August 1990 to January 1991, he served as the assistant deputy chief of staff, Engineer, United States Army, Europe, and Seventh Army. In January 1991 General Joe N. Ballard was assigned as the assistant commandant of the United States Army Engineer School and deputy commanding general of Fort Leonard Wood. His awards and decorations include the Legion of Merit (oak leaf cluster), the Bronze Star Medal (oak leaf cluster), the Defense Meritorious Service Medal, the Meritorious

Service Medal (second oak leaf cluster), the Army Commendation Medal (oak leaf cluster), and the Army Staff Identification Badge. He was appointed brigadier general on October 1, 1991.

William C. Banton II

★ ———————————————————— ★

Brigadier General

Born on November 9, 1922, in Washington, D.C. He earned a B.S. degree from Howard University's College of Liberal Arts and Science. He also received an M.D. degree from Howard University, College of Medicine, and an M.P.H. from the Johns Hopkins School of Hygiene and Public Health.

General Banton was commissioned in the United States Air Force in World War II. He went on to serve in the Korean War, the Cuban conflict, and the Vietnam War. While serving in the United States Air Force Reserve, general officer–mobilization augmentee to the Strategic Air Command (SAC), he established a medical management system for SAC's medical reserves whereby reserve active duty time was utilized to support United States active force manpower shortages at SAC bases on a year-round basis and worldwide. This system was subsequently adopted at other United States major air commands. He retired from the United States Air Force Reserve as a brigadier general in 1979.

He has devoted the practice of medicine to the citizens of the St. Louis area for over 46 years; has committed himself to public service in the health and medical field by serving as director of tuberculosis control, city of St. Louis, 1964–1970, and health commissioner for the city of St. Louis, 1970–1972; designed the innovative public health care system in St. Louis County, which integrated the Department of Community Health and Medical Care (DOCHMC), and served as its first director, 1973–1979; contributed to academic medicine by serving on the faculties of both Washington University School of Medicine and St. Louis University School of Medicine.

He devoted his Missouri Public Health Association presidency (1984–1985) to the strategic planning and implementation of a movement to extract the Missouri Division of Health from the multidivisional Department of Social Services and establish health in Missouri as a separate cabinet-level department (successful enabling legislation was effective September 28, 1985). He retired from the part-time private practice of internal medicine in 1985 and retired after 31 years as an aviation medical examiner, Federal Aviation Administration, in 1991.

Brig. Gen. William C. Banton II

Dr. Banton, has served as a member of the Centers for Disease Control's Advisory Committee for Elimination of Tuberculosis, 1987–1990, and was appointed its chairman from 1989 to 1990. In 1991 he served as medical consultant to the Missouri Department of Health, assistant clinical professor of internal medicine and assistant clinical professor of community medicine at St. Louis University School of Medicine. He is a life board member of the American Lung Association of Eastern Missouri and has actively served with it since 1965. He has also served as a representative director on the newly reorganized National Board of Directors of the American Lung Association and is chairman of the Missouri Advisory Committee for the Elimination of Tuberculosis.

He is a member of numerous other professional and civic organizations, among them the American Medical Association, Missouri State Medical Association, American and Missouri Public Health associations, Mound City Medical Forum, American Thoracic Society, and American College of Chest Physicians. He has received numerous medical and civic awards for his contributions to the health profession and his community. Dr. Banton was elected to the presidency of the 150-year-old St. Louis Metropolitan Medical Society for the year 1987. His military awards and decorations include World War II Victory Medal, Am Campaign Medal, Armed Forces Longevity Service Award, Armed Forces Reserve Medal, South Vietnam Campaign Medal, National Defense Service Medal, and the Expert Marksman Medal. He was appointed brigadier general on April 6, 1973.

Julius W. Becton, Jr.

★★★ ——————————————————— ★★★

Lieutenant General

Born June 29, 1926, Bryn Mawr, Pennsylvania, he married the former Louise Thornton, and they have five children—Shirley, Karen, Joyce, Renee, and Wesley. They also have six grandchildren. General Becton's public service career includes two key federal positions after nearly 40 years of active commissioned service in the United States Army, rising to the rank of lieutenant general. He is the first graduate of Prairie View A&M University to attain star rank in the military. In November 1989, the Texas A&M University System Board of Regents unanimously elected him president of Prairie View A&M University. After receiving his B.S. degree in mathematics from Prairie View A&M University in 1960, he earned his M.A. in economics from the University of Maryland in 1967. He is also a graduate of top military schools, including the United States Army Command and General Staff College, the Houston-Tillotson College in Austin, and Muhlenberg College in Pennsylvania.

He enlisted in the United States Army in July 1944 and graduated from Officers Candidate School in 1945. A veteran of World War II and the Korean and Vietnam conflicts, he served in various positions at scores of posts in this country. Overseas duties carried him to Germany, the Philippines, France, the southwest Pacific, Korea, and Japan. His active duty assignments included deputy commanding general, United States Army Training and Doctrine Command; commander, VII Corps, in Germany; and commander, 1st Cavalry Division. He served 22 months as director of the Office of United States Foreign Disaster Assistance before being nominated by President Ronald Reagan and confirmed by the Senate as director of the Federal Emergency Management Agency, a position he held for nearly four years before moving into the private sector.

Prior to his acceptance of the position of president of Prairie View A&M University, he served as chief operating officer for American Coastal Industries. President Becton has also been asked by the United States government to serve as chairman of the New Select Group of the Senior Civil Emergency Planning Committee of NATO in Brussels, Belgium. The native of Bryn Mawr serves as secretary on the World Board of Governors for the United Services Organization (USO). He is first vice president of the United States Armor Association, a member of the Federal Emergency Management Agency Advisory Board, the Board of Trustees for Valley Forge Military Academy and Junior College, and the Defense Equal Opportunity Management Institute Board of Visitors. He has been listed in several

Lt. Gen. Julius W. Becton, Jr.

Who's Who directories and was named by *Ebony* magazine several times as "one of the 100 most influential blacks in America." He was awarded the Distinguished Service Award (Federal Emergency Management Agency); the Distinguished Knight (Gold), Order of St. George; and honorary colonel, 17th Cavalry Regiment.

Leroy Crawford Bell

★ ———————————————————— ★

Brigadier General

Born May 3, 1932, in Tampa, Florida. He received his educational training from Florida A&M University, Shippensburg State College; Air Defense Artillery School, Airborne School, Field Artillery School, Command and General Staff College, and U.S. Army War College.

His military career began in 1955, when he was commissioned as a second lieutenant, field artillery, through the ROTC program at Florida A&M University. His early assignments included duty with the 32nd Air Defense Brigade in Langerkoph, Germany, and command of A Battery, 2nd Battalion, 42nd Field Artillery at Fort Benning, Georgia from 1964 to 1965. From 1965 to 1966, he served in Vietnam where he commanded A Battery, 2nd Battalion, 19th Field Artillery, with the 1st Air Cavalry Division.

He returned to the United States and served from 1966 to 1969 as chief

Brig. Gen. Leroy C. Bell

instructor for the fire support coordinator, 108th Field Artillery Group, 24th Corps Artillery. Following graduation from Command and General Staff College in 1971, he was assigned to Officer Personnel Directorate, Military Personnel Carter. There, he served as personnel management officer, field artillery branch, from 1971 to 1973. From October 1973 until October 1974, he commanded the 2nd Battalion, 17th Field Artillery, 2nd Infantry Division in Korea.

Upon his subsequent return to the United States, he was assigned to the Washington, D.C. area and served as chief, military personnel team in the Office of the Deputy Chief of Staff for Research, Development and Acquisition, Department of Army. He held this position until July 1975, when he attended the Army War College. He graduated from the U.S. Army War College in 1976 and was assigned as chief, manpower survey team, Inspections and Surveys Division, Department of the Army Inspector General Agency, Washington, D.C. from September 1976 to January 1979. In 1979, Leroy Crawford Bell was promoted to the one star rank of brigadier general, and assigned as the adjutant general for the District of Columbia Army National Guard.

Rufus L. Billups

★★ ———————————————————— ★★

Major General

Born January 7, 1928, Birmingham, Alabama. He married the former Margaret C. Talton of New Orleans. They have three children—Eric,

Maj. Gen. Rufus L. Billups

Geraldine, and Robert. He graduated from Parker High School in Birmingham, Alabama, and earned a bachelor of science degree from Tuskegee Institute, Alabama, in 1949. He received a master of science degree in business from the University of Colorado in 1957. He has an honorary doctorate degree from Guadalupe College of Texas.

General Billups was commissioned in the Regular Air Force as a distinguished graduate of the Air Force Reserve Officers Training Corps program at Tuskegee Institute. He completed the Air Tactical School at Tyndall Air Force Base, Florida, in May 1950 and served briefly at Norton Air Force Base, California. In January 1951 he began pilot training at Goodfellow Air Force Base, Texas.

During the Korean War, General Billups was Air Force liaison officer at the Army ports of Pusan and Inchon. From January 1953 to December 1955, he served as a transportation officer in various units at New Castle County Airport, Wilmington, Delaware. He then entered the University of Colorado under the Air Force Institute of Technology program and graduated with a master of science degree in business in 1957. General Billups left for Germany in July 1957 for an assignment with the 7100th Transportation Squadron at Lindsey Air Station, Germany. He returned to the United States in August 1961 for duty with the 803rd Transportation Squadron at Davis-Monthan Air Force Base, Arizona. He completed a transportation executive training course at Hughes Aircraft Company, Culver City, California, in July 1964. He was then assigned as a staff officer in the Air Force inspector general's office at Norton Air Force Base, California.

In August 1968 he was assigned at Tan Son Nhut Air Base, Vietnam, as director of aerial port operations, 2nd Aerial Port Group. During this one-year tour of duty, he flew 56 combat missions. In September 1969 General Billups was transferred to Headquarters, United States European Command, Vaihingen, Germany. He served there as staff transportation officer until August 1970 when he became director of transportation, Headquarters, United States Air Forces, Europe, at Lindsey Air Station. He returned to the United States in May 1973 to become commander of the 12th Air Base Group at Randolph Air Force Base, Texas. In August 1974 he assumed duties as deputy director of transportation in the Office of the Deputy Chief of Staff, Systems and Logistics, Headquarters, United States Air Force. He was appointed commander of the Defense General Supply Center, Defense Supply Agency, in Richmond, Virginia, in September 1975. He became the director of logistics plans, programs, and transportation in the Office of the Deputy Chief of Staff, Logistics, and Engineering, Headquarters, United States Air Force, Washington, D.C., in August 1978.

He was appointed major general on July 1, 1978, with date of rank September 1, 1974. His military decorations and awards include the Defense Superior Service Medal, the Legion of Merit, the Bronze Star, the Meritorious Service Medal, the Air Medal, the Air Force Commendation Medal, and the Air Force Outstanding Unit Award ribbon.

Roger Reckling Blunt

★★ ——————————————————— ★★

Major General

Born October 12, 1930, in Providence, Rhode Island, he married the former DeRosette Yvonne Hendricks, and they have four children — Roger, Jr., Jennifer Mari, Jonathan Hendricks, and Amy Elizabeth. He was graduated from the United States Military Academy in 1956 with a B.S. degree and was the only black in his class. He also received an M.S. degree from the Massachusetts Institute of Technology in 1962. He entered the United States Army Corps of Engineers as an engineer officer in 1956 and served in numerous assignments until 1969, when he transferred to the United States Army Reserves. He was appointed major general in the United States Army Reserves in 1983, received the Distinguished Service Medal in 1986. He has served as CEO and chairman of the Tyroc Construction Company and chairman of the board and president of Blunt Enterprises, Inc. He has received numerous awards and honors.

Maj. Gen. Roger Reckling Blunt

James T. Boddie, Jr.

★ ————————————————— ★

Brigadier General

Born October 18, 1931, Baltimore, Maryland. He married the former Mattye Dwiggins of Tuskegee, Alabama, and they have five sons. General Boddie, known by his friends and associates as "Tim," was graduated from Frederick Douglass High School, Baltimore, in 1949. He received his bachelor's degree from Howard University in Washington, D.C., in 1954. He is a graduate of the Academic Instructors School and Squadron Officer School, both located at Maxwell Air Force Base, Alabama. He is also a graduate of the Industrial College of the Armed Forces, Fort Lesley J. McNair, Washington, D.C., and the Air War College at Maxwell. He earned a master of public administration degree from Auburn University in Alabama.

He received his commission through the Air Force Reserve Officers Training Corps program and was awarded the Convair Aviation Association Award for his outstanding accomplishments as a cadet. General Boddie entered primary pilot training in March 1955 at Bartow Air Force Base, Florida, where he flew PA-18s and T-6Gs. From there he went to single-engine basic pilot training at Laredo Air Force Base, Texas, flying T-28s and T-33s, earning his wings in March 1956. His first operational

Brig. Gen. James T. Boddie, Jr.

assignment was with the 560th Strategic Fighter Squadron at Bergstrom Air Force Base, Texas, which was equipped with F-84F Thunderstreaks.

In May 1957 he was assigned to Nellis Air Force Base, Nevada, for gunnery weapons delivery training in the F-100 Super Sabre. Upon completion in September 1957, he was assigned to the United States Air Forces in Europe Weapons Center, Wheelus Air Base, Tripoli, Libya. For the next 45 months he performed instructor-pilot, flight-test, and standardization duties, requiring that he be simultaneously qualified in T-33s, F-86s, F-100s, and B-57s.

He returned to the Air Force Reserve Officers Training Corps program in February 1961 was commandant of cadets at Tuskegee Institute, Alabama. He also taught military aspects of world political geography and international relations to senior cadets. In June 1965 General Boddie joined the 4453rd Combat Crew Training Wing at Davis-Monthan Air Force Base, Arizona, where he flew and instructed in F-4s.

The following year he volunteered for combat duty in Southeast Asia and was assigned to the 559th Tactical Fighter Squadron at Cam Ranh Bay Air Base, Vietnam, in October 1966. In addition to his duties as operations and scheduling officer, he flew 201 F-4 combat missions, including 57 missions over North Vietnam. General Boddie returned to the 4453rd at Davis-Monthan Air Force Base in August 1967 and commanded the F-4 replacement training unit weapons school of the 4457th Tactical Training Squadron until July 1971. During this tour of duty, he was also appointed provisional squadron commander of the 40th Tactical Fighter Squadron, which was being formed to receive A-7D's.

The general's next assignment took him to Headquarters, Air Force

Military Personnel Center, Randolph Air Force Base, Texas, as chief of the Flying Status Branch in the Directorate of Personnel Program Actions until August 1974 when he entered the Air War College. Following his studies at the Air War College, in July 1975 he was assigned to Headquarters, Tactical Air Command, Langley Air Force Base, Virginia, as chief of the Maintenance Standardization and Evaluation Division of the Directorate of Maintenance Engineering. He led a 27-member team that evaluated the aircraft maintenance management effectiveness of all the command's units.

In August 1976 he moved to Moody Air Force Base, Georgia, where he served as deputy commander for operations of the 347th Tactical Fighter Wing. The next year he became vice commander of the wing. In June 1978 he became 51st Composite Wing (Tactical) vice commander at Osan Air Base in South Korea and took command in June 1979. In June 1980 Brig. Gen. James T. Boddie, Jr., was assigned as deputy director for operations, J-3, National Military Command Center, Organization of the Joint Chiefs of Staff, Washington, D.C.

General Boddie is a command pilot with more than 4,000 hours in jet fighter aircraft. His military decorations and awards include the Legion of Merit, the Distinguished Flying Cross, the Meritorious Service Medal (with two oak leaf clusters), the Air Medal (13 oak leaf clusters), the Air Force Commendation Medal, the Air Force Outstanding Unit Award ribbon (three oak leaf clusters and "V" device), the Combat Readiness Medal, the National Defense Medal (with service star), the Armed Forces Expeditionary Medal, the Vietnam Service Medal (with three service stars), the Republic of Vietnam Gallantry Cross (with palm) and Vietnam Campaign Medal, and the Joint Chiefs of Staff badge. He was appointed brigadier general August 1, 1980, with date of rank July 25, 1980.

Marvin Delano Brailsford

★★★ ———————————————————— ★★★

Lieutenant General

Born January 30, 1939, Burkeville, Texas. He received a bachelor of science degree in biology from Prairie View A&M University and a master of science degree in bacteriology from Iowa State University.

In August 1959 he entered the United States Army as a second lieutenant and student in the Armor Officer Basic Course at the United States Army Armor School, Fort Knox, Kentucky. From October 1959 to July 1961, he served as a platoon leader of the 3rd Armored Cavalry Regiment,

Lt. Gen. Marvin Delano Brailsford

Fort Meade, Maryland. He was promoted to first lieutenant on December 15, 1960. From August 1961 to May 1962, he was a student in the Chemical Officer Advanced Course at the United States Army Chemical School, Fort McClellan, Alabama. From May 1962 to November 1962, he served as a platoon leader for the 12th Chemical Company of the 100th Chemical Group, Fort McClellan, Alabama. From November 1962 to December 1963, he was a chemical adviser for the 22nd Infantry Division of the United States Military Assistance Group in Vietnam.

He was promoted to captain on June 17, 1963. From March 1964 to February 1966, he was a student at Iowa State University in Ames, Iowa. From February 1966 to July 1969, he served as the deputy chief of the Special Operations Division, later the executive officer, and later the deputy commander of the United States Army Biological Laboratories, Fort Detrick, Maryland.

He was promoted to major on August 1, 1967. From August 1969 to June 1970, he was a student at the United States Army Command and General Staff College, Fort Leavenworth, Kansas. From June 1970 to June 1972, he served as chief of the Academic Operations Division, later deputy director of instruction, at the United States Army Chemical Center and School, Fort McClellan, Alabama. From June 1972 to January 1973, he served as a staff officer in the Chemical Division of the Chemical and Nuclear Operation Directorate at the Office of the Assistant Chief of Staff for Force Development, United States Army, Washington, D.C. From January 1973 to December 1974, he served as a logistics staff officer in the Operations Division, where he worked on logistics plans, operations, and systems in the Office of the Deputy Chief of Staff for Logistics, United States Army, Washington, D.C.

He was promoted to lieutenant colonel on May 30, 1973. From December 1974 to August 1976, he was the commander of the 101st Ordnance Battalion, 60th Ordnance Group, VII Corps, United States Army, Europe. From August 1976 to May 1977, he served as deputy commander of Kaiserslautern Army Depot, United States Army, Europe. From August 1977 to June 1978, he was a student at the United States Army War College, Carlisle Barracks, Pennsylvania. From June 1978 to May 1982, he served first as assistant project manager for logistics, later assistant development project officer for select ammunition, then chief of systems evaluation, then deputy chairman for operations, Division Air Defense Gun Source Selection Board, and later as chief of the Program Management Office in the United States Army Armament Research and Development Command, Dover, New Jersey.

He was promoted to the rank of colonel on January 1, 1980. From 1982 to October 1984, he was the commander of the 60th Ordnance Group, 21st Support Command, United States Army, Europe. From October 1984 to June 1987, he was the commanding general of the 59th Ordnance Brigade, United States Army, Europe. He was promoted to brigadier general on August 1, 1985. From June 1987 to October 1987, he served as the deputy commanding general for armaments and munitions, United States Army Armament, Munitions, and Chemical Command/Commanding General, United States Army Armament Research and Development Center, Picatinny Arsenal, Dover, New Jersey. From October 1987 to June 1990, he was the commanding general of the United States Army Armament, Munitions, and Chemical Command at Rock Island, Illinois.

He was promoted to major general on August 1, 1988. On June 11, 1990, he was promoted to lieutenant general and named the deputy commanding general, materiel readiness, executive director for conventional ammunition, United States Army Materiel Command, Alexandria, Virginia. He has received numerous awards and decorations: the Distinguished Service Medal, the Legion of Merit, the Bronze Star, the Meritorious Service Medal (with four oak leaf clusters), the Army Commendation Medal, the Parachutist Badge, and the Army Staff Identification Badge. The source of his commission was the ROTC.

Carl E. Briscoe

★ ———————————————————— ★

Brigadier General

Born August 22, 1924, in Atlantic City, New Jersey, he was drafted into the United States Army Air Corps on August 28, 1943. He served as

Brig. Gen. Carl E. Briscoe

chief clerk at Headquarters, McClellan Field, California, and on February 5, 1946, he was discharged as a sergeant.

General Briscoe joined the New Jersey Army National Guard on March 1, 1948, as a sergeant and was later promoted to sergeant major of the 122nd AW Battalion. In January 1951 he accepted an appointment as warrant officer, junior grade. After completion of the 10 Series, he was commissioned a second lieutenant on June 29, 1953, and assigned as adjutant of the 122nd AAA Gun Battalion. He served in that capacity until April 1955, at which time he was transferred to the 116th AAA Gun Battalion (On-Site) in the Camden area as the battalion adjutant. The unit was reorganized to a Nike-Ajax on-site unit, and on June 29, 1956, he was promoted to first lieutenant. He completed the 20 and 30 series air defense and on May 22, 1958, he was promoted to captain.

He attended the Nike-Ajax Officer Orientation Course at Ft. Bliss, Texas. On May 2, 1962, General Briscoe was reassigned to the 5th Battalion, 112th Field Artillery, in Atlantic City, New Jersey, as adjutant and completed the Officer Familiarization Field Artillery extension course. On January 24, 1966, he was promoted to major, field artillery, and assigned as S-3. General Briscoe was reassigned as battalion executive officer on July 1, 1970, and on December 7, 1971, he was promoted to lieutenant colonel and assumed command of the 5th Battalion, 112th Field Artillery. On December 13, 1974, he completed Command and General Staff College.

On February 1, 1976, General Briscoe was appointed commanding officer of the 50th Armored Division Artillery and was promoted to colonel on February 7, 1976. On September 1, 1977, he was transferred to Headquarters, New Jersey Army National Guard as executive officer, and on

May 1, 1979, he was appointed director of the State Area Command. He was promoted and federally recognized as brigadier general on August 23, 1979. General Briscoe was appointed adjutant general, United States Virgin Islands, St. Croix, USVI, in December 1982. He exercised the supervision and direct command of the National Guard of the Virgin Islands, promulgating in the name of the governor orders, directives, and regulation to maintain the National Guard of the Virgin Islands trained, disciplined, uniformed, and equipped at all times. He was responsible for the 132 federal technician and 10 territory employees.

He retired from the National Guard on July 15, 1983. From March 14, 1984, to July 1, 1991, he was employed as business administrator for Atlantic City, New Jersey. He was responsible for coordinating all administrative activities within the various subelements in city government: budget responsibilities in excess of $120 million; fiscal policy and procedures relating to $5 billion dollars of property assessment within city limits; personnel activities involving 2,000 employees; staff coordination including police and fire; facility management, fleet management, purchasing, and general ledger oversight; coordination with city council and the 12 casinos operating in the city. His military decorations and awards: the Meritorious Medal, Army Commendation Medal, National Defense Service Medal, American Campaign, World War II Victory, Armed Forces Reserve Medal, Army Reserve Components Achievement Medal, New Jersey Medal of Merit, New Jersey Medal of Honor, New Jersey Recruiting Award.

Elmer T. Brooks

★ ———————————————————— ★

Brigadier General

Born December 30, 1932, Washington, D.C. He married the former Kathryn M. Casselberry of Dayton, Ohio. They have one daughter, Karen, and three sons — Victor, Eric, and Mark. He received a bachelor of arts degree in zoology from Miami University, Oxford, Ohio, in 1954. He was commissioned through the Air Force Reserve Officer Training Corps program.

In 1973 he received a master of science degree from George Washington University in Washington, D.C., and was graduated from the Industrial College of the Armed Forces at Fort Lesley J. McNair, Washington, D.C. General Brooks completed the executive program of the Colgate Darden Graduate School of Business Administration at the University of Virginia under the Air Force's Advanced Management Program in 1978.

Brig. Gen. Elmer T. Brooks

He entered the United States Air Force in April 1955 and was assigned to a Continental Air Command Air Reserve Flying Center, Greater Pittsburgh, Pennsylvania, Airport, as unit adjutant, then as base director of personnel. The general then went to the Philippines as a radar station commander and later as a personnel division chief at Headquarters, 13th Air Force, Clark Air Base. In July 1961 General Brooks returned to the United States and was assigned as a missile combat crew commander and instructor missile crew commander with the Atlas F intercontinental ballistic missile system at Lincoln Air Force Base, Nebraska.

From November 1965 to May 1968, he served in Houston, Texas, as a flight control technologist for Gemini and Apollo space missions at the National Aeronautics and Space Administration's Manned Spacecraft Center. He then became a resource manager and section chief at the Force Military Personnel Center, Randolph Air Force Base, Texas, until August 1972. After completing the Industrial College of the Armed Forces in August 1973, General Brooks remained in Washington, D.C., where he was assigned to the Office of the Secretary of the Air Force, Space Systems Office, as executive officer. He became the military assistant to the special assistant to the secretary and deputy secretaries of defense in June 1975. He later served as military assistant to secretaries of defense.

General Brooks became vice commander of the 381st Strategic Missile Wing, a Titan II intercontinental ballistic missile unit at McConnell Air Force Base, Kansas, in July 1978 and commanded the wing from January 1979 until October 1981. He then returned to Washington, D.C., as assistant deputy director, international negotiations, Organization of the Joint Chiefs of Staff, and was appointed by the president as deputy commissioner of the U.S.-USSR Standing Consultative Commission. In September 1982 he became deputy director, international negotiations, Organization of the Joint Chiefs of Staff.

Brig. Gen. Elmer T. Brooks was assigned as assistant deputy, Under Secretary of Defense for Strategic and Theater Nuclear Forces, in Washington, D.C., in August 1983. He was appointed brigadier general on September 1, 1981, with same date of rank. The general's military decorations and awards: Defense Superior Service Medal (with two oak leaf clusters), Legion of Merit, Meritorious Service Medal (with one oak leaf cluster), Joint Service Commendation Medal, Air Force Commendation Medal, Air Force Outstanding Unit Award Ribbon (with two oak leaf clusters), Readiness Medal, Master Missile Badge, and the Space Badge.

George M. Brooks

★ ——————————————————— ★

Brigadier General

Retired from the Army National Guard after serving over 30 years. The source for this fact was *Black Americans in Defense of Our Nation* (1985) published by the Department of Defense, Office of Deputy Assistant Secretary of Defense for Equal Opportunity and Safety Policy. No other information could be obtained.

Harry William Brooks, Jr.

★★ ——————————————————— ★★

Major General

Born on May 17, 1928, Indianapolis, Indiana. He is the son of Harry W. Brooks, Sr., and Nora E. Brooks. He married the former June Hezekiah, and they have three children: Harry W. III, Wayne L., and Craig E. He received a B.S. degree in business administration from the University of Omaha, then an M.A. from the University of Oklahoma. His military education included the Quartermaster School, Basic Course; the Artillery and Guided Missile School, Basic and Advanced Courses; United States Army Command and General Staff College; United States Army War College.

His military career began as a private in 1947, and on July 1, 1949, he

Maj. Gen. Harry William Brooks, Jr.

was commissioned a second lieutenant in the United States Army. General Brooks's major permanent duty assignments during his last ten years to service were: from February 1962 to October 1963, he served as an adviser to United States Army Reserve units in the northern New York Sector, II United States Army Corps, in Syracuse, New York; commanding officer, United States Army Reserve Center, northern New York Sector, II United States Army Corps, Syracuse, New York, from October 1963 to August 1965. From August 1965 to June 1966, he was a student at the United States Command and General Staff College, Fort Leavenworth, Kansas. From June 1966 to November 1967, he was assigned first as commanding officer of the 2nd Battalion, 40th Artillery, 199th Infantry Brigade, then as a special assistant to the deputy commanding officer of the 199th Infantry Brigade in Vietnam. From December 1967 to July 1969, he served as a staff officer in the Doctrine Branch of the Doctrine and Concepts Division, Doctrine and Systems Directorate, Assistant Chief of Staff for Force Development, United States Army, Washington, D.C.

From August 1969 to July 1970, he was a student at the United States Army War College at Carlisle Barracks, Pennsylvania. From July 1970 to January 1972, he served as commanding officer of the 72nd Field Artillery Group, United States Army, Europe. From January 1972 to January 1973, he served as director of equal opportunity programs, in the Office of the Deputy Chief of Staff for Personnel, United States Army, Washington, D.C. From January 1973 to June 1974, he was assigned as the assistant division commander for the 2nd Infantry Division in Korea.

In June 1974 he was appointed major general and assigned as the commanding general of the 25th Infantry Division in Korea. General Brooks retired on August 31, 1976. His military awards and decorations include: Legion of Merit (with oak leaf cluster), Bronze Star Medal (with oak leaf cluster), Meritorious Service Medal, Air Medal (seven awards), Army Commendation Medal.

Leo Austin Brooks

★ ———————————————— ★

Brigadier General

Born August 9, 1932, in Washington, D.C., he married the former Naomi Ethel Lewis, and they have three children: Leo, Jr., Vincent Keith, and Marquita Karen. He received a B.S. degree from Virginia State University in 1954. He began his military career in 1954.

General Brooks has held a wide variety of important command and staff positions, culminating in his most recent assignments, which include congressional coordinator with the Department of the Army in Washington, D.C., from 1967 to 1970. He was assigned as the Cambodian desk officer for the Joint Chiefs of Staff in Washington, D.C., from 1972 to 1974. In 1974, he was assigned as the commanding officer of the Sacramento Army Depot. From 1976 to 1978, he served as commanding officer of the 13th Corps Support Command at Fort Hood, Texas. In 1978, he was appointed commanding general of the United States Army Troop Support Agency at Fort Lee, Virginia. General Brooks's military awards include the Legion of Merit (with two oak leaf clusters), the Bronze Star Medal, the Meritorious Service Medal, the Army Commendation Medal.

Brig. Gen. Leo Austin Brooks

Dallas Coverdale Brown, Jr.

★ ——————————————————— ★

Brigadier General

Born August 21, 1932, in New Orleans, Louisiana, the son of Dallas
C. Brown and Sydney Taylor Brown. He and his wife, Dr. Elizabeth T.
Brown, have five children: Dallas C. III, Leonard G., Jan B., Karen L., and
Barbara A. He received a B.A. degree in history from West Virginia State
College. He earned an M.A. degree in government from Indiana Univer-
sity. Military schools attended include Infantry School, Basic Course; Ar-
tillery School, Battery Officer and Advanced Courses; Defense Language
Institute, Russian; United States Army Command and General Staff Col-
lege; United States Naval War College.

He began his 30-year career in the Regular Army as an infantry platoon leader in the 82nd Airborne Division. Subsequently, he served in
various troop units in Korea, Germany, and the United States. In Vietnam
he commanded the 519th Military Intelligence Battalion. This battalion
received a Meritorious Unit Commendation for General Brown's period of
command. He later commanded the United States Army Field Station in
Berlin. After being designated a foreign area officer (Russian) in 1970, he
served as a specialist on Soviet affairs in various positions in the Defense
Intelligence Agency, including deputy vice director for foreign intelligence.
General Brown also served as a United States delegate and chief delegate
at five NATO intelligence conferences involving all of Europe and the

Brig. Gen. Dallas Coverdale Brown, Jr.

Middle East. His final assignment was deputy commandant of the United States Army War College. He has written and lectured extensively on Soviet, Communist, and military affairs throughout the United States. He was appointed brigadier general on September 1, 1978. His awards and decorations include the Defense Superior Service Medal, Master Parachutist Badge, Army Commendation Medal, Joint Service Commendation Medal, Meritorious Service Medal, and Aircraft Crewman Badge.

He was the West Virginia State College alumnus of the year in 1978, inducted into the West Virginia State College ROTC Hall of Fame in 1980. He is also a member of the Military Advisory Council of the Center for Defense Information, the Army War College Foundation, the West Virginia State College Board of Advisors (1990–1991), and the Retired Officers Association of West Virginia (vice president). He retired from active duty in 1984 and served as an associate professor of history at West Virginia State College.

John Mitchell Brown, Sr.

★★ ———————————————————— ★★

Major General

Born December 11, 1929, in Vicksburg, Mississippi, he is the son of Joeddie Fred Brown and Ernestine Helen Foster Brown. He married the former Louise (Lou) Yvonne Dorsey. They have four children: Ronald Quinton, Jan Michelle, John Mitchell, and Jay Michael.

He was commissioned a second lieutenant and awarded a bachelor of science degree in engineering by the United States Military Academy. He also holds a master's degree in comptrollership and has completed the Advanced Management Program at the University of Houston. His military education includes completion of the basic and advanced courses of the Infantry School, the United States Army Command and General Staff College, and the Industrial College of the Armed Forces.

He has held a wide variety of important command and staff positions, culminating in his current assignment as deputy commanding general, III Corps, Fort Hood, Texas. Other key assignments held recently include assistant division commander, 2nd Infantry Division, Korea; deputy director of materiel plans and programs, Office of the Deputy Chief of Staff for Research, Development, and Acquisition in Washington, D.C.; and deputy chief of staff, comptroller, United States Army Forces Command, Fort McPherson, Georgia.

General Brown served in a variety of important career-building assignments preparatory to his most recent duties. He was operations research analyst, later chief, Cost Methodology Branch, Cost Research Division, and later executive officer, Directorate of Cost Analysis, Office of the Comptroller of the Army in Washington, D.C. He was then assigned as assistant secretary of the general staff (Staff Action Council), Office of the Chief of Staff, United States Army, Washington, D.C. He then departed for Europe where he commanded the 1st Battalion, 87th Infantry, 8th Infantry Division, United States Army, Europe. After completion of the Industrial College of the Armed Forces at Fort Lesley J. McNair in Washington, D.C., he served as executive to the Comptroller of the Army, Washington, D.C. He then departed for Korea where he commanded the 3rd Brigade, 2nd Infantry Division, and subsequently became the assistant chief of staff comptroller, United Nations Command, United States forces in Korea, Eighth United States Army.

He was appointed major general in 1985, and he retired in 1988. General Brown's awards and decorations include the Legion of Merit, Bronze Star Medal, Meritorious Service Medal, Army Commendation Medal with (two oak leaf clusters), Combat Infantryman Badge, Parachutist Badge, Ranger Tab, and Army General Staff Identification Badge. He received a city of Atlanta proclamation designating June 19, 1985, as "John M. Brown Day" in the state of Georgia.

William E. Brown, Jr.

★★★ ——————————————————— ★★★

Lieutenant General

Born December 5, 1927, Bronx, New York. He married the former Gloria Henry of Plainfield, New Jersey. They have three children: Nancy, Louis, and Bill. He was graduated from Dwight Morrow High School in Englewood, New Jersey, in 1945 and received a bachelor of science degree from Pennsylvania State University in 1949. He has done graduate work in systems management at the University of Southern California and attended the Harvard Business School's advanced management program. The general was graduated from Squadron Officer School at Maxwell Air Force Base in Alabama in 1956; Armed Forces Staff College, Norfolk, Virginia, in 1966; and the Industrial College of the Armed Forces, Fort Lesley J. McNair, Washington, D.C., in 1973.

He was commissioned in December 1951 at Craig Air Force Base, Alabama. After completing pilot training as a distinguished graduate, his first assignment was to Williams Air Force Base, Arizona, as a student in

Lt. Gen. William E. Brown, Jr.

the F-80 Shooting Star jet transition program. From 1952 to 1970, General Brown served principally in fighter aircraft in various squadron, wing, and numbered Air Force positions. He flew 125 combat missions in F-86 Sabrejets with the 4th Fighter-Interceptor Wing in South Korea and another 100 combat missions in F-4 Phantoms during tours of duty in Thailand at Ubon Royal Thai Air Force Base in 1966 and Udorn Royal Thai Air Force Base in 1969. He also served overseas in Spain and Germany.

In January 1971 he was assigned to the Department of Defense Manpower and Reserve Affairs Office at the Pentagon, serving as special assistant for domestic actions to the Assistant Secretary of Defense. From June 1973 to April 1974 he served as deputy commander of operations, 64th Flying Training Wing, Reese Air Force Base, Texas. He was subsequently assigned to Williams Air Force Base, first as base commander and then as commander of the 82nd Flying Training Wing. In February 1975 he took command of the 1st Composite Wing, Military Airlift Command, at Andrews Air Force Base in Maryland. From June 1977 to October 1978, he served as chief of Air Force Security Police at the headquarters of the United States Air Force in Washington, D.C. From October 1978 to August 1980, he served as commander of the Air Defense Weapons Center at Tyndall Air Force Base in Florida. From August 1980 to September 1982, he was the commander of the 17th Air Force, Sembach Air Base, in Germany. In September 1982 he was commander of the Allied Air Forces, Southern Europe, and deputy commander in chief, United States Air Forces in Europe, Southern Area, Naples, Italy.

He was appointed brigadier general on August 1, 1975; major general April 1, 1979; and lieutenant general on September 15, 1982.

Lt. Gen. William E. Brown, Jr., is a command pilot with more than 5,100 flying hours. His military decorations and awards include the Distinguished Service Medal, Legion of Merit (two oak leaf clusters); Distinguished Flying Cross (one oak leaf cluster); Air Medal (four oak leaf clusters); Air Force Commendation Medal (one oak leaf cluster); and the Purple Heart. He received a Distinguished Alumni award from Pennsylvania State University in 1981.

Albert Bryant

★ ──────────────────────── ★

Brigadier General

Born in Glen Allen, Mississippi. Bryant is a graduate of Xavier University, receiving a B.S. degree. He earned a M.A. degree from Central Michigan University. His military service included: executive officer of the 253rd General Hospital; deputy commander of the 220th Military Police; commander of the 220th Military Police Brigade; and as deputy director of pharmacy service at the Veteran's Administration in Washington, D.C. He was promoted to the one star rank of brigadier general in the Army Reserves.

Brig. Gen. Albert Bryant

Alvin Bryant

★★ ——————————————— ★★

Major General

Born February 27, 1937, Miami, Florida. He earned a bachelor's degree in biology from Florida A&M University in 1959. Bryant's next academic degree was a master's in zoology from Purdue University in 1966, which he attended on a National Science Foundation scholarship that allowed him to study for several summers.

His degrees gave Bryant a broad science background from which to draw when he enrolled in medical school at Howard University in Washington, D.C. After earning his medical degree in 1977 and completing his residency in general surgery, Newport News General (then Whittaker Hospital) recruited him to practice in the predominantly black east end of Newport News, Virginia. His military schooling includes Infantry School, Infantry Officer Basic Course; Airborne Course; Ordnance Officer Advanced Course; Army Command and General Staff College; Army War College; Tactical Nuclear Awareness; and the Combat Service Support Command Refresher.

After he received an ROTC Commission to second lieutenant on June 1, 1959, he served as an infantry officer, later ordnance officer. "I knew I was going into the Army and spend two years on active duty when I finished college," General Bryant commented, remembering how well ROTC helped him develop leadership and discipline skills.

General Bryant has 33 years of service as a commissioned officer, and with the exception of a few weeks work with a National Guard unit, he has never used his medical skills in the Reserve. He has served as a research member of the 3372nd Research and Development (REINF). At the 300th Inventory Control Center, he has been chief, Installations and Construction; chief, Repair Parts Management Materiel Division. He also has been chief, Missile and Munitions Division, 55th Materiel Management Center. At 310th TAACOM, he served as chief, Training Plans and Programming, Logistics Readiness Office; assistant chief of staff, Services Division; commander, 300th Support Group (Area); and deputy commander.

He serves as general surgeon and president of Alvin Bryant, M.D. Corporation (civilian occupation). He has the overall responsibilities for management of a surgical corporation, supervises a staff of seven employees, delivers medical surgical care to 120–140 outpatients per week, and is responsible for the preoperative, operative, and postoperative care of 20–30 inpatients per week. He has overall responsibility, as board chairman, for the Peninsula Institute for Community Health, which serves

Maj. Gen. Alvin Bryant

15,000 to 20,000 residents of southeastern Newport News, Virginia. A past board chairman of the Newport News General Hospital, serving on the regional Board of Directors of the Medical Society of Virginia Review Organization, a professional standards review organization, which controls the cost of services and quality of care for patients in the 21 area hospitals in eastern Virginia, he also served as coadministrator for Hampton University's Nurse Practitioner Clinic. General Bryant had wanted to use his medical skills in the Army Reserve. While a lieutenant colonel, he asked to switch to the Medical Corps. The Army gave approval on condition that he drop back in rank to major, and Bryant declined. Later, Bryant asked for a second skills specialty listing and again was told he could have it if he dropped back to major. He refused again.

With the exception of his first two years of medical school, General Bryant has been in the Army Reserve since completing two years of activity duty in 1961. Following active duty, he put medical school on hold so that he could work and help put his five brothers through college. Four of those brothers also went to Florida A&M. For five years he taught general science, biology, chemistry, and math in high school.

He spearheaded a $250,000 grant that was funded to establish PICH. It focuses on recruiting doctors to serve minorities in the east end of Newport News and surrounding communities. His military decorations and awards include the Meritorious Service Medal, the Army Commendation Medal (with oak leaf cluster), Army Reserve Components Achievement Medal (with three oak leaf clusters), the National Defense Service Medal, the Army Service Ribbon, Army Reserve Components Overseas Training Ribbon with eight numerals, Parachutist Badge. He was appointed major general on May 15, 1991.

Cunningham C. Bryant

★★ ——————————————————— ★★

Major General

Born on August 8, 1921, in Clifton, Virginia, he attended Howard University from 1940 to 1943. In 1943 he joined the United States Army and after completion of the Infantry Officer Candidate School in 1944, he was commissioned a second lieutenant with the United States Army during World War II. At the end of that war he transferred to the Washington, D.C., National Guard. In 1968 he was appointed adjutant general for the D.C. National Guard, the first federally recognized black general officer in the National Guard. In 1974, he was appointed commanding officer of the Washington, D.C., National Guard. In 1975, he was appointed major general.

He has received numerous awards and decorations: the Bronze Star, Army Commendation Medal, Purple Heart Medal, Army of Occupation Medal (Germany), World War II Victory Medal, National Defense Service Medal, European-African-Middle Eastern Campaign Medal (with two stars), Combat Infantry Badge, and American Campaign Medal.

Maj. Gen. Cunningham C. Bryant

Harold Eugene Burch

★ ──────────────────────────────── ★

Brigadier General

Born August 19, 1941, Lake Wales, Florida. He married the former Jewelle Cheek, and they have two children, Karla and Daryl. He was graduated from Tuskegee University with a bachelor of science degree in 1964 and a master of science degree in agronomy in 1966.

After completing the Infantry Officer Basic Course, he served as executive officer for Company C, 3rd Battalion, 199th Infantry Brigade (Separate) (Light), Fort Benning, Georgia. Assigned to Vietnam from December 1966 through December 1967, he held positions as executive officer, Company C, and S-1 detachment commander, 7th Support Battalion (DISCOM), 199th Infantry Brigade. Graduating from the Quartermaster Officer Advanced Course, he commanded A Company, 24th Supply and Transportation Battalion, 24th Infantry Division, from October 1968 through December 1969, with a follow-on assignment through May 1970 as division property book officer for the 1st Infantry Division at Fort Riley, Kansas. From May 1970 through May 1971, he served as a senior advisor for the 90th Parachute Maintenance and Aerial Delivery Base Depot, Military Assistance Command, United States Army, Vietnam.

From May 1971 to May 1974, he was assigned to V Corps, United States Army, Europe, Federal Republic of Germany, as assistant G-4 (logistics). Returning from overseas, he taught at the United States Army Armor School at Fort Knox, Kentucky, from May 1974 through June 1977. After graduation from the United States Army Command and General Staff College, he was assigned as the division parachute officer, Company E, and later as executive officer, 407th Support and Supply Battalion (Airborne), 82nd Airborne Division, at Fort Bragg, North Carolina, from July 1978 through October 1980.

Reassigned to Japan, he served as chief, Maintenance and Services Division, Directorate of Industrial Operations, Honshu Sagami Depot, from October 1980 through May 1983. He commanded the 75th Support Battalion, 194th Armored Brigade, Fort Knox, Kentucky, from May 1983 through May 1985. Assigned to Korea, he served as the assistant chief of staff, G-4 (logistics), 2nd Infantry Division, Eighth United States Army, from May 1985 through May 1986.

After attending the Industrial College of the Armed Forces, Fort McNair, Washington, D.C., he was appointed as the deputy executive director, Technical Services and Logistics Directorate, Defense Logistics Agency, Cameron Station, Virginia, from June 1987 through June 1988.

Brig. Gen. Harold Eugene Burch

From August 1988 through November 1990, he served as the commander of the Division Support Command, 1st Cavalry Division, Fort Hood, Texas. He was reassigned to the 21st Theater Army Area Command, Federal Republic of Germany, on January 11, 1991, as deputy commander.

Brig. Gen. Harold Eugene Burch was appointed to his rank on October 1, 1991. His decorations and awards include the Legion of Merit (one oak leaf cluster), Bronze Star Medal (one oak leaf cluster), Meritorious Service Medal (three oak leaf clusters), Army Commendation Medal (one oak leaf cluster), Army Achievement Medal, National Defense Service Medal, Senior Parachutist Badge, Parachute Rigger Badge, and Combat Badge.

Charles D. Bussey

★★ ———————————————— ★★

Major General

Born December 8, 1933, in Edgefield, South Carolina, and raised in Washington, D.C., he is the son of Alex William Bussey, Sr., and Mattie Lou Bussey. He married the former Eva Lois Gray. They have three children: Terri Lyn, Tonia Marie, and Charles Frederick. He received a bachelor of science degree in English and a commission as a second lieutenant of infantry from the Agricultural and Technical College of North

Maj. Gen. Charles D. Bussey

Carolina in June 1955. He also has a master of arts in journalism from Indiana University and a master of science in communication science from Shippensburg State College. His military schooling includes completion of the Infantry Officer Basic and Advanced Courses, Army Information School, Armed Forces Staff College and War College.

General Bussey has held varied command and staff posts, including troop assignments with eight combat divisions and a separate brigade. In Washington, D.C., he was chief of personnel actions in Legislative Liaison and chief, Policy and Plans Division, Office of the Chief of Public Affairs. He also was professor of military science for the Indianapolis public schools Junior ROTC program.

He commanded a rifle company in the 1st Cavalry Division in Korea, an infantry battalion in the 82nd Airborne Division, and an infantry brigade in the 2nd Infantry Division in Korea. For two years, he was deputy commander and chief of staff of the 172nd Infantry Brigade in Alaska. His overseas service includes two tours in Korea and one each in Vietnam, Germany, and Alaska.

In July 1982 he was reassigned to Washington, D.C., as the deputy chief of public affairs. General Bussey became the chief of public affairs, Office of the Secretary of the Army, on August 13, 1984. In 1987 he was assigned as chief of staff for personnel. He retired on May 31, 1989. His military awards and decorations include two Legions of Merit, two Bronze Star Medals, three Meritorious Service Medals, three Army Commendation Medals, the Air Medal, the Combat Infantryman Badge, the Parachutist Badge, and the Army General Staff Identification Badge.

Melvin Leon Byrd

★ ───────────────── ★

Brigadier General

Born November 1, 1935, Suffolk, Virginia. He received a bachelor of arts degree in accounting from Howard University and a master's in business administration from Babson College. From February 1959 to March 1959, he was a student at the Infantry Officer Basic Course at the United States Army Infantry School Fort Benning, Georgia. From March 1959 to September 1959, he was an administration officer for the United States Army Garrison at Camp Drum, New York. From September 1959 to November 1961, he served as a platoon leader for the 5th Ordnance Company, Aberdeen Proving Ground, Maryland, with duty station Camp Drum, New York. He was promoted to first lieutenant on November 26, 1960. From December 1961 to May 1963, he was the repair parts supply officer for Company B, 801st Maintenance Battalion, 101st Airborne Division, Fort Campbell, Kentucky. On May 27, 1963, he was promoted to captain. From June 1963 to October 1964, he served as an ordnance adviser with the Military Advisor Group of the United States Army Element in Iran.

From October 1964 to March 1965, he was a student at the Ordnance Officer Advanced Course at the United States Army Ordnance Center and School, Aberdeen Proving Ground, Maryland. From March 1965 to May 1966, he was an ordnance adviser with the United States Military Assistance Command, Vietnam. From May 1966 to November 1967, he was chief of welding, Metal Body Division, and maintenance officer at the United States Army Ordnance Center and School, Aberdeen Proving Ground, Maryland. On June 20, 1967, he was promoted to major. From November 1967 to September 1968, he served as a civilian affairs officer with the 199th Infantry Brigade, United States Army, Vietnam. From September 1968 to June 1969, he was the executive officer of the 7th Combat Support Battalion, 199th Infantry Bridge, United States Army, Vietnam. From June 1969 to July 1972, he was chief, Maintenance Management Branch, United States Army Quartermaster School, Fort Lee, Virginia.

From July 1972 to June 1973, he was a student at the Marine Corps Command and Staff College at Quantico, Virginia. From June 1973 to December 1974, he was a student at Babson College, Babson Park, Massachusetts. From December 1974 to July 1976, he served as a logistics staff officer in the Materiel Management Division, Office of the Deputy Chief of Staff for Logistics, United States Army, Washington, D.C. From September 1976 to September 1977, he was commander of the 702nd Maintenance

Brig. Gen. Melvin Leon Byrd

Battalion, 2nd Infantry Division, United States Army, Korea. From September 1977 to July 1979, he served as an inspector general in the Assistance Division, United States Army Inspector General Agency, Washington, D.C.

On September 30, 1979, he was promoted to lieutenant colonel. From July 1979 to June 1980, he was a student at the United States Army War College Carlisle Barracks, Pennsylvania. From June 1980 to January 1981, he served as the deputy director for joint actions, plans, Force Structure and Systems Directorate, Office of the Deputy Chief of Staff for Logistics, United States Army, Washington, D.C. He was promoted to colonel on July 1, 1980. From March 1981 to June 1983, he was the commander of Division Support Command, 82d Airborne Division, at Fort Bragg, North Carolina. From June 1983 to July 1986, he was the commander of the United States Army Electronics Materiel Readiness Activity at Vint Hill Farms Station, Warrenton, Virginia. From July 1986 to July 1988, he was the commanding general of the United Army Materiel Command in Europe. He was promoted to brigadier general on October 1, 1986. He has received numerous decorations, badges and awards.

Alfred Jackal Cade

★ ————————————————— ★

Brigadier General

Born February 4, 1931, Fayetteville, North Carolina. He received a bachelor of science degree in general psychology from Virginia State

Brig. Gen. Alfred Jackal Cade

College, then a master of business administration, comptrollership, from Syracuse University. His military schooling includes Field Artillery Officer Basic Course, United States Army Command and General Staff College, and he is a graduate of the Industrial College of the Armed Forces at Fort Lesley J. McNair, Washington, D.C.

He was commissioned a second lieutenant in 1954. From 1966 through 1967, he served as an assistance sector advisor and sector advisor with the United States Military Command, Phu Yen Province, Vietnam. He served as commander of the 1st Battalion, 92nd Artillery, United States Army, Vietnam, from 1967 to 1968. He returned to the United States in 1968 serving as first budget operations officer until 1970 with the Director of Army Budget in Washington, D.C., then as executive officer with the Army's Materiel Command and assistant comptroller for budget, Washington, D.C., until 1973. From 1973 through 1974, he served as commander of the 210th Field Artillery Group in Europe. He was appointed brigadier general on April 1, 1975, and retired December 31, 1978.

Brigadier General Cade's decorations include Legion of Merit (two oak leaf clusters), Bronze Star Medal (three oak leaf clusters), Meritorious Service Medal, Air Medal, Army Commendation Medal, Parachutist Badge.

Sherian Grace Cadoria

★ ───────────────────────────── ★

Brigadier General

Born on January 26, 1940, Marksville, Louisiana. She received a bachelor of science in business education from Southern University A&M College and a master's from the University of Oklahoma.

She received a commission by direct appointment, and from January 1962 to May 1963, she was a platoon officer for Company B, Women's Army Corps Training Battalion, Fort McClellan, Alabama. From June 1963 to May 1965, she served as executive officer, Women's Army Corp Company, and assistant adjutant, United States Army Communications Zone, Europe. From June 1965 to July 1966, she served as adjutant of special troops, United States Army Quartermaster Center, Fort Lee, Virginia.

She was promoted to captain on May 17, 1965. From July 1966 to December 1966, she was a student at the Adjutant General School, Fort Benjamin Harrison, Indiana. From January 1967 to December 1967, she was the administrative officer in the Provost Marshal's Office, United States Army, Vietnam. From January 1968 to October 1969, she served as the protocol officer in Qui Nhon Support Command, Vietnam. She was promoted to major on August 1, 1968. From November 1969 to July 1970, she served as chief, Personnel Division/Adjutant, United States Army Ordnance Center and School, Aberdeen Proving Ground, Maryland.

From July 1970 to June 1971, she was a student at the United States Army Command and General Staff College, Fort Leavenworth, Kansas. From June 1971 to June 1973, she was an instructor at the Officer Education and Training Branch, United States Army Women's Army Corps Center and School, Fort McClellan, Alabama. From June 1973 to June 1975, she served as a personnel management officer, later executive officer, Women's Army Corps Branch, Officer Personnel Directorate, United States Army Military Personnel Center, Alexandria, Virginia. From June 1975 to December 1976, she served as a personnel staff officer with the Law Enforcement Division, Human Resources Development Directorate, Office of the Deputy Chief of Staff for Personnel, United States Army, Washington, D.C.

On July 1, 1976, she was promoted to lieutenant colonel. From December 1976 to July 1978, she was commander, Student Battalion, Training Brigade, United States Army Military Police School, Fort McClellan, Alabama. From July 1978 to June 1979, she was a student at the United States Army War College, Carlisle Barracks, Pennsylvania. From June 1979 to May 1982, she served as a special assistant to the provost marshal,

Brig. Gen. Sherian Grace Cadoria

later chief, Physical Security Division, Office of the Provost Marshal, United States Army, Europe, and Seventh Army.

On September 1, 1980, she was promoted to colonel. From May 1982 to July 1984, she was the commander of the First Region, United States Army Criminal Investigation Command, Fort George G. Meade, Maryland. From July 1984 to July 1985, she served as chief, the Law Enforcement Division, Human Resource Development Directorate, Office of the Deputy Chief of Staff for Personnel, United States Army, Washington, D.C. From August 1985 to September 1987, she served as director, Manpower and Personnel, J-1, Organization of the Joint Chiefs of Staff, Washington, D.C. On October 1, 1985, she was promoted to brigadier general. In September 1987, she was assigned as deputy commanding general, Total Army Personnel Command, Alexandria, Virginia. She has received numerous decorations and badges: the Defense Superior Service Medal, the Legion of Merit, the Bronze Star Medal (two oak leaf clusters), Meritorious Service Medal (oak leaf cluster), Air Medal, Army Commendation Medal (three oak leaf clusters), Joint Chiefs of Staff Identification Badge.

Roscoe Conklin Cartwright

★ ————————————————————— ★

Brigadier General

Born May 27, 1919, Kansas City, Kansas. He received a B.A. degree in social science from San Francisco College. He earned an M.B.A. in

Brig. Gen. Roscoe Conklin Cartwright

business administration from the University of Missouri. His military education includes completion of the Artillery School, Advanced Course; United States Army command and General Staff College; and Industrial College of the Armed Forces.

He has held a wide variety of important command and staff positions, culminating in the following major permanent duty assignments (the last 10 years of a 31-year career): comptroller, United States Army Garrison, Fort Leavenworth, Kansas, from November 1963 to August 1966; from August 1966 to July 1968, management analyst, later chief, Research and Development Division, Office of the Director of Management, Office, Comptroller of the Army, Washington, D.C. From August 1968 to June 1969, he was a student at the Industrial College of the Armed Forces, Fort Lesley J. McNair, Washington, D.C. After completion of the Industrial College, he was assigned as commanding officer of the 108th Artillery Group, then as deputy commanding officer of the United States Army Support Command at Cam Ranh Bay, Pacific-Vietnam, from August 1969 to July 1970.

In August 1970 he returned to the United States and was assigned as chief, Budget and Five-Year Defense Program, Coordination Division, Manpower and Forces Directorate, Office of the Assistant Chief of Staff for Force Development, United States Army, Washington, D.C. From July 1971 to November 1971, he served as special assistant, Assistant Chief of Staff for Force Development, United States Army, Washington, D.C. In November 1971 he was assigned as director of management, review, and analysis, Comptroller of the Army, Washington, D.C. From February 1972 to July 1973, he served as assistant division commander, 3rd Infantry

Division, United States Army, Europe. In August 1973 he was assigned as deputy chief of staff, Office of the Comptroller, United States Army, Europe, and Seventh Army.

He retired on August 31, 1974. His military awards and decorations include the Legion of Merit (with oak leaf cluster), Bronze Star Medal (with two oak leaf clusters), Meritorious Service Medal, Air Medal (three awards), and Army Commendation Medal (with two oak leaf clusters). He was appointed to brigadier general on August 1, 1971.

Andrew P. Chambers

★★★ ─────────────────────────── ★★★

Lieutenant General

Born on June 30, 1931, in Bedford, Virginia, he married the former Norita E. (Rita) Garner. They have four children: Kathy, Linda, Steven, and David. Upon completion of the Reserve Officers Training Corps curriculum and the educational course of study at Howard University in 1954, he was commissioned a second lieutenant and awarded a bachelor of science degree in physical education. He also holds a master of science in communications from Shippensburg State College. His military education includes completion of the Basic and Advanced Officer Courses at the Infantry School, the United States Army Command and General Staff College, and the United States Army War College.

He has held a wide variety of important command and staff positions, culminating in his current assignment as commanding general, VII Corps, United States Army, Europe. Other key assignments include assistant deputy chief of staff for personnel, United States Army, Washington, D.C.; commanding general, Readiness and Mobilization Region VII, deputy commanding general, Fifth Army, Fort Sam Houston, Texas; and commanding general, 1st Cavalry Division, Fort Hood, Texas. General Chambers served in a variety of important career-building assignments preparatory to his most recent duties. He served as an instructor-author at the United States Army Command and General Staff College, Fort Leavenworth, Kansas, followed by assignment to Europe in the Office of the Deputy Chief of Staff for Personnel. While in Europe, he served as a deputy infantry brigade commander and an infantry battalion commander.

General Chambers assumed duty as chief, Force Programs Analysis, Chief of Staff, United States Army, in Washington, D.C. While in Washington, he also served as deputy, later director, of the Army Equal Employment Opportunity Program. Upon reassignment, he was commander of the

Lt. Gen. Andrew P. Chambers

9th Infantry Division Support Command, Fort Lewis, Washington, and director of personnel, J1, inspector general, Pacific Command, Hawaii. He then served as assistant division commander, 1st Cavalry Division, Fort Hood, Texas. His next assignment was commanding general, VII Corps, United States Army, Europe.

He retired on March 31, 1989. His awards and decorations include the Bronze Star Medal (with "V" device), Distinguished Service Medal, Soldier's Medal, Defense Superior Service Medal, Legion of Merit, Meritorious Service Medal (with oak leaf cluster), Air Medal, Army Commendation Medal (two oak leaf clusters), Combat Infantryman Badge, Senior Parachutist Badge.

Lawrence Cleveland Chambers

★★ ———————————————————— ★★

Rear Admiral

Born June 10, 1929, Bedford, Virginia. He entered the United States Naval Academy as a midshipman on June 30, 1948.

On June 6, 1952, he was appointed an ensign, and from June 1952 to November 1952, he was assigned to the USS *Columbus* (CA-74). From November 1952 to October 1953, he was a student at NABTC, NAS, Pensacola, Florida. From October 1953 to March 1954, he was a student at NAAS, Kingsville, Texas. He was designated a naval aviator (HTA) on

Rear Adm. Lawrence Cleveland Chambers

June 9, 1954. From March 1954 to June 1954, he was a student at NABTC, NAS, Pensacola, Florida. From June 1954 to June 1955, he served in Air Anti-Submarine Squadron 37. From June 1955 to April 1957, he was assigned to Attack Squadron 215.

On July 1, 1956, he was promoted to lieutenant. From April 1957 to August 1959, he was a student at the Naval Postgraduate School, Monterey. From August 1959 to September 1960, he was a student at the NROTC Unit, Stanford University, Stanford, California. From September 1960 to July 1961, he was assigned to Attack Squadron 125. From July 1961 to December 1963, he was assigned to Attack Squadron 22 (OIC).

On September 1, 1961, he was promoted to lieutenant commander. From December 1963 to January 1967, he served as assistant curriculas officer in the Aeronautical Engineering Programs, Naval Postgraduate School, Monterey. He was promoted to commander on July 1, 1966. From January 1967 to August 1968, he served on the USS *Ranger* (CVA-34). From August 1968 to November 1971, he served as a PCO, Attack Squadron 67, later commander, Attack Squadron 67, then commander, Attack Squadron 15, and USS *Oriskany* (CVA-34).

From November 1971 to June 1973, he served as the deputy project manager at A-7E Project Office, Naval Air Systems Command. He was promoted to captain on July 1, 1972. From June 1973 to January 1975, he was the commander of the USS *White Plains* (AFS-4). From January 1975 to December 1976, he was the commander of the USS *Midway* (CVA-41).

In December 1976 he was designated rear admiral while serving in billets commensurate with that grade. From December 1976 to November 1978, he was assistant chief of naval personnel for enlisted personnel development and distribution at the Bureau of Naval Personnel. On August 1, 1977, he was promoted to rear admiral. From November 1978 to April 1979, he served as chief of naval personnel, Naval Military Personnel Command. From April 1979 to August 1979, he was a student in the Senior Officers Ships Material Readiness Course, Idaho Falls, Idaho. From August 1979 to May 1981, commander, Carrier Group 3; from May 1981 to March 1, 1984, deputy commander, ASW, Naval Air System Command.

He has received numerous medals and awards: the Bronze Star Medal, Meritorious Service Medal, China Service Medal, Vietnam Service Medal with three bronze stars.

Allen E. Chandler

★★ —————————————————————— ★★

Major General

Born September 16, 1935, in Hagerstown, Maryland, he married the former Barbara Hardiman, and they are the parents of three children. Their oldest son, Allen, is deceased. Their second son, Rodney, was a UH-1 (Huey gunship) pilot with Troop D, 104th Armored Cavalry Squadron, PAARNG. Their youngest son, Roderick, is a prelaw student.

Chandler was graduated from North Street High School in Hagerstown in 1953. He began his military career as a private on May 18, 1955, in the United States Army Reserve. He continued his enlisted service until he was commissioned on June 3, 1957. He was a Distinguished Military Graduate of the ROTC program and graduated summa cum laude with a bachelor of science degree in chemistry from Morgan State College, Baltimore, Maryland. Chandler served as a supervisory nurse with the 30th General Hospital from October 15, 1957, to June 13, 1959, while attending Jefferson Medical College in Philadelphia. He was promoted to first lieutenant, Medical Service Corps, on June 5, 1959, while serving with the 361st General Hospital.

Chandler received his doctorate in medicine in 1961, graduating with honors from Jefferson Medical College. Chandler served a rotating internship at the Fitzgerald Mercy Hospital, Darby, Pennsylvania, during 1961 and 1962 and completed a pediatric residency at Jefferson Medical College from June 1962 through May 1964.

He served on active duty as chief, Pediatric Department, General Leonard Wood Army Hospital, Fort Leonard Wood, Missouri, from 1964 through 1966. He performed this duty as a captain, Medical Corps. He was certified by the American Board of Pediatrics in 1966. He joined the

Maj. Gen. Allen E. Chandler

Pennsylvania Army National Guard on September 14, 1976, as the chief of medical services for the 108th Combat Support Hospital.

He was promoted to lieutenant colonel on March 10, 1977, and assumed command of the 108th Combat Support Hospital on October 1, 1977. He took a reorganized unit that had formerly been a field artillery battalion and developed it into a high-priority hospital. Chandler completed the Army Medical Department Command and General Staff College on April 4, 1980. He was promoted to colonel on May 13, 1980, continuing his service as commander of the 108th Combat Hospital.

Until his selection as state surgeon, Headquarters State Area Command, Pennsylvania, Chandler was responsible for the development of medical plans, policies, and training, utilizing all medical assets of the state, both military and domestic. He also served as the FUSA advisor to the National Guard Bureau Surgeon from 1984 to 1988.

He was assigned as the assistant adjutant general in July 1987 and promoted to his current rank on March 24, 1988. In this capacity, his duties include supervision of personnel, logistics, maintenance, medical, chaplain, judge advocate, provost marshal, safety, and selective service activities.

He is a medical doctor of pediatrics in private practice in Philadelphia, Pennsylvania. He is also the senior pediatrician in the Philadelphia Health Department and serves responsibilities relative to the overall wellness of the youth of Philadelphia. Chandler is also the medical director of the Childhood Lead Poisoning Program of Philadelphia and has years of experience in the area of heavy-metal intoxication. He develops, manages, and monitors all programs that affect the health of all children in Philadelphia from birth to 18. He directly supervises 45 board-certified pediatricians and four senior pediatric consultants, with a budget of $7.5 million, and has over 300,000 patient visits per year.

Academically, Chandler has served on the professorial staff of Thomas Jefferson University since 1964. He served as a member of the Admissions Committee there from 1971 to 1979. From 1972 to 1978, he was the director of Minority Admissions at Jefferson Medical College. On March 24, 1988, Allen E. Chandler's promotion to brigadier general made him the first black American to hold that position in the Pennsylvania Army National Guard at Fort Indiantown Gap, Pennsylvania. Brig. Gen. Allen E. Chandler serves as assistant adjutant general, Headquarters, State Area Command.

In 1992, General Chandler was promoted to major general. He was nominated by President Bush and confirmed by the Senate to serve as the Department of the Army deputy surgeon general for National Guard Affairs and Mobilization.

Thomas E. Clifford

★★ ———————————————————— ★★

Major General

Born March 9, 1929, Washington, D.C. He and his wife, Edith, have four children: Maria, Edwin, Larry, and Mark. He attended school in Washington, D.C., graduating from Paul Lawrence Dunbar High School in June 1945. He then entered Howard University where he majored in accounting and was a cadet in the Air Force Reserve Officers Training Corps program.

In June 1949 he graduated cum laude with a bachelor of arts degree in business administration. He also completed the Reserve Officers' Training Corps program as a distinguished military graduate and was commissioned a second lieutenant in the United States Air Force. He entered active military service in September 1949 as a supply officer in the 225th Overseas Replacement Depot, Camp Kilmer, New Jersey. In August 1950 he completed the Air Tactical School (forerunner of Squadron Officer School) at Tyndall Air Force Base, Florida. In November 1950 he entered pilot training at Connally Air Force Base, Waco, Texas. He earned his wings in December 1951, then received combat crew training in fighter-interceptor operations at Moody Air Force Base, Georgia, and Tyndall Air Force Base, Florida.

In April 1952 General Clifford was assigned as an F-94 pilot in the 5th

Maj. Gen. Thomas E. Clifford

Fighter-Interceptor Squadron at McGuire Air Force Base, New Jersey. In June 1953 he went to the 449th Fighter-Interceptor Squadron at Ladd Air Force Base, Fairbanks, Alaska, where he was elevated to the position of flight commander and flew F-94 and F-89 aircraft. In January 1956 he moved to the 437th Fighter-Interceptor Squadron, Oxnard Air Force Base, California, and was again assigned as a flight commander in F-89 aircraft. A year later he was selected as the first chief of the 27th Air Division Jet Instrument School, which he organized at Oxnard Air Force Base and commanded for two years.

In May 1959 he was assigned to the 329th Fighter-Interceptor Squadron, George Air Force Base, California, where he served successively as flight commander, weapons training officer, and assistant operations officer while flying F-102 and F-106 aircraft. He left the squadron in June 1962 to commence in-residence graduate study at George Washington University, Washington, D.C. Upon graduation in June 1963 with a masters of business administration in management, he was assigned to Headquarters, United States Air Forces, Europe (USAFE), Lindsey Air Station, Wiesbaden, Germany, Directorate of Management Analysis. During this tour he became chief of the Progress Analysis Division, which tracked the status of all major programs being implemented throughout USAFE.

In July 1966 General Clifford went to the Pentagon, where he served for 18 months in the Directorate of Aerospace Programs under the deputy chief of staff for programs and resources. In December 1967 he was selected to be a military assistant in the Directorate of Organizational and Management Planning, Office of the Assistant Secretary of Defense for Administration. He completed his Pentagon tour in July 1969 and entered the

Industrial College of the Armed Forces at Fort McNair, Washington, D.C. Upon graduation (with honors) in June 1970, he proceeded to George Air Force Base for F-4 training.

Upon completion, he went to Vietnam, where he served from March to November 1971 in the 366th Tactical Fighter Wing at Da Nang Air Base, first as deputy commander for operations, then as wing vice commander, flying in more than 90 combat missions. He was then sent directly from Vietnam to Germany to become the first commander of the 52nd Tactical Fighter Wing at Spangdahlem Air Base. General Clifford commanded the wing from December 1971 until July 1973 when he was transferred to Sembach Air Base, Germany, to become vice commander of the 17th Air Force.

In July 1974 he returned to the United States for duty as the United States Air Force director of inspection, Norton Air Force Base, California. This was followed in April 1976 by his assignment as commander of the 26th North American Air Defense Command, Region/Air Division, with headquarters at Luke Air Force Base, Arizona. In September 1978 he was assigned as deputy assistant secretary of defense for public affairs, with offices in the Pentagon. He assisted in the formulation of policies and directives covering public affairs and community relations throughout the Department of Defense (DOD).

His military decorations and awards include the Legion of Merit (two oak leaf clusters), Distinguished Flying Cross, Air Medal (four oak leaf clusters), Air Force Commendation Medal (one oak leaf cluster), Air Force Outstanding Unit Award, Republic of Vietnam Gallantry Cross (with palm).

He was appointed major general on January 18, 1977, with date of rank November 1, 1973.

Jerome Gary Cooper

★★ ——————————————— ★★

Major General

Born October 2, 1936, in Lafayette, Louisiana, he has three children: a son, Patrick, and two daughters, Joli and Shawn. He received a bachelor of science in finance from the University of Notre Dame. He has completed a special program for senior managers in government at the Harvard University School of Business.

He was commissioned upon graduation from Notre Dame as a second lieutenant in the United States Marine Corps in June 1958. Upon graduation from the Basic School, he reported for duty with the 1st Marine

Maj. Gen. Jerome Gary Cooper

Brigade. He served on active duty 12 years, commanding a number of units, including the Marine detachment aboard the guided missile cruiser *Chicago*.

While in Vietnam in 1967, he became the first black Marine Corps officer to lead an infantry company into combat. Upon release from active duty, he joined the Individual Ready Reserve in January 1970. He has commanded the 13th Force Reconnaissance Company and the 4th Battalion, 14th Marines Division. His distinction as the first black officer to command a Marine reserve unit is noted in the Marine Corps historical calendar. He was appointed major general on June 3, 1988, and returned to active duty to serve as director, Personnel Procurement Division, Headquarters, United States Marine Corps, Washington, D.C., from June to October 1988. He then transferred to the Standby Reserve.

In December 1989 he became assistant secretary of the Air Force for manpower, reserve affairs, installations, and environment. He is responsible for management and policy regarding all matters pertaining to the formulation, review, and execution of plans and programs related to manpower, military and civilian personnel, reserve and guard forces, installations, environment, safety and occupational health, medical care, and drug interdiction for the Air Force. While in a civilian capacity, he has twice received the highest award given by the secretary of the Navy for public service. He has been particularly noted for his work as a personal consultant to the Marine Corps commandmant in equal opportunity and human relations.

General Cooper, in Mobile, Alabama, was twice elected to the Alabama legislature and as commissioner of the Alabama Department of Human

Resources, and was a member of the governor's cabinet. He was vice president for marketing with David Volkert and Associates, an engineering and architectural firm with offices in six cities. He was recognized as Omega Psi Phi fraternity's Citizen of the Year in 1974, and was named Man of the Year by the Nonpartisan Voters League in 1977. In 1979 he was awarded the M. O. Beale Scroll of Merit for good citizenship in Mobile and was named Man of the Year by the Notre Dame Club of Mobile. He received the John J. Cavanaugh Award from the Alumni Association of the Notre Dame Club in 1987 and the Roy Wilkins Meritorious Service Award from the National Association for the Advancement of Colored People in 1989. His military decorations and awards include the Legion of Merit, Bronze Star Medal, two Purple Hearts, Republic of Vietnam Gallantry Cross (with palm), Silver Star, and Bronze Star.

John Sherman Cowings

★ ———————————————————— ★

Brigadier General

Born August 11, 1943, New York City. He received a bachelor of arts degree in civil government from New York University, a master's in business administration from Golden Gate University.

He entered the United States Army with a ROTC commission as second lieutenant in November 1965. From November 1965 to January 1966, he was a student in the Ordnance Office Basic Course, United States Army Ordnance School, Aberdeen Proving Ground, Maryland. From January 1966 to March 1967, he was a platoon leader in Company C, later Company D, 702nd Maintenance Battalion, 2nd Infantry Division, United States Army, Korea. From August 1967 to September 1968, he served as shop officer, later acting commander, Company C, and later commander, Company D, 701st Maintenance Battalion, in Vietnam. From October 1968 to September 1969, he was a student in the Ordnance Officer Advanced Course, United States Army Ordnance School, Aberdeen Proving Ground, Maryland.

He was promoted to captain on February 7, 1968. From September 1969 to April 1971, he was commander, Maintenance Company, General Support Group, Fort Ord, California. From April 1971 to May 1972, he served as a special assistant to the commanding general, United States Army Combat Development Experimentation Command, Fort Ord, California. From May 1972 to September 1975, he was a student at Golden Gate University in San Francisco. From September 1973 to June 1975, he served

Brig. Gen. John Sherman Cowings

as the historical officer, later student, United States Army Command and General Staff College, Fort Leavenworth, Kansas.

He was promoted to major on June 5, 1975. From June 1975 to June 1977, he served as a research and development coordinator at the United States Army Institute for the Behavioral and Social Sciences, Far East Field Unit, Korea. From June 1977 to September 1978, he served as a staff officer in the Manpower Coordination Branch, Allocation and Documents Division, Office of the Deputy Chief of Staff for Personnel, United States Army, Washington, D.C. From October 1978 to October 1979, he served as the executive officer, Office of Director of Manpower, Plans and Budget, Office of the Deputy Chief of Staff for Personnel, United States Army, Washington, D.C.

He was promoted to lieutenant colonel on August 12, 1979. From November 1979 to May 1982, he was commander, 708th Maintenance Battalion, 8th Infantry Division (Mechanized), United States Army, Europe. From June 1982 to June 1983, he served as a logistics staff officer and North Atlantic Treaty Organization team chief in the Office of the Deputy Chief of Staff for Logistics, United States Army, Washington, D.C. From June 1983 to June 1984, he was a student at the Industrial College of the Armed Forces, Fort Lesley J. McNair, Washington, D.C. From July 1984 to June 1986, he served as director, Maintenance Directorate, United States Army Munitions and Chemical Command, Rock Island, Illinois.

He was promoted to colonel on October 1, 1985. From June 1986 to June 1988, he served as the commander of the Rock Island Arsenal, Rock Island, Illinois. From July 1988 to September 1989, he served as chief of staff, Tank-Automotive Command, Warren, Michigan. He was promoted to brigadier general in October 1989, then assigned as the commanding general of the 3rd Support Command (Corps), United States Army, Europe, and Seventh Army. He has received numerous awards and decorations: the Legion of Merit (with oak leaf cluster), Army Commendation Medal (with two oak leaf clusters), Meritorious Service Medal (with six oak leaf clusters), Bronze Star Medal.

Eugene Rufus Cromartie

★★ ———————————————————— ★★

Major General

Born October 3, 1936, Wabasso, Florida. He received a bachelor of science degree in social science from Florida A&M University, a master of science degree in education, guidance, and counseling from the University of Dayton.

He received an ROTC commission to the rank of second lieutenant on June 3, 1957, was promoted to first lieutenant on January 14, 1959. On January 15, 1962, he was promoted to captain, on September 21, 1966, to major.

From June 1971 to November 1972, he served as chief, Elective Branch, Office of the Director of Graduated Studies and Research, United States Army Command and General Staff College, Fort Leavenworth, Kansas. He was promoted to lieutenant colonel on August 9, 1971. From December 1972 to July 1974, he was the commander of the 503rd Military Police Battalion, Fort Bragg, North Carolina. From July 1974 to June 1975, he was appointed provost marshal for the 82nd Airborne Division, Fort Bragg, North Carolina. From June 1975 to July 1976, he served as the personnel management officer, Assignments Branch, Lieutenant Colonels' Division, Officer Personnel Management Directorate, United States Army Military Personnel Center, Alexandria, Virginia. From August 1976 to June 1977, he was a student at the National War College, Fort Lesley J. McNair, Washington, D.C. From June 1977 to May 1978, he served as an special assistant to the commanding general, United States Army Criminal Investigation Command, Falls Church, Virginia.

He was promoted to colonel on August 5, 1977. From June 1978 to November 1979, he was commander, First Region, United States Army Criminal Investigation Command, Fort Meade, Maryland. From January 1980 to October 1983, he first served as the deputy provost marshal, later provost marshal, United States Army, Europe, and the Seventh Army.

He was promoted to brigadier general in April 1982. In November 1983

Maj. Gen. Eugene Rufus Cromartie

he was promoted to major general, then assigned as the commanding general of the United States Criminal Investigation Command, Falls Church, Virginia.

Awards and decorations: Bronze Star Medal (with oak leaf cluster), Meritorious Service Medal (with two oak leaf clusters), Army Commendation Medal (with oak leaf cluster), and Parachutist Badge.

Jerry Ralph Curry

★★ —————————————————— ★★

Major General

Born September 7, 1932, in McKeesport, Pennsylvania, he and his wife, Charlene, are the parents of four children: Charlein, Jerry, Toni, and Natasha.

He received a bachelor's degree in education from the University of Nebraska, Omaha, a master's degree in international relations from Boston University, and a doctorate from Luther Rice Seminary. He is a graduate of the United States Army War College and the Command and General Staff College, and a fellow in the Oxford Society of Scholars.

He began his military career in 1950 as a private during the Korean War. In 1952 he was commissioned a second lieutenant. He worked his way through the ranks and in 1984 retired as a major general. During his 34-year military career, General Curry gained experience in aviation, research and

Maj. Gen. Jerry Ralph Curry

development, management, international relations, and public affairs as a senior defense official in Europe, the Far East, and the United States.

He is a decorated combat veteran and pilot who served two tours of duty in Vietnam. His major Army assignments included deputy commanding general press secretary, Secretary of Defense; commanding general, United States Army Test and Evaluation Command and White Sands Missile Range. Following his retirement in 1984, General Curry became president and publisher of the National Perspectives Institute. He then became vice president of Systems Management America Corporation. In 1988, he unsuccessfully ran for the United States Congress from Virginia against an incumbent.

General Curry is a member of Delta Phi Alpha, the national honorary German society; Phi Alpha Theta, the international honor society in history; and the National Eagle Scout Association. His military honors include the Defense Distinguished Service Medal, Army Distinguished Service Medals, Legion of Merit (with oak leaf clusters), Meritorious Service Medals, Bronze Star (with "V" device), Cross of Gallantry (with palm) (Vietnam), Master Army Aviator Badge, Combat Infantryman Badge, Parachutist Badge, Ranger, Army Commendation Medals, Navy Commendation Medal, Navy Unit Commendation Ribbon, Air Medals, Queen Beatrix of the Netherlands Order of Orange-Nassau, and other decorations.

He has served on the boards of directors of the Greater Washington, D.C., Board of Trade and the American Red Cross and was a federal trustee of the Federal City Council. In 1982, Curry was honored by *Washingtonian* magazine as Washingtonian of the Year for his leadership in building better relations between the military and the Washington, D.C.

community. Maj. Gen. Jerry Ralph Curry retired from the United States Army in 1984.

Benjamin O. Davis, Jr.

★★★ ——————————————— ★★★

Lieutenant General

Born December 18, 1912, in Washington, D.C. His father was Brig. Gen. Benjamin O. Davis, Sr., United States Army, Retired; his mother, Sadie Overton Davis. He was graduated from Central High School, Cleveland, Ohio, in 1929, attended Western Reserve University at Cleveland and the University of Chicago. He entered the United States Military Academy in July 1932 and graduated in June 1936 with a commission as a second lieutenant of infantry.

In June 1937, after a year as commander of an infantry company at Fort Benning, Georgia, he entered the Infantry School there and a year later was graduated and assumed duties as professor of military science at Tuskegee Institute, Tuskegee, Alabama. In May 1941, he entered Advanced Flying School at nearby Tuskegee Army Air Base and received his wings in March 1942. Davis transferred to the Air Corps in May 1942. As commander of the 99th Fighter Squadron at Tuskegee Army Air Base, he moved with his unit to North Africa in April 1943 and later to Sicily.

He returned to the United States in October 1943, assumed command of the 332nd Fighter Group at Selfridge Field, Michigan, and returned to Italy with the group two months later. In 1945 he returned to the United States to command the 477th Composite Group at Godman Field, Kentucky, and later assumed command of the field. In March 1946, he went to Lockbourne Army Air Base, Ohio, as commander of the base, and in July 1947 he became the commander of the 332nd Fighter Wing there.

In 1949, Davis went to the Air War College, at Maxwell Air Force Base, Alabama. After graduation, he was assigned to the Deputy Chief of Staff Operations, Headquarters, United States Air Force, Washington, D.C. He served in various capacities with the headquarters until July 1953 when he went to the advanced jet fighter gunnery school at Nellis Air Force Base, Nevada.

In November 1953 he assumed duties as commander of the 51st Fighter Interceptor Wing, Far East Air Forces (FEAF), Korea. He served as director of operations and training at FEAF Headquarters, Tokyo, from 1954 until 1955 when he assumed the position of vice commander, Air Task Force 13 (Provisional), Taipei, Formosa. In April 1957, General Davis arrived at

Lt. Gen. Benjamin O. Davis, Jr.

Ramstein, Germany, as chief of staff, 12th Air Force. In December 1957, he assumed new duties as deputy chief of staff for operations, Headquarters, USAFE, Wiesbaden, Germany.

In July 1961 he returned to the United States and Headquarters, United States Air Force, where he served as the director of the manpower and organization, deputy chief of staff for programs and requirements. In February 1965 he was assigned as assistant deputy chief of staff, Programs and Requirements. He remained in that position until his assignment as chief of staff for the United Nations Command and United States Forces in Korea in April 1965. He assumed command of the 13th Air Force at Clark Air Base in the Philippines in August 1967. He was assigned as deputy commander in chief, United States Strike Command, with headquarters at MacDill Air Force Base, Florida. He had additional duty as commander in chief, Middle East, Southern Asia, and Africa.

He was the second black United States general and first black Air Force general. He was also the first black American to obtain the rank of lieutenant general. He retired from active duty February 1, 1970, and was appointed by the president of the United States to serve as assistant secretary, United States Department of Transportation. He also served as director of public safety for the city of Cleveland, Ohio.

Benjamin Oliver Davis, Sr.

★ ——————————————————— ★

Brigadier General

Born July 1, 1877, in Washington, D.C. He entered the military service on July 13, 1898 during the Spanish-American War as a temporary first lieutenant of the 8th United States Infantry. He was mustered out on March 6, 1899, and on June 14, 1899, he enlisted as a private in Troop I, 9th Cavalry, Regular Army. He then served as corporal and squadron sergeant major, and on February 2, 1901, he was commissioned a second lieutenant of cavalry in the Regular Army.

He was promoted to first lieutenant on March 30, 1905; captain on December 24, 1915; major (temporary) on August 5, 1917; and lieutenant colonel (temporary) on May 1, 1918. He reverted to his permanent rank of captain on October 14, 1919, and was promoted to lieutenant colonel on July 1, 1920; colonel on February 18, 1930. In the early part of 1931, he was assigned to duty as professor of military science and tactics at Tuskegee, Alabama, where he remained until August 1937 when he was transferred to Wilberforce University.

After a year at Wilberforce, he was assigned as instructor and commanding officer of the 369th Infantry, New York National Guard. He was promoted to brigadier general (temporary) on October 25, 1940. He retired on July 31, 1941, and was recalled to active duty in the rank of brigadier general the following day. He became the first black to be promoted to the

Brig. Gen. Benjamin Oliver Davis, Sr.

rank of general in the regular Army. He was assigned to the European theater of operations in September 1942 on special duty as adviser on Negro problems, and upon completion of this special duty he returned to the United States and was assigned to the Inspector General's office in Washington, D.C., in 1946.

On June 14, 1948 General Davis retired from active duty with over 50 years service at a White House ceremony hosted by President Harry S Truman. His military decorations and awards include the Distinguished Service Medal, Bronze Star Medal, French Croix de Guerre (with palm), and an honorary Ll.D. degree from Atlanta University. After his retirement, General Davis served as a member of the Citizens Advisory Committee to the District of Columbia Commissioners. He later moved to Chicago, Illinois, where he resided until his death at the age of 93 on November 26, 1970.

Russell C. Davis

★★ ——————————————————— ★★

Major General

Born on October 22, 1938, in Tuskegee, Alabama, he married the former Shirley A. Kimble of Aberdeen, Maryland. They have two children: Tyree and Pamela. He was graduated from Tuskegee Institute High School in 1956 and attended Tuskegee University from 1956 to 1958. He earned a bachelor of general education degree from the University of Nebraska at Omaha in 1963. He later attended graduate and law schools at Drake University, receiving his law degree (J.D.) in 1969. His military education includes Squadron Officer School, 1964; Air Command and Staff College, 1973; and Industrial College of the Armed Forces, 1979.

He began his military career when he joined the United States Air Force as an aviation cadet. Upon completion of undergraduate pilot training at Graham Air Base, Florida, and Vance Air Force Base, Oklahoma, he received his wings and was commissioned a second lieutenant in March 1960. His next assignment was at Lincoln Air Force Base, Nebraska, where he served until his release from active duty in April 1965.

In 1965 he joined the Iowa Air National Guard in Des Moines, Iowa, serving in numerous positions of increased authority and responsibility, ranging from squadron pilot to director of operations, State Headquarters, until 1979. After graduating from the Industrial College of the Armed Forces in June 1979, he remained on active duty as the deputy chief, Manpower and Personnel Division, for the Air National Guard Readiness

Maj. Gen. Russell C. Davis

Center at Andrews Air Force Base, Maryland. In February 1980 the general became the executive officer to the chief of the National Guard Bureau, Pentagon, Washington, D.C. Following this assignment, he joined the District of Columbia Air National Guard in January 1982 and assumed duties as wing commander in February 1982. He became air commander, his civil service position, one month late.

He served in both positions, wing and air commander, until July 1990. He then served as the Air National Guard assistant to the commander, Tactical Air Command, until December 1991 when he assumed the position of commanding general, District of Columbia National Guard, Washington, D.C. He was appointed to major general on August 3, 1990.

The general is a command pilot with more than 4,700 flying hours in B-47, T-33, F-89, F-84, F-100, A-7, F-4, and F-16 aircraft. His awards and decorations include the Legion of Merit (one oak leaf cluster), Air Force Meritorious Service Medal (one oak leaf cluster), Air Force Commendation Medal (one oak leaf cluster), Army Commendation Medal, Air Force Outstanding Unit Award Ribbon (four oak leaf clusters), Combat Readiness Medal, National Defense Service Medal (with star), Air Force Longevity Service Award Medal (with one silver and two bronze oak leaf clusters), Armed Forces Reserve Medal (with two hourglass devices), Air Force Training Ribbon, and the Small Arms Expert Marksmanship Ribbon. In addition, he wears a number of District of Columbia and Iowa National Guard awards, including the Distinguished Service Medal (one oak leaf cluster), Meritorious Service Medal, Community Service Ribbon (with two stars), Outstanding Unit Award, and the Iowa National Guard Longevity Service Ribbon (two oak leaf clusters).

Walter Jackson Davis, Jr.

★★ ─────────────────── ★★

Rear Admiral

Born on August 1, 1936, in Winston-Salem, North Carolina, he married the former Constance P. Surles of Pensacola, Florida, and they have two daughters, Sharon P. Davis Clayton and Kimberly D. Davis. He received a bachelor of science degree in electrical engineering from Ohio State University in 1959, a master's of science in aeroelectronics from the Naval Post Graduate School, Monterey, in 1967.

On August 1, 1959, he was commissioned an ensign in the United States Naval Reserve. From August 1959 to December 1960, he was a student at NABTC, NAS, Pensacola, Florida. From June 1960 to December 1960, he was a student at NAAS, Kingsville, Texas. He was promoted to the rank of lieutenant (junior grade), on December 3, 1960. On December 19, 1960, he was designated naval aviator (HTA).

From December 1960 to October 1961, he was assigned to the Fighter Squadron 121 (DUINS). From October 1961 to March 1962, he was assigned to the Fighter Squadron 53. From March 1962 to July 1964, he was assigned to Fighter Squadron 143. From July 1964 to June 1967, he was a student at the Naval Postgraduate School, Monterey. From June 1967 to May 1970, he was first assigned to the Fighter Squadron 121 (DUINS), later as assistant operation officer, maintenance officer, Fighter Squadron 143.

He was promoted to the grade of lieutenant commander on May 1, 1968. From May 1970 to February 1971, he attended the Naval Test Pilot School, NATC Patuxent River (project officer). From February 1971 to July 1973, he was appointed project officer, Weapons Systems Test Division, NATC Patuxent River. From July 1973 to July 1974, he was a student at the Naval War College (DUINS).

He was promoted to the grade of commander on July 1, 1973. From July 1974 to May 1977, he was assigned to Fighter Squadron 121 (DUINS), then as deputy commander of Fighter Squadron 114, later as commander of Fighter Squadron 114. From May 1977 to February 1979, he was appointed assistant project manager for the F-14s at the Naval Air Systems Command Headquarters. From February 1979 to June 1979, he was a student at the Surface Warfare Officer's School Command in Newport (DUINS). From June 1979 to December 1980, he was assigned as the deputy commander of the USS *Kitty Hawk* (CV-63).

He was promoted to captain on July 1, 1980. From December 1980 to May 1981, he was chief of Naval Personnel (DUINS). From May 1981 to December 1981, he served as staff, COMNAVSURFPAC (DUINS). In May 1981 he was the commander of USS *Sacramento* (AOE-1).

Rear Adm. Walter Jackson Davis, Jr.

From August 1984 to June 1985, he was a student at the Industrial College of the Armed Forces (DUINS). From June 1985 to May 1987, he was the commander of the USS *Ranger* (CV-61). On August 1988 he was appointed commandant of the Naval District in Washington. He was promoted to rear admiral (lower half) on December 1, 1988.

He has received numerous awards and medals: the Legion of Merit, Meritorious Service Medal, Air Medal (with numeral 10), Navy Commendation Medal (with combat V), Sea Service Deployment Ribbon (with one bronze star), Vietnam Service Medal (with one silver and one bronze star).

Frederic Ellis Davison

★★ ————————————————— ★★

Major General

Born September 28, 1917, the son of Albert Charles Davison and Sue (Bright) Davison, he married the former Jean E. Brown, and they have four children: Jean M., Andrea S., Dayle A., and Carla M. He is a native of Washington, D.C., and attended the all-black Dunbar High School there, earning membership in the National Honor Society. After graduating from Dunbar, in 1934 he entered Howard University where he starred in track. He received a bachelor of science degree from Howard University, cum laude, in 1938 and his master of science degree there two years later.

Having completed ROTC training, he was commissioned a lieutenant in

Maj. Gen. Frederic Ellis Davison

the United States Army Reserve in 1939. He was ordered to active duty in 1941, a few months before America entered World War II. During the war, as a captain, he led the all-black B Company, 371st Infantry, 92nd Division, in fighting from Sicily through Italy. Between 1947, when he was training an ROTC unit at South Carolina Agricultural and Mechanical College, and the early 1950s, when he was a battalion operations officer in Germany, the United States Army gradually rid itself of segregation.

In 1954, Davison entered the Command and General Staff College at Fort Leavenworth, Kansas. In 1957, after a stint as a personnel management officer in Washington, he was promoted to lieutenant colonel, and in 1959 was sent to Korea as chief of personnel services with the Eighth Army. Back in the United States, he enrolled at the Army War College in 1962–1963 and received a master of arts degree in international affairs at George Washington University in 1963. During the following two years, he was in charge of manpower and reserve matters at the Pentagon. From 1965 to 1967 he commanded the 3rd Training Brigade at Fort Bliss, Texas.

At his request, Davison was sent to Vietnam in November 1967 as deputy commander of the 199th Light Infantry Brigade, which was deployed in the defense perimeter around Saigon. When the North Vietnamese and National Liberation Front demonstrated their military and popular power in the astounding Tet offensive of February 1968, the brigade's commander was absent. Davison led the defense of the base at Long Binh in such close rapport with the men under him that they continued to treat him as their de facto leader, even after their commander returned.

In August 1968 Davison, then a full colonel, was made brigade commander, and the following month General Creighton W. Abrams, the United States commander in South Vietnam, pinned the silver stars of a brigadier general on his collar in a promotion ceremony at Binh Chanh. From September 1971 to May 1972, he was deputy chief of staff for United States Army personnel in Europe. Meanwhile, in April 1971, he had been promoted to the rank of major general. Davison returned to his native city to take command of the Military District of Washington on November 12, 1973. He retired in 1974.

General Davison's military awards and decorations include the Distinguished Service Medal, Legion of Merit (with oak leaf cluster), Bronze Star Medal, Air Medal (nine awards), Army Commendation Medal (with two oak leaf clusters), Combat Infantryman Badge (two awards).

Arthur Truman Dean

★ ───────────────────────── ★

Brigadier General

Born January 6, 1946, Wadesboro, North Carolina. He received a bachelor of arts degree from Morgan State University in 1967 and he earned a master of arts degree from Central Michigan University in 1977. His military schooling includes the Field Artillery Officer Basic Course (1968); Adjutant General Officer Advanced Course (1971); United States Army Command and General Staff College (1976); United States Army War College (1986).

General Dean has held a wide variety of important command and staff positions. He began his military career in August 1967 as a student in the Field Artillery Basic Course at the United States Army Artillery and Missile School, Fort Sill, Oklahoma. From January 1968 to March 1968, he was a student in the Ranger Course, United States Army Infantry School, Fort Benning, Georgia. From March 1968 to December 1969, he served first as a forward observer, Battery A, 320th Artillery, 82nd Airborne Division, then as assistant personnel management officer, Adjutant General Section, 82nd Airborne Division, Fort Bragg, North Carolina.

From December 1969 to February 1971 he served as chief, Administrative Services Branch, later chief, Classified Control, Publications Supply and Records Branch, United States Military Assistance Command, Vietnam. He returned to the United States after he was selected to attend the Adjutant General Advanced Course at the United States Army Adjutant General School, Fort Benjamin Harrison, Indiana. After he completed that course, he remained at Fort Benjamin Harrison as an instructor for the

Communicative Arts Division of the United States Army Adjutant General School from October 1971 to January 1973.

His next assignment in January 1973 was also at Fort Benjamin Harrison in Indiana. He served as the commander of Company B, United States Army Administration Center and Fort Benjamin Harrison, until October 1973. In the eighties General Dean was military assistant, Office of the Assistant Secretary of the Army; assistant chief of staff, personnel, 1st Corps Support Command; commander, 18th Personnel and Administration Battalion; commander, Task Force Victory, 1st Corps Support Command, XVIII Airborne Corps, Fort Bragg, North Carolina; adjutant general, V Corps, United States Army, Europe, and Seventh Army; commander, United States Army Postal Group, 1st Personnel Command, Europe; commander, United States Army 1st Recruiting Brigade, Fort Meade, Maryland; assistant to the commanding general, Postal Operations for Desert Storm, Saudi Arabia, from February 1991 to April 1991.

He was appointed to brigadier general in April 1992. His military awards and decorations include the Legion of Merit (one oak leaf cluster), Bronze Star Medal, Meritorious Service Medal (four oak leaf clusters); Joint Service Commendation Medal, Army Commendation Medal (two oak leaf clusters), Army Achievement Medal (one oak leaf cluster), Senior Parachutist Badge, Ranger Tab, Army Staff Identification Badge.

Donald J. Delandro

★ ─────────────────────────── ★

Brigadier General

Born July 20, 1935, New Orleans, Louisiana. He received a B.S. degree from Southern University in 1956 and earned an M.B.A. in 1966 from the University of Chicago. General Delandro completed the Command and General Staff College in 1971 and the United States Army War College in 1974.

His military career highlights: from 1957 to 1958, platoon leader, 3rd Brigade, and United States Army Training Center, Fort Ord, California; from 1959 to 1962, AG administrative officer, G-1, Headquarters, Fifth United States Army, USARAL; from 1963 to 1967, first administrative officer, G-1, Headquarters, Fifth United States Army, then action officer, G-1, Headquarters, Fifth Army, Chicago, Illinois.

His next assignment was G-1 adviser for the 1st Imperial Iranian Army in Iran from 1967 to 1968. From there he was reassigned as chief, Msg. Con. Branch, NMCC/MCO, Joint Chiefs of Staff, Washington, D.C., 1968

Brig. Gen. Donald J. Delandro

to 1970. He served next as the AG for the 23rd Infantry Division, United States Army, Vietnam. In 1972 he returned to the United States and was the executive officer, WSA, Office of the Assistant Vice Chief of Staff of the Army, Washington, D.C. In 1973 he served as the administrative executive, Office of the Deputy Chief of Staff Officer Personnel Section, Department of the Army, Washington, D.C.

From 1974 to 1975, General Delandro served as chief, Enlisted Distribution, Enlisted Personnel Management Directorate, United States Army Military Personnel Center. His military awards and decorations include the Legion of Merit, Bronze Star Medal, Air Medal, Joint Service Commendation Medal, Army Commendation Medal (with oak leaf cluster), Meritorious Service Medal. He was appointed brigadier general in 1974 and retired on September 30, 1985.

Oliver Williams Dillard

★★ ——————————————— ★★

Major General

Born September 28, 1926, Margaret, Alabama. He and his wife, Helen, have four children: Oliver, Jr., Stephen, Diane, and Dennis. He received a B.G.E. degree from the University of Omaha, an M.S. degree in international affairs from George Washington University.

He has held a wide variety of important command and staff positions, which include the following assignments from his last ten years of service: from August 1963 to August 1964, chief, Europe, Africa, and Middle East Section, later chief, Foreign Intelligence Assistance Section, Special Warfare and Foreign Assistance Branch, Combat Intelligence Development Division, Assistant Chief of Staff for Intelligence, United States Army, Washington, D.C.; from August 1964 to June 1965, student, National War College, Washington, D.C. After completion of the War College, he was assigned as operations and training staff officer, Special Studies Division, later operation training staff officer, Analysis Division, and later chief, Analysis/Coordination Branch, Study Division 3, Special Studies Directorate, United States Army Combat Developments Command Institute of Special Studies, Fort Belvoir, Virginia, from July 1965 to January 1967.

In January 1967 he was assigned as the commanding officer of the 5th Combat Support Training Brigade, Fort Dix, New Jersey. From December 1968 to July 1969, he was a student at the Vietnam Training Center, Foreign Service Institute, Department of State, in Washington, D.C. From July 1969 to June 1971, he was senior military adviser, Advisory Team 41, Military Region II, United States Military Assistance Command, Vietnam. General Dillard returned to the United States in July 1971 and was assigned as the deputy assistant chief of staff for intelligence, United States Army, in Washington, D.C. In February 1973 he returned to Vietnam and served as director of intelligence, United States Military Assistance Command. From May 1973 to June 1973, he served as special assistant to the commanding general, Continental Army Command, Fort McPherson, Georgia. In July 1973 he was first assigned as deputy chief of staff, intelligence, the United States Army Forces Command, Fort McPherson, then deputy chief of staff, intelligence, United States Army, Heidelberg, Germany.

He retired on January 31, 1980. General Dillard's awards and decorations include the Purple Heart, Distinguished Service Medal, Legion of Merit (with two oak leaf clusters), Bronze Star Medal (with oak leaf cluster), Air Medal, Army Commendation Medal (with oak leaf cluster), Combat Infantryman Badge, Silver Star.

Henry Doctor, Jr.

★★★ ─────────────────────────── ★★★

Lieutenant General

Born on August 23, 1932, in Oakly, South Carolina, he married the former Janie M. Manigault (Jane). They have three children: Lori, Kenneth, and Cheryl. Upon completion of the Reserve Officers Training Corps

Lt. Gen. Henry Doctor, Jr.

curriculum and the educational course of study at South Carolina State College, he was commissioned a second lieutenant and awarded a bachelor of science degree in agriculture in 1954. He also earned a master of arts degree in counseling and psychological services from Georgia State University. His military education includes completion of the Infantry School, the United States Army Command and General Staff College, and the United States Army War College.

General Doctor has held a wide variety of important command and staff positions, including commander of the 1st Brigade, 25th Infantry Division, Schofield Barracks, Hawaii; assistant division commander, 24th Infantry Division (Mechanized), Fort Stewart, Georgia. He was assigned as the director of personnel training and force development, later chief of staff, United States Army Materiel Command, Alexandria, Virginia. He served as commanding general of the 2nd Infantry Division with the Eighth United States Army, Korea.

General Doctor served in a wide variety of important career-building assignments preparatory to his most recent duties. He was executive officer of the 1st Battalion, 4th Infantry Division, and later served as the assistant G-3 (operations and training), 4th Infantry Division, in Vietnam. Upon his return to the United States, General Doctor served as the personnel management officer and later chief, Personnel Actions Section, Infantry Branch, Office of Personnel Operations, Washington, D.C. General Doctor commanded the 1st Battalion, 29th Infantry, with a follow-on assignment as deputy brigade commander, 197th Infantry Brigade, Fort Benning, Georgia.

General Doctor remained at Fort Benning to serve as chief, Modern

Volunteer Army Control Group, United States Army Infantry Center. Following his studies at Georgia State University and the United States Army War College, General Doctor served as the director of psychometrics at the United States Army War College. His last assignment was deputy inspector general for investigations, assistance, training, and information management. His military awards and decorations include the Legion of Merit, Bronze Star Medal, Meritorious Service Medal, Air Medal, Army Commendation Medal (with three oak leaf clusters). He is also authorized to wear the Combat Infantryman Badge.

Alonzo D. Dougherty, Jr.

★ ———————————————— ★

Brigadier General

Born July 19, 1926, Leavenworth, Kansas. He and his wife, Ellen, are the proud parents of six children (four boys, two girls). He entered the military service on May 12, 1955, at Leavenworth, Kansas, when he enlisted in Company A, 174th Military Police Battalion, Kansas Army National Guard. By February 1959, he had advanced to the rank of sergeant when his unit was reorganized as infantry.

On June 18, 1962, he was commissioned a second lieutenant in the infantry with Company A, 2nd Battalion, 137th Infantry, Leavenworth, Kansas. Lieutenant Dougherty continued his career serving as a platoon leader and executive officer. On February 8, 1968, he was promoted to captain and assigned as company commander, headquarters, Headquarters Company, 2nd Battalion, 137th Infantry, 69th Infantry Brigade. In May 1968 Captain Dougherty was ordered to extended active duty and reported with his command to Fort Carson, Colorado. It was in November of the same year that Captain Dougherty reported as an individual replacement to the South Vietnam. He was assigned to the 3rd Battalion, 7th Infantry, 199th Infantry Brigade, where he commanded Company D and later served as S-3, air, for the same battalion.

Following his tour in Vietnam, Captain Dougherty returned to the Kansas Army National Guard and the 69th Infantry Brigade, serving in various assignments, including company commander, battalion and brigade staff officer. He was promoted to major in May 1973, and in January 1974 he left the 69th Infantry Brigade to serve on the state headquarters staff as equal employment opportunity officer, later as the assistant G-3.

He was promoted to lieutenant colonel in May 1977 while continuing in his assignment as assistant G-3. In December 1979, Lieutenant Colonel

Brig. Gen. Alonzo D. Dougherty, Jr.

Dougherty became commander of the 2nd Battalion, 137th Infantry, and served in that assignment until December 1981. Lieutenant Colonel Dougherty was promoted to full colonel in December 1981 and assigned as the assistant G-3 in STARC headquarters until September 19, 1983. On September 19, 1983, Colonel Dougherty assumed the duties of deputy brigade commander for the 69th Infantry Brigade (Mechanized) and assumed command of the 69th Infantry Brigade on November 19, 1984. His military awards include the Bronze Star Medal (two oak leaf clusters), Air Medal (two oak leaf clusters), Army Commendation Medal, National Defense Service Medal, Vietnamese Campaign Medal, Combat Infantryman's Badge.

Louis Duckett

★★ ———————————————— ★★

Major General

Born January 1, 1929, a native of Chicago, Illinois. He was graduated from the City College of New York. He entered the NYNG on June 23, 1948 as a Private. General Duckett has served in a variety of important career building assignments preparatory to his last assignment. He served as the executive officer for the Battery C, 879th AAA Gun Battalion. In November 1967 he was assigned as group operations and training officer for the 187th Artillery Group. Duckett became commander of the 369th Transportation Battalion. He was appointed to the one star rank of brigadier general in the New York Army National Guard March 13, 1979. He was promoted to the rank of Major General July 16, 1984.

Maj. Gen. Louis Duckett

Archer L. Durham

★★ ──────────────── ★★

Major General

Born June 9, 1932, in Pasadena, California, he married the former Sue M. Harrison of Los Angeles. They have four children: Debra, Beverly, David, and Steven. He graduated from Utah State University with a bachelor of science degree in political science in 1960 and earned a master of science degree in international affairs from George Washington University in 1975. He completed Squadron Officer School in 1960, Air Command and Staff College in 1961, Industrial College of the Armed Forces in 1973, National War College as a distinguished graduate in 1975, the advanced management program at Columbia University, and the program for senior executives in national and international security at the John F. Kennedy School of Government, Harvard University.

He began his military career in January 1953, as an aviation cadet and in April 1954 received his commission and wings at Laredo Air Force Base, Texas. In August 1954 he was assigned as a pilot with the 744th Troop Carrier Squadron, Charleston Air Force Base, South Carolina, and in October 1955 he transferred with the squadron to Kadena Air Base, Okinawa. From June 1956 to June 1958, the general was assigned to the 2720th Maintenance Group, an Air Force logistic command unit, at Clark Air Base in the Philippines as a flight test maintenance officer.

Maj. Gen. Archer L. Durham

He then served with the 28th Logistics Support Squadron, Hill Air Force Base, Utah, as an aircraft commander and squadron plans and mobility officer (the squadron was redesignated as the 28th Air Transport Squadron and assigned to the Military Airlift Command in 1962). In August 1963 General Durham transferred to the 1622nd Support Squadron, Paris, France, where he performed duties as an airlift command post controller until the squadron was disestablished in June 1964. From July 1964 through September 1966, he was assigned to the 322nd Air Division, Chateauroux Air Station, France, as a plans officer in the Directorate of Plans and Programs.

Returning to the United States in October 1966, he served at Headquarters, Military Airlift Command, Scott Air Force Base, Illinois, then chief, Advanced Programming and Policy Division, Office of the Deputy Chief of Staff for Plans, until December 1968. General Durham was assigned to Headquarters, United States Air Force, Washington, D.C., in the Directorate of Plans, Office of the Deputy Chief of Staff for Plans and Operations, in January 1969. During this tour of duty, he served as a plans action officer and assistant deputy director for plans and policy for Joint Chiefs of Staff matters.

From June 1973 to June 1974, he was assigned to the 314th Air Division, Osan Air Base, South Korea, as director of plans and programs for United States Air Forces, Korea. He then returned to the United States to attend the National War College. General Durham transferred to McGuire Air Force Base, New Jersey, in August 1975, as deputy base commander and became base commander in February 1976. He commanded the 1606th Air Base Wing, Kirtland Air Force Base, New Mexico, from July 1977 to

February 1979 when he transferred to Dover Air Force Base, Delaware, as commander of the 436th Military Airlift Wing, the only all-C-5 wing in the Air Force.

In February 1980 the general assumed command of the 76th Military Airlift Division, Andrews Air Force Base, Maryland. In February 1982 he was assigned as vice commander, Military Traffic Management Command, Washington, D.C. General Durham became the director of plans, programs, and policy (J-5) and inspector general, United States Readiness Command, MacDill Air Force Base, in March 1984. He was assigned as director of deployment, Joint Deployment Agency, MacDill, in April 1985. In June 1987 he was assigned as director of deployment, United States Transportation Command, MacDill Air Force Base, Florida. He was appointed to major general on June 1, 1984, with a date of rank September 1, 1980.

The general is a command pilot with more than 6,000 flying hours. His military decorations and awards include the Defense Superior Service Medal, Legion of Merit (two oak leaf clusters), Meritorious Service Medal (one oak leaf cluster), Air Force Commendation Medal (one oak leaf cluster), Air Force Outstanding Unit Award (three oak leaf clusters).

Samuel Emanuel Ebbesen

★★★ ——————————————— ★★★

Lieutenant General

Born September 15, 1938, Saint Croix, Virgin Islands. He received a bachelor of science in political science from the City College of New York. He received a master's in public administration from Auburn University.

Ebbesen enlisted in the Army in September 1961, and until March 1962, he was a platoon leader in Company D, 1st Training Regiment, Fort Dix, New Jersey. He went on to serve the Army in numerous assignments. In March 1963 he was the commander of Company F, 1st Training Regiment, Fort Dix, New Jersey; in July 1965, commander of Headquarters Company, 1st Battalion, 15th Infantry, 3rd Infantry Division, United States Army, Europe; in 1969, headquarters commandant, 4th Infantry Division, United States Army, Vietnam; in August 1971, student, Command and General Staff College, Fort Leavenworth, Kansas; in July 1977, commander, 2nd Battalion, 32nd Infantry, 7th Infantry Division, Fort Ord, California; in May 1983, commander, 1st Brigade, 101st Airborne Division (Air Assault), Fort Campbell, Kentucky.

By April 1990, he had been promoted to major general and assigned as

Lt. Gen. Samuel Emanuel Ebbesen

the commanding general of the 6th Infantry Division (Light), Fort Wainwright, Alaska. He has received numerous medals and badges: the Legion of Merit (with three oak leaf clusters), Bronze Star medal (with "V" device), Air Medal, Combat Infantryman Badge, Parachutist Badge, Air Assault Badge.

Albert J. Edmonds

★★ ———————————————— ★★

Major General

Born January 17, 1942, in Columbus, Georgia, he married the former Jacquelyn Y. McDaniel of Biloxi, Mississippi. They have three daughters: Gia, Sheri, and Alicia. He was graduated from Spencer High School in Columbus in 1960, earned a bachelor of science degree in chemistry from Morris Brown College in Atlanta in 1964 and received a master of arts degree in counseling psychology from Hampton Institute in 1969. He was graduated from Air War College as a distinguished graduate in 1980 and completed the National Security program for senior officials at Harvard University in 1987.

He entered the Air Force in August 1964 and was commissioned upon graduation from Officer Training School, Lackland Air Force Base, Texas, in November 1964. After completing the basic communications-electronics course at Keesler Air Force Base, Mississippi, in February 1966, Edmonds

Maj. Gen. Albert J. Edmonds

was assigned as a data systems officer to Tactical Communications Area, Langley Air Force Base, Virginia. In February 1969, he was assigned to Pacific Communications Area, Hickam Air Force Base, Hawaii. While there, he served successively as an inspection team chief, Office of the Inspector General, contributing editor, Project Corona Harvest, and director of emergency mission support.

He later served as chief of operations, 2083rd Communications Squadron (Provisional), Takhli Royal Thai Air Force Base, Thailand. He was assigned to Air Force Headquarters in May 1973 as an action officer, Directorate of Command, Control, and Communications, responsible for managing air communications programs in the continental United States, Alaska, Canada, South America, Greenland, and Iceland.

In June 1975 the general was assigned to the Defense Communications Agency and headed the Commercial Communications Policy Office, responsible for establishing Department of Defense policies for the acquisition of long-line communications and overseeing the procurement activities of the Defense Commercial Communications Office. Edmonds was assigned to Anderson Air Force Base, Guam, in 1977, as director of communications-electronics for Strategic Air Command's 3rd Air Division and as commander of the 27th Communications Squadron.

After completing Air War College in June 1980, he returned to Air Force headquarters as chief, Joint Matters Group, Directorate of Command, Control and Telecommunications, Office of the Deputy Chief of Staff, Plans and Operations. From June 1, 1983, to June 14, 1983, he served as director of plans and programs for the assistant chief of staff for information systems. He was assigned to Headquarters, Tactical Air Command,

Langley Air Force Base, as assistant deputy chief of staff communications and electronics and vice commander, Tactical Communications Division. In January 1985, he became deputy chief of staff, Communications-Computer Systems, Tactical Air Command, Headquarters, and commander, Tactical Communications Division, Air Force Communications Command, Langley. In July 1988 he became director of command and control, Communications and Computer Systems Directorate, United States Center Command, MacDill Air Force Base, Florida.

He was promoted brigadier general on July 1, 1988, with same date of rank. In May 1989 he assumed the command responsibility for United States military and security interests in a 19-country area in the Persian Gulf, Horn of Africa, and southwest Asia. His military decorations and awards include the Defense Distinguished Service Medal, Legion of Merit, Meritorious Service Medal (with two oak clusters), Air Force Commendation Medal (with three oak leaf clusters).

He was promoted to major general on February 1, 1991, with same date of rank. In September 1991 he was assigned as vice director, Command, Control, Communications, and Computer Systems Directorate (J-6), and deputy director, Defense-Wide C-4 Support, Joint Staff, Washington, D.C. He was responsible for establishing C-4 systems policy throughout the Department of Defense.

Larry Rudell Ellis

★ ———————————————— ★

Brigadier General

Born June 30, 1946, in Cambridge, Maryland. He received a B.S. degree in physical education from Morgan State University in 1969. He earned an M.S. degree in physical education from Indiana University in 1975. His military education includes: the Infantry Officer Basic (1969) and Advanced (1974) courses; Armed Forces Staff College (1979); and the United States Army War College (1986).

His military career began in February 1969 as a student in the Infantry Officer Basic Course at Fort Benning, Georgia as a second lieutenant. He has held a wide variety of important command and staff positions. He was assistant secretary of the General Staff with the Command Group in Europe and the Seventh Army (May 1980–May 1981). From May 1981 to June 1982, he was assigned as executive officer for the 2nd Battalion of the 13th Infantry (Mechanized) with the 8th Infantry Division. From June 1982 to May 1983, he served as the executive officer for the Devil Troop Bridge at Fort

Polk, Louisiana. From May 1983 to August 1985, he was assigned as the commander of the 3rd Battalion of the 6th and 5th Infantry Divisions (Mechanized) at Fort Polk, Louisiana.

He was a student in the Army War College from August 1985 to June 1986. In June 1986, he was assigned as a manpower analyst, at the Program Analysis and Evaluation Division in the Office of the Chief of Staff, United States Army in Washington, D.C. In May 1987, he served as the chief of the Manpower and Force Analysis Division, Washington, D.C. In September 1988, he was assigned as the commander of the 1st Brigade of the 3rd Infantry Division with the United States Army in Europe and the Seventh Army. In October 1990, he was assigned as the deputy director of the Military Personnel Management in the Office of the Deputy Chief of Staff for Personnel in Washington, D.C.

In July 1992, Larry Rudell Ellis was promoted to the one star rank of brigadier general. His awards and decorations include the Legion of Merit (with oak leaf cluster), Bronze Star Medal, Meritorious Service Medal (with two oak leaf clusters), Air Medal, Army Commendation Medal (with oak leaf cluster), Combat Infantryman Badge, Senior Parachutist Badge, Army Staff Identification Badge.

Alonzo L. Ferguson

★ ———————————————————— ★

Brigadier General

Born January 10, 1931, in Washington, D.C., he married the former Frances Thorne of Washington, D.C. They have four daughters: Theresa, twins Pamela and Cynthia, and Lisa. He was graduated from Dunbar High School in 1947 and from Howard University in June 1952 with a bachelor of science degree in psychology. He was commissioned a second lieutenant in the United States Air Force through the ROTC program and is a graduate of the Armed Forces Staff College at Norfolk, Virginia.

He began active duty in July 1952. After completion of flight and jet fighter training, he served in Korea as a T-6 Mosquito forward air controller from July 1954 to June 1955. He was then assigned to the 4520th Combat Crew Training Wing at Nellis Air Force Base, Nevada, where he instructed in T-33s, F-86s and F-100s. From June 1961 through September 1964, he served at Wheelus Air Base, Libya, as an F-105 weapons instructor. He also acted as liaison officer for the 36th Tactical Fighter Wing, Bitburg Air Base, Germany, which conducted weapons qualification training at Wheelus.

Brig. Gen. Alonzo L. Ferguson

Following this assignment, he returned to Nellis as an F-105 instructor pilot and operations officer for the 4523rd Combat Crew Training Squadron. In August 1966 General Ferguson entered the Armed Forces Staff College. In April 1967 he was assigned to Takhli Royal Thai Air Force Base, Thailand. He flew 103 combat missions with the 355th Tactical Fighter Wing in F-105s over North Vietnam. General Ferguson returned to South Korea in February 1974 and served until February 1975 at Osan Air Base as vice commander and commander of the 51st Air Base Wing and commander, 51st Combat Support Group, 51st Composite Wing (Tactical).

He was named vice commander of the 355th Tactical Fighter Wing, Davis-Monthan Air Force Base, Arizona, in March 1975 and took command of the wing in February 1976. He became deputy director, J-3, National Military Command Center, Joint Staff, Organization of the Joint Chiefs of Staff, in August 1977. General Ferguson was appointed deputy director for readiness development, Directorate of Operations and Readiness, under the deputy chief of staff for operations and plans, Headquarters, United States Air Force, in September 1978. In June 1979 he assumed command of the 21st North American Air Defense Command Region, Hancock Field, New York. He also served as commander, 21st Aerospace Defense Command Region, and commander, 21st Air Division, the air defense component of the Tactical Air Command.

He was responsible for air defense operations in the northern United States and portions of Canada. A command pilot, General Ferguson's military decorations and awards include the Silver Star (one oak leaf cluster), Legion of Merit, Defense Meritorious Service Medal (one oak leaf cluster), Air Medal (three oak leaf clusters), Air Force Commendation

Medal (one oak leaf cluster). He is a member of the Daedalians, the Air Force Association, and the Red River Valley Fighter Pilots Association. He was appointed to brigadier general August 1, 1977, with date of rank July 28, 1977.

Johnnie Forte, Jr.

★ ———————————————— ★

Brigadier General

Born December 20, 1936, in New Boston, Texas, he married the former Delores B. Bowles Johnson (Dee). They have three children: Denise M., Mitchell C. Johnson, and Shermaine L. Johnson. Upon completion of the Reserve Officers Training Corps curriculum and the educational course of study at Prairie View A&M University, he was commissioned a second lieutenant and awarded a bachelor of science degree in political science. He also holds a master of science degree in public administration from Auburn University. His military education includes completion of the Field Artillery School, the Air Defense Artillery School, the United States Army Command and General Staff College, and the Air War College.

His key assignments include deputy commanding general, 32nd Army Air Defense Command, United States Army, Europe; commander, 108th Air Defense Command, United States Army, Europe; director of personnel, J-1, Inspector General, United States European Command. He served as director of personnel, plans and systems, Office of the Deputy Chief of

Brig. Gen. Johnnie Forte, Jr.

90   *Johnnie Forte, Jr.*

Staff for Personnel, Washington, D.C., and he served as assistant division commander of the 8th Infantry Division (Mechanized), United States Army, Europe.

General Forte served in a variety of important career-building assignments preparatory to his most recent duties. In Vietnam he commanded the 41st Civil Affairs Company, 1st Field Force, and subsequently became the assistant inspector general of the 1st Field Force. He returned from overseas as personnel management officer in the Air Defense Artillery Branch, Officer Personnel Directorate, Office Personnel Operations, Washington, D.C. He commanded the 4th Battalion, 61st Air Defense Artillery, 4th Infantry Division (Mechanized), Fort Carson, Colorado. After completing the Air War College at Maxwell Air Force Base, Alabama, he returned to the European theatre to serve as the liaison officer to the United States Air Force, Europe, United States Army, Europe, Liaison Group, Germany. His military awards and decorations include the Defense Superior Service Medal, Legion of Merit (with oak leaf cluster), Meritorious Service Medal, Army Commendation Medal (with two oak leaf clusters), Air Force Commendation Medal, Aircraft Crewman Badge, Army General Staff Identification Badge.

Calvin G. Franklin

★★ ——————————————————— ★★

Major General

Born on March 31, 1929, in DeQueen, Arkansas, he married the former Betty Marzett of Los Angeles, California. They have three children: Gail, Steven, and Kevin. He was graduated from Sevier County High School in 1947 and received an associate of arts degree in industrial electronics from San Diego City College. He was graduated magna cum laude with a bachelor of technology degree in industrial engineering from National University in 1972. In 1974, he earned a master of arts degree in human behavior from the United States International University of San Diego. His military education includes the Transportation Officer Basic Course, 1955; Signal Officers Career Course, 1961; Command and General Staff College, 1970; Industrial College of Armed Forces, 1972; United States Army War College, 1977; and the Harvard University Program for Senior Managers in Government, 1986.

He began his military career on November 30, 1948, by enlisting in the California Army National Guard. Mobilized with the 1402nd Engineer Battalion, he served on active duty from September 1950 to June 1952 at Fort

Maj. Gen. Calvin G. Franklin

Lewis, Washington, and in West Germany. Upon his release from active duty, he returned to the California National Guard. On September 18, 1954, he was commissioned a second lieutenant, transportation, after graduating from the California National Guard Officer Candidate School. His assignments included platoon leader; company commander, 118th Signal Battalion and 240th Signal Battalion; communications officer, intelligence officer (S-2), and training officer (S-3), 111th Armor Group.

In November 1971 he assumed command of the 3rd Battalion, 185th Armor. In 1974 he was assigned as the civil–military affairs officer (G-5), 40th Infantry Division, where he served until November 1975 when he became commander of the 240th Signal Battalion. In 1976 he entered active duty to attend the Army War College. After his graduation in 1977, he was assigned as chief, Mobilization Improvement, and director, Nifty Nugget Mobilization Exercise 78, Headquarters, United States Army Forces Command. In May 1979 he was assigned to the District of Columbia Army National Guard as the operations and training officer (G-3).

In October 1979 he returned to active duty as director of an Army study group with a charter to determine the minimum requirements needed by reserve components to train for required readiness levels. In May 1980 he was appointed assistant adjutant general of the California Army National Guard and was federally recognized as a brigadier general on August 18, 1980. He also served as the assistant division commander for the 40th Division until assuming his present position as commanding general of the District of Columbia National Guard on December 4, 1981.

He was appointed major general, Adjutants General Corps, on March 2, 1982. His military awards and decorations include the Legion of

Merit, Meritorious Service Medal (two oak leaf clusters), Army Commendation Medal, Army Achievement Medal, Good Conduct Medal, Army of Occupation Medal, National Defense Service Medal, Humanitarian Service Medal, Armed Forces Reserve Medal (with 10-year device), Reserve Components Achievement Medal (three oak leaf clusters), Army Service Ribbon, Reserve Components Overseas Service Ribbon. He also received the Selective Service Exceptional Service Award, the District of Columbia Distinguished Service Medal, and the National Guard Association of the United States Distinguished Service Medal.

General Franklin is a member of the Greater Washington Board of Trade, Federal City Council, Kiwanis Club of Washington, D.C., Community Foundation of Greater Washington, D.C., and the D.C. Armory Board. He is also a member of the United Negro College Fund Advisory Board and the Air-Space America National Advisory Council. He retired on December 31, 1991.

William S. Frye

★ ———————————————— ★

Brigadier General

Born September 8, 1924, Montclair, New Jersey. He graduated from Rutgers University in 1947. General Frye entered active service in March 1943 at Fort Dix, New Jersey. After serving in the 429th Medical Battalion in Mississippi and California, he was transferred to the 590th Ambulance Company and served with that unit in the European theatre of operation from March 1944 through September 1945, during which time he participated in the campaigns of Ardennes-Alsace, central Europe, Normandy, Northern France, and the Rhineland. He was discharged as a staff sergeant in October 1945.

He was appointed as a second lieutenant, Medical Service Corps, in the 311th AAA Battalion, New Jersey Army National Guard, on February 2, 1948, changed branches to Coast Artillery Corps on December 8, 1949, and was promoted to first lieutenant, Coast Artillery Corps, March 9, 1950. He continued to serve in the 311th AAA Battalion, was assigned as battalion S-2, 109th AAA Gun Battalion, on July 1, 1954, and as a major, artillery, in June 1957 as S-3 of the 109th (later redesignated as the 1st Missile Battalion, 245th Artillery). He was reassigned to battalion commander of that unit on February 10, 1964, and promoted to lieutenant colonel on February 24, 1964. He served as battalion commander for over five years.

In November 1969 he was assigned as inspector general, 50th Armored

Brig. Gen. William S. Frye

Division, a position he held until April 1972, at which time he was promoted to colonel and assigned as commander, 44th Area Headquarters. On June 1, 1976, he was reassigned to Headquarters Detachment as inspector general. He was promoted and federally recognized as brigadier general on June 30, 1977.

He was assigned as commander, State Area Command, Headquarters Detachment, New Jersey Army National Guard. His military decorations and awards include the Meritorious Service Medal, Army Commendation Medal, American Campaign Medal, European-African-Middle Eastern Campaign Medal (with five bronze stars), World War II Victory Medal, Army of Occupation Medal Germany, Armed Forces Reserve Medal (with hourglass device), Army Reserve Components Achievement Medal, New Jersey Medal of Honor (25 years).

Robert Clarence Gaskill

★★ ——————————————————— ★★

Major General

Born April 12, 1931, Yonkers, New York. He received a bachelor of arts degree from Howard University, a master's of business administration from George Washington University.

Gaskill was commissioned in 1952, a second lieutenant in the United States Army after completing with distinction the Army Reserve Officers

Maj. Gen. Robert Clarence Gaskill

Training Course (ROTC) at Howard University. Initially he served in various infantry positions. Following assignment to the Quartermaster Center, Fort Lee, Virginia, he has held numerous key Army logistical positions. He served as deputy commanding general, 1st Support Brigade, United States Army, Europe, which he helped organize. He served as commanding general, 21st Support Command, United States Army, Europe. He served as the commanding general of Letterkenny Army Depot in Pennsylvania. He has served in staff positions with the Military Assistance Command in Vietnam and in the office of the deputy chief of staff for logistics, Department of the Army, Washington, D.C.

He is a graduate of the United States Army Command and General Staff College, the Army Forces Staff College, the Army Logistics Management Center, the Army Institute for Military Assistance and Navy Postgraduate School. From 1971 to 1972, he was a student at the Army War College and became a faculty member, teaching command management and executive development until 1974. In 1977 he was promoted to major general. In October 1978 he was assigned as the deputy director of the Defense Logistics Agency. As the deputy director of the Defense Logistics Agency, his responsibilities encompassed the agency's worldwide activities, which provide all the armed forces with a vast range of supplies and logistic support services.

He has received numerous awards and decorations: the Distinguished Service Medal, Legion of Merit, Meritorious Service Medal (with oak leaf cluster), the Honor Medal 1st class (Republic of Vietnam).

Mack Charles Gaston

★★ ———————————————————— ★★

Rear Admiral

Born on July 17, 1940, in Dalton, Georgia, he married the former Lillian Bonds of Dalton, and they have a daughter, Sonja. He received a bachelor of science in electrical engineering, from Tuskegee Institute in 1964, a master of science in business administration from Marymount College of Virginia in 1984.

On August 20, 1964, he enlisted in the United States Navy. From 1965 to 1967, he served on the USS *Buck* (DD-761). He attended Naval Destroyer School, Newport, Rhode Island, from March 1967 to September 1967. He served on the USS *O'Brien* (DD-725) from September 1967 to May 1969. Then, until May 1971, he served on the staff of the commander of Destroyer Squadron 5.

From May 1971 to December 1972, he was assigned to the Office of CNO (personal aide to the director, Research, Development, Test and Evaluation). He had numerous assignments until December 1985 when he was assigned to the Surface Warfare Officers School Command (DUINS). In February 1986, he became commander of USS *Josephus Daniels* (CG-27). In July 1988, Gaston was assigned to the Office of CNO as director, Surface Warfare Manpower and Training Requirement. In June 1990 he became commander of Field Command, Defense Nuclear Agency.

In 1990, Mack Charles Gaston, was selected rear admiral (lower half).

Rear Adm. Mack Charles Gaston

He has received numerous medals and awards: the Meritorious Service Medal (with one gold star), Navy E Ribbon, Vietnam Campaign Medal (with device), Vietnam Service Medal (with one bronze star), Navy Commendation Medal (with combat "V").

Fred Augustus Gorden

★★ ──────────────────────── ★★

Major General

Born February 22, 1940, Anniston, Alabama. He received a bachelor of science degree from the United States Military Academy, a master of arts in foreign language literature from Middlebury College. From August 1962 to October 1962, he was a student at the Field Artillery Officer Basic Course, United States Army Artillery and Missile School, Fort Sill, Oklahoma. From November 1962 to January 1963, he was a student in the Ranger Course at the United States Army Infantry School, Fort Benning, Georgia.

From January 1963 to November 1965, he served as a forward observer, later liaison officer, later assistant executive officer, and later executive officer of Battery B, 22nd Artillery, 193rd Infantry Brigade, Fort Kobbe, Canal Zone, Panama. He was promoted to first lieutenant on December 6, 1963. From November 1965 to March 1966, he served as assistant S-3, 193rd Infantry Brigade, Fort Kobbe, Canal Zone, Panama.

He was promoted to captain, on November 9, 1965. From March 1966 to December 1966, he was a student in the Artillery Officer Advanced Course, United States Army Air Defense School, Fort Bliss, Texas. From December 1966 to January 1968, he first served as the assistant S-3 (operations), later liaison officer, later commander of Battery C, then as assistant S-3 of 2nd Howitzer Battalion, 320th Artillery, 1st Brigade, 101st Airborne Division, United States Army, Vietnam.

From May 1968 to August 1969, he was a student at Middlebury College, Middlebury, Vermont. He was promoted to major on December 31, 1968. From August 1969 to June 1972, he was appointed instructor of Spanish, later assistant professor (Spanish), Department of Foreign Language, United States Military Academy. From June 1972 to January 1973, he was a student in the Armed Forces Staff College, Norfolk, Virginia. From January 1973 to May 1975, he was an assignment officer, later personnel management officer, Field Artillery Branch, United States Army Military Personnel Center, Alexandria, Virginia. From May 1975 to July 1976, he was executive officer, 1st Battalion,

Maj. Gen. Fred Augustus Gorden

15th Field Artillery, 2nd Infantry Division, Korea. On June 7, 1976, he was promoted to lieutenant colonel. From July 1976 to March 1977, he served as special assistant to the commander, later S-3, Division Artillery, 25th Infantry Division, Schofield Barracks, Hawaii. From March 1977 to September 1978, he was the commander of the 1st Battalion, 8th Field Artillery, 25th Infantry Division, Schofield Barracks, Hawaii.

From September 1978 to June 1979, he served as inspector general, 25th Infantry Division, Schofield Barracks, Hawaii. From August 1979 to June 1980, he was a student at the National War College, Fort McNair, Washington, D.C. From June 1980 to August 1982, he served as executive officer, Office of the Chief of Legislative Liaison, United States Army, Washington, D.C.

He was promoted to colonel on August 7, 1980. From August 1982 to October 1984, he was commander of the Division Artillery, 7th Infantry Division, Fort Ord, California. From October 1984 to October 1986, he served as director of the Inter-American Region, Office of the Assistant Secretary of Defense (international security affairs), Washington, D.C. He was promoted to brigadier general on October 1, 1985. From October 1986 to August 1987, he served as assistant division commander, 7th Infantry Division, Fort Ord, California. From August 1987 to January 1990, he was commandant of cadets, United States Military Academy.

On July 1, 1989, he was promoted to major general. In January 1990, he was assigned as commanding general, 25th Infantry Division (Light), Schofield Barracks, Hawaii. He has received numerous awards and decorations: the Defense Distinguished Service Medal, Legion of Merit, Bronze Star Medal (with "V" device and oak leaf cluster), Meritorious Service Medal (with oak leaf cluster), Air Medal, Army Commendation Medal (with oak leaf cluster), Parachutist Badge, Ranger Tab.

Edward Orval (Ned) Gourdin

★ ———————————————— ★

Brigadier General

Born on August 10, 1897, in Jacksonville, Florida. He is son of Walter Holmes and Felicia Garvin Gourdin. He married the former Amalia Ponce and they had four children: Elizabeth, Ann Robinson, Amalia Lindal and Edward O., Jr. He attended Stanton and Cambridge Latin High Schools. He received a B.A. degree from Harvard University and earned a L.L.B. degree from Harvard Law School.

He gained fame as an athlete during his college career. After he passed the bar, Gourdin practiced law in Boston, Massachusetts. While at Harvard he joined the Student Army Training Corps to be commissioned a second lieutenant in October 1925. On March 3, 1941, he became commander of the all black 3rd Battalion of the 372nd Infantry Regiment with the rank of lieutenant colonel. In December 1941, he assumed command of the entire regiment with the rank of colonel.

For several months the regiment was assigned to guard duty in New York City and its metropolitan area. A training battalion was rotated at Fort Dix, N.J., from 1941 to 1944. Not only basic military training was taught to some 1200 troops, but also literacy, basic education and citizenship. Gourdin took an active role in these programs. From 1943 to 1944, he participated in postcollege workshops and seminars in counseling, law, communications and Negro history.

From April 23, to November 8, 1944, the chief of army ground forces assigned the regiment to Camp Breckenridge, Kentucky. In November 1944, Colonel Gourdin and the 372nd were assigned to Fort Huachuca, Arizona. In April 1945, the regiment left this staging area, as part of the Fourth Army, from Fort Lawton, Washington, for the Pacific theater. When the war in Europe officially came to an end on May 8, 1945, there were celebrations aboard transports bound for Honolulu. The Middle Pacific Command retested Gourdin's 372nd for the "Jungle Training Combat Command." The regiment was assigned to ground defense of Oahu and other Hawaiian islands from May to September 2, 1945, when the Japanese officially surrendered. This event changed the nature of Gourdin's assignment to one of rehabilitation, education and coordination of the return of eligible personnel to civilian life.

Colonel Gourdin became a member of the Mid Pacific Sociology and Psychiatry Board. In February 1946, the 372nd reassembled at Schofield Barracks, was deactivated, and returned to National Guard status. Colonel Gourdin returned to the United States on February 11, 1946, and until 1947 served on the Discharge and Review Board under the secretary of war. When he returned to the Massachusetts National Guard, he served as acting chief of staff, acting judge advocate general, and as plans and training general staff officer for defense of the Boston area as well as aide to the governor of Massachusetts.

When he retired in 1959, he was a brigadier general. He resumed his law position as assistant U.S. district attorney. In 1952, he was appointed to be a special justice of the Roxbury District Court, the third African American to serve on the state bench. In 1958, Governor Fosler Furcolo appointed him to the Massachusetts Superior Court. Gourdin was elected president of the National Olympic Athletes Association in 1965.

While at Harvard, Gourdin had won the silver medal and added points to the American team victory in the broad jump at the Olympic Games in Paris (1924). This was accomplished in spite of final law exams, lack of training and leg injuries. He also was a member of the National Championship Rifle Team.

Gourdin died of cancer on July 22, 1966, in City Hospital, Quincy, Massachusetts. In 1969, the Harvard Varsity Club placed in its Hall of Fame, a plaque, the Edward O. "Ned" Gourdin Memorial Award, honoring him for his accomplishments as a track jumper, for exemplary character and for his Harvard community contributions. The Colonel Edward O. Gourdin Post 5298, Veterans of Foreign Wars of the United States, was chartered in Springfield Gardens, Queens County, New York in 1968.

Samuel Lee Gravely

★★★ ──────────────────────────── ★★★

Vice Admiral

Born June 4, 1922, in Richmond, Virginia, he married the former Alma Clark, having three children — Robert, David, and Tracey. He is a graduate of Virginia Union University (A.B., 1948). He enlisted in the U.S. Naval Reserve (1942) and completed Midshipmen School at Columbia University (1944), becoming the first black man to be commissioned an ensign in World War II.

He was assigned to the submarine chaser PC-1264, on which he served successively as communications officer, electronics officer, and personnel

Vice Adm. Samuel Lee Gravely

officer. Released from active duty in 1946, he completed college in 1948. In August 1949, the Navy recalled him to active duty, and he saw both sea and shore duty during the Korean War. He transferred from the Navy Reserve to the Regular Navy in 1955.

In February 1961, as temporary skipper of the destroyer USS *Chandler,* he became the first black man ever to command a Navy ship. Rising to lieutenant commander, he was given his own ship, the radar picket destroyer USS *Falgout.* Two other ship commands followed. He was promoted to captain in 1967 and to rear admiral and director, Naval Communications, in 1971.

In 1973 he was named commander of a flotilla of 30 ships. He distinguished himself as a naval communications expert, shop captain, and eventually commander of the Third Fleet. He was the navy's first black three-star naval officer as well as the first black ever to obtain the rank of admiral. He retired from the Navy in 1980. Since that time he has served on several corporate boards and as a consultant to defense contractors while living in rural Haymarket, Virginia.

Vice Admiral Gravely has been awarded the Legion of Merit, Bronze Star Medal, Meritorious Service Medal, Joint Services Commendation Medal, Navy Commendation Medal (with bronze star and combat "V"). He is also authorized to wear the World War II Victory Medal, Naval Reserve Medal (for 10 years' service in the U.S. Naval Reserve), American Campaign Medal, Korean Presidential Unit Citation, National Defense Medal (with one bronze star), China Service Medal (extended), Korean Service Medal (with two bronze stars), United Nations Service Medal, Armed Forces Expeditionary Medal, Vietnam Service Medal (with six bronze stars),

Vietnamese Campaign Medal, Antarctica Service Medal, Venezuelan Order of Merit Second Class.

Kenneth D. Gray

★ ———————————————— ★

Brigadier General

Born April 27, 1944, in Excelsior, West Virginia, he married the former Carolyn Jane Trice of Glen Jean, West Virginia. They have two sons, Christopher, and Michael. He received his bachelor of arts degree from West Virginia State College in 1966 and his law degree from West Virginia University in 1969.

He was commissioned a second lieutenant in 1966 from ROTC and entered active duty with the Judge Advocate General's Corps in June 1969. He has completed the JAGC Basic Course, the Military Judge's Course, the JAGC Graduate Course, Command and General Staff College, and the Industrial College of the Armed Forces.

General Gray has served in extensive assignments in the JAGC. His initial tour of duty was in the Office of Staff Judge Advocate, Fort Ord, California, where he served as a defense counsel and legal assistance officer. He was then assigned to the Danang Support Command, Vietnam, from June 1970 to August 1971, where he served in various assignments, including part-time military judge, trial and defense counsel, legal assistance officer, deputy command judge advocate, and command judge advocate.

After his tour in Vietnam, from January 1972 to May 1974, he was assigned to the Office of Judge Advocate General as a personnel management officer, Personnel, Plans, and Training Office. After graduation from the JAGC Advanced Course, he served from May 1975 to June 1978 as an instructor and senior instructor, Criminal Law Division, Judge Advocate General's School, Charlottesville, Virginia. From June 1978 to June 1980 he served as deputy staff judge advocate, 1st Armored Division, Ansbach, Germany. Upon completion of Command and General Staff College, he served as staff judge advocate, 2nd Armored Division, Fort Hood, Texas, from June 1981 to June 1984. From June 1984 to July 1987, he served as chief, personnel, plans, and training officer, Office of Judge Advocate General, Washington, D.C.

Following completion of the Industrial College of the Armed Forces, he was assigned as staff judge advocate, III Corps, Fort Hood, in June 1988. From September 1989 to March 1990 he served as special assistant, Office of Judge Advocate General, United States Army, Washington, D.C.

Brig. Gen. Kenneth D. Gray

In March 1990 he was assigned as acting commander, United States Army Legal Services Agency, Associate Judge, Army Court of Military Review, Falls Church, Virginia; in March 1991, commander.

He was appointed brigadier general on April 1, 1991. Brigadier General Gray's decorations and awards include the Legion of Merit, Bronze Star Medal, Meritorious Service Medal (two oak leaf clusters), Army Commendation Medal, Army Achievement Medal, Army General Staff Identification Badge.

Robert E. Gray

★★ ————————————————— ★★

Major General

Born October 18, 1941, Algoma, West Virginia. He and his wife, Annie, have three children: Frances, Edith, and Parker. He graduated from Ohio State University with a bachelor's degree in computer and information science. He was also awarded a master's of military arts and sciences from the United States Army Command and General Staff College.

General Gray first enlisted in the United States Army as a private in 1959. He remained in the enlisted service until 1966 when he received his commission as a second lieutenant in the United States Army, May 1966. He is a graduate of the Signal Officer Advanced Course and the Army War College. From 1966 to 1967, he was a student in the Signal Officer Basic

Maj. Gen. Robert E. Gray

Course, United States Army Signal School, Fort Monmouth, New Jersey.

From March 1967 to October 1968 he served as a communications officer, 56th Artillery Group, United States Army, Europe. He was promoted to first lieutenant on May 26, 1967, and promoted to captain on May 26, 1968. From October 1968 to May 1969, he was the commander of Company C, 97th Signal Battalion, Seventh United States Army Communications Command, Europe. From May 1969 to June 1970, he served as S-4 (logistics officer) and commander of Company A, 501st Signal Battalion, 101st Airborne Division (Airmobile), United States Army, Vietnam. From June 1973 to November 1974, he served as an automatic data processing officer in the Computer Security Element, Counterintelligence and Security Division, Defense Intelligence Agency, Washington, D.C. From November 1974 to July 1976, he was assigned as a communications-electronics staff officer in the Plans and Policy Branch, Systems Management Division, Information Systems Directorate, Defense Intelligence Agency, Washington, D.C.

He was promoted to major on August 19, 1975. From July 1976 to June 1977, he was a student at the United States Army Command and General Staff College, Fort Leavenworth, Kansas. From June 1977 to August 1978, he served as the executive officer, 50th Signal Battalion, 35th Group, XVIII Airborne Corps, Fort Bragg, North Carolina. From August 1978 to April 1980, Gray served as tactical plans officer, G-3 (operations), Contingency Plans Division, XVIII Airborne Corps, Fort Bragg, North Carolina.

He was promoted to lieutenant colonel on August 13, 1979. From May 1980 to June 1983, he served as commander of the 82nd Signal Battalion,

82nd Airborne Division, Fort Bragg, North Carolina. From June 1983 to June 1984, he was a student at the United States Army War College, Carlisle Barracks, Pennsylvania. From June 1984 to February 1986, he served as chief, Command, Control, and Communications Division, United States Army Combined Arms Combat Development Activity, Fort Leavenworth, Kansas. From February 1986 to June 1988, he was the commander of the 35th Signal Brigade, XVIII Airborne Corps, Fort Bragg, North Carolina.

He was promoted to colonel on November 1, 1984. From July 1988 to October 1988, he served as special assistant to the commanding general, XVIII Airborne Corps, Fort Bragg, North Carolina. In October 1988 he was promoted to brigadier general and was assigned as deputy commanding general, United States Army Signal Center, Fort Gordon, assistant commandant, United States Army Signal School, Fort Gordon, Georgia. In August 1990 he was assigned as the deputy director for plans, programs, and systems, Office of the Director of Information Systems for Command, Control, Communication, and Computers, Office of the Secretary of the Army, Washington, D.C.

He has received numerous awards and decorations: the Legion of Merit, Bronze Star, Air Medal, Meritorious Service Medal (with two oak leaf clusters), Army Commendation Medal (with oak leaf cluster), Master Parachutist Badge.

Edward Greer

★★ ——————————————————————— ★★

Major General

Born on March 8, 1924, in Gary, West Virginia, he married the former Jewell Means. They have three children: Gail Lyle, Michael, and Kenneth. He received a B.S. degree (biological science) from West Virginia State College in 1948, an M.S. degree from George Washington University in Washington, D.C., in 1967.

General Greer's military career began following his eighteenth birthday when he joined the Army Reserve. Called to active duty on May 12, 1943, he attained the grade of master sergeant during World War II. Upon receipt of his honorable discharge at the end of the war, he resumed his education at West Virginia State College. As a member of the Reserve Officer Training Corps, he continued his interest in the military while a student.

He was commissioned a second lieutenant of artillery in the Regular

Maj. Gen. Edward Greer

Army upon graduation in 1948. On July 12, 1948, he was called to active duty, his first duty station Fort Riley, Kansas. The outbreak of the Korean War in 1950 found General Greer serving on the front lines during some of the most decisive battles. He acquitted himself with valor and distinction while accomplishing combat missions involving great personal risk. His exemplary and heroic service during this period was recognized by awards of the Silver Star and Bronze Star medals.

A series of important assignments following the Korean War gave every indication that the Army had identified General Greer as a rising star in the officer corps. He was rapidly promoted to captain. After advanced schooling in 1955, he was selected for assignment to the Department of the Army General Staff in Washington, D.C. Three years later, he was selected for accelerated promotion to major. Important military schooling followed—Command and General Staff College at Fort Leavenworth, Kansas. After graduation, a year of service at Fort Lewis, Washington, as second in command of a combined rocket and howitzer battalion further prepared him for higher-level command. During the next three years, General Greer again served on the Army General Staff in Washington as a personal planner and manager of assignments for artillery officers.

He was promoted to lieutenant colonel in January 1963. In 1964 he returned to Korea where he first served as an artillery operations officer in a major headquarters and subsequently was assigned to the most coveted position available for a lieutenant colonel—command of a battalion. In 1965 he was again assigned to the Command and General Staff College, this time as an author-instructor. His normal tour was interrupted, however, by selection for the highest military schooling available in the Army, the

National War College. While a student at the National War College, General Greer also earned his master's degree from George Washington University. He then returned to Washington as an operations officer in the Office of the Joint Chiefs of Staff. During his assignment, he was promoted to colonel.

In April of 1970, General Greer was assigned to Vietnam where he served initially as deputy commander of artillery, United States Army XXIV Corps. Further acknowledgment of the special trust and confidence placed in General Greer by the Army came when he was selected to command an entire artillery group. He was honored for his service in the war by awards including the Legion of Merit and the Vietnamese Cross of Gallantry with gold star. Combat service in his third war ended in March 1971 when he was reassigned to the Office of the Assistant Secretary of Defense. During this assignment, he was selected for promotion to brigadier general. He then moved to Fort Leonard Wood, Missouri, where he became the deputy commanding general.

In 1974 General Greer was reassigned to the Washington, D.C., area as deputy commanding general, United States Army Military Personnel Center. Less than a year later, his rapid rise continued when he received a second star as major general. On November 1, 1976, General Greer requested that he be placed on the United States Army retired list. His request was granted, and on November 30, 1976, one of the Army's most distinguished soldiers retired with honor. Besides his many citations for valor on the battlefield and meritorious achievement in peacetime, General Greer was awarded the Distinguished Service Medal, Silver Star, Legion of Merit (with oak leaf cluster), Bronze Star Medal (with oak leaf cluster), Air Medal, Joint Service Commendation Medal, Army Commendation Medal (with oak leaf cluster).

Arthur James Gregg

★★★ ——————————————————— ★★★

Lieutenant General

Born May 11, 1928, Florence, South Carolina. He received a B.S. degree in business administration from Benedict College. His military schooling included completion of the Quartermaster School, Basic and Advanced Courses; the United States Army Command and General Staff College; the United States Army War College.

His military career began on May 19, 1950, and expanded over 31 years of service, during which time his career was characterized by a succession of

Lt. Gen. Arthur James Gregg

demanding assignments in both staff and command positions. From February 1960 to August 1963, he served as operations officer, 95th Quartermaster Battalion, United States Army, Europe. From August 1963 to July 1964, he was a student in the United States Army Command and General Staff College, Fort Leavenworth, Kansas. In January 1965 he was assigned as logistics plans officer, United States Army Materiel Command, then as assistant secretary, General Staff, United States Materiel Command, Washington, D.C., until February 1966.

From February 1966 to July 1967, he served commanding officer, 96th Quartermaster Battalion (later redesignated 96th Supply and Service Battalion), Fort Riley, Kansas, later Vietnam. He returned to the United States in July 1967 and was selected a student in the United States Army War College, Carlisle Barracks, Pennsylvania. After graduating from the War College, he was assigned first as logistics officer, J-4, United States European Command, then commanding officer, Nahbollenbach Army Depot, United States Army, Europe.

In March 1972 General Gregg returned to the United States and was assigned as deputy director, Troop Support, Office of the Deputy Chief of Staff for Logistics, United States Army, Washington, D.C., from July 1971 to March 1972. In March 1972 he served as director, Troop Support, Office of Deputy Chief of Staff for Logistics, United States Army, Washington, D.C. From September 1972 to March 1973 he served first as special assistant, Director of Supply and Maintenance Office; deputy chief of staff, logistics; then deputy director, Supply and Maintenance Office, Deputy Chief of Staff for Logistics, United States Army, Washington, D.C.

After this assignment, General Gregg was reassigned to Europe as commander, European Exchange System in March 1973. He retired on July 31, 1981. His military awards and decorations include the Legion of Merit (with oak leaf cluster), Meritorious Service Medal, Joint Service Commendation Medal, Army Commendation Medal (with two oak leaf clusters).

Benjamin T. Hacker

★★ ——————————————— ★★

Rear Admiral

Born September 19, 1935, in Washington, D.C., he married the former Jeanne House of Springfield, Ohio, and they have three children: Benjamin, Jr., Bruce, and Anne. He attended high school in Daytona Beach, Florida, and Dayton, Ohio. Following completion of Aviation Officer Candidate School in Pensacola, Florida, he was commissioned an ensign in September 1958.

Hacker's operational assignments have included serving concurrently as commander, Fleet Air Mediterranean; commander, Maritime Surveillance and Reconnaissance Forces, United States Sixth Fleet; and commander, Maritime Air Forces Mediterranean, Naples, Italy, from 1982 to 1984. In 1973 he reported to Patrol Squadron 24, Jacksonville, Florida, where he served as executive officer and later commanding officer. During this tour, the squadron made highly successful deployments to Keflavik, Iceland, and was heavily tasked in major operational exercises in the northern and central Atlantic.

Hacker reported in 1970 to Patrol Squadron 47, Moffett Field, California, where the squadron completed numerous deployments in the P3C Orion aircraft to Adak, Alaska, and the western Pacific. His first operational assignment was to Patrol Squadron 21, Brunswick, Maine, where he flew the P2V Neptune antisubmarine warfare aircraft. His shore assignments have included serving on the staff of the Chief of Naval Operations in 1984 as director, Total Force Training and Education Division.

In 1972 he established the NROTC unit at Florida A&M University in Tallahassee, Florida, where he served as its first commanding officer and professor of naval science. He served as the Commanding Officer of the United States Naval Facility, Argentia, Newfoundland, and personnel officer and instructor in the P-3A aircraft while attached to Patrol Squadron 31, Naval Air Station, Moffett Field.

In 1975, he was assigned to the Bureau of Naval Personnel as a division director and special assistant to the chief of naval personnel in Washington,

Rear Adm. Benjamin T. Hacker

D.C. In 1980, he assumed duties as commander, United States Military Enlistment Processing Command, Fort Sheridan, Illinois.

He is the son of the Rev. C. Leroy Hacker and Alzeda C. Hacker. After two years at the University of Dayton, he transferred to the University of Wittenberg in Springfield, Ohio, where he received a bachelor of arts degree in 1957. In September 1958 he graduated from the United States Naval Aviation Officer Candidate School, Pensacola, Florida.

On March 1, 1981, he was promoted to rear admiral. His last assignment was commander, Naval Training Center, commander, Naval Base, San Diego, California.

David M. Hall

★ ——————————————————— ★

Brigadier General

Born June 21, 1928, in Gary, Indiana, he married the former Jacqueline Branch of Washington, D.C. They have two sons: Glen and Gary. He was graduated from Roosevelt High School in Gary, Indiana, in 1946. He graduated from Howard University with a bachelor's degree in business administration in 1951. He earned a master's in educational sociology from Agricultural and Technical State University of North Carolina, Greensboro, in 1966. He is a graduate of Squadron Officer School, Air Command and Staff College, and Air War College, all located at Maxwell Air Force

Brig. Gen. David M. Hall

Base, Alabama, and the Industrial College of the Armed Forces, Fort Lesley J. McNair, Washington, D.C. In 1976 he attended the advanced management program at Massachusetts Institute of Technology.

He enlisted in the Air Force in August 1951 and received his commission as a second lieutenant in June 1953 through the Air Force Officer Candidate School. Early in his career General Hall served in a variety of career fields, which included supply, accounting and finance, data processing, and instructor in the Air Force Reserve Officers Training Corps program. In 1958 General Hall cross-trained into the data processing career field while stationed at Oxnard Air Force Base, California. He was assigned to Clark Air Base, the Philippines, in July 1960 as a data processing officer.

He became assistant professor of aerospace science in the Reserve Officers Training Corps program at the Agricultural and Technical State University of North Carolina in June 1962. In August 1966 he returned to the data processing career field concurrent with his assignment to Ubon Royal Thai Air Force Base, Thailand, where he also served as comptroller of the 8th Tactical Fighter Wing. General Hall was assigned to the Air Force Accounting and Finance Center, Denver, in September 1967. He was chief, Computer Operations Division, Directorate of Data Automation, until 1969 when he joined a software development division as an analyst programmer.

In March 1971 he was assigned to Scott Air Force Base, Illinois, where he became chief, Computer Operations Division for Military Airlift Command, and in March 1972 he became the assistant for social actions in the Office of the Deputy Chief of Staff for Personnel at Scott. He became the deputy base commander for Scott Air Force Base in May 1974 and base commander in February 1975. General Hall was assigned to Headquarters, Air Force Logistics Command, Wright-Patterson Air Force Base, in June 1976 as assistant deputy chief of staff, comptroller (data automation). In August 1977 he was assigned as deputy chief of staff, comptroller, Air Force Logistics Command, Wright-Patterson Air Force Base, Ohio.

He was appointed to Brigadier General on August 1, 1980, with date of rank July 23, 1980. His military decorations and awards include the Legion of Merit, Meritorious Service Medal (one oak leaf cluster), Air Force Commendation Medal (one oak leaf cluster).

James Reginald Hall, Jr.

★★★ ———————————————————— ★★★

Lieutenant General

Born July 15, 1936, Anniston, Alabama, he married the former Helen A. Kerr, and they have three children: Sheila, James, and Cheryl. Upon completion of work toward a bachelor of arts degree in political science at Morehouse College, he enlisted in the Army. Following basic training at Fort Chaffee, Arkansas, and advanced individual training at Fort Carson, Colorado, Hall attended Officer Candidate School, where he was commissioned a second lieutenant in 1958. He also holds an advanced degree in public administration from Shippensburg State College.

His military schooling includes completion of the Armed Forces Staff College and the United States Army War College. Among his command and staff positions, he has served as commander, Company C, 2nd Battalion (Airborne), 503rd Infantry, 173rd Airborne Brigade, United States Army, Okinawa and Vietnam; 1st Battalion, 9th Infantry, 2nd Infantry Division, Eighth United States Army, Korea; 4th Regiment, United States Military Academy Corps of Cadets, West Point; 197th Infantry Brigade, Fort Benning, Georgia; assistant division commander, 4th Infantry Division (Mechanized), Fort Carson, Colorado; commanding general, United States Army Military Personnel Center, Alexandria, Virginia; commanding general, 4th Infantry Division (Mechanized), Fort Carson, Colorado; commanding general, Fourth United States Army, Fort Sheridan, Illinois.

On January 22, 1982, he was promoted to brigadier general; on June 1, 1986, major general; on May 31, 1989, lieutenant general.

General Hall's staff assignments include subsector adviser, Advisory Team 91, and joint planner, Joint Planning Group II Field Force, United States Military Assistance Command, Vietnam; personnel management officer, Assignment Section, Infantry Branch, Officer Personnel Directorate,

Lt. Gen. James Reginald Hall, Jr.

Office of Personnel Directorate, Office of Personnel Operations, Washington, D.C.; assistant executive officer, deputy chief of staff for personnel, Department of the Army, Washington, D.C.; executive officer, Office of the Deputy Chief of Staff for Training, United States Training and Doctrine Command, Fort Monroe, Virginia; assistant deputy chief of staff for personnel and assistant deputy chief of staff for operations, United States Forces Command, Fort McPherson, Georgia; director of enlisted personnel management, United States Army Military Personnel Center, Alexandria, Virginia; and deputy inspector general, Department of the Army, Washington, D.C.

His military decorations and awards include the Legion of Merit, Bronze Star Medal, Meritorious Service Medal (one oak leaf cluster), Army Commendation Medal (one oak leaf cluster), Combat Infantryman Badge, Parachutist Badge, Army Staff Identification Badge.

Titus C. Hall

★★ ——————————————————————— ★★

Major General

Born May 8, 1928, in Pflugerville, Texas, he married the former Clarissa Douglas of Hastings, Florida. They have three children: Sandra, a graduate of Howard University in Washington, D.C.; Pamela, a 1978 graduate of Ohio State University; and a son, Titus, Jr.

Maj. Gen. Titus C. Hall

He was graduated from I. M. Terrell High School in Fort Worth, Texas, in 1944. He received a bachelor of science in electrical engineering from Tuskegee Institute, Alabama, in 1952. He was a distinguished graduate of the Reserve Officers Training Corps program. He also earned a master's in systems engineering management from the University of Southern California, Los Angeles, in 1971.

He entered active duty with the United States Air Force in March 1952. After completing communications officers training at Scott Air Force Base, Illinois, in June 1953, he was assigned as a communications intelligence operations officer with the United States Air Force Security Service in Japan, serving at Johnson and Shiroi Air Bases. The general attended Basic Navigator Flying School at Ellington Air Force Base, Texas, and Advanced Bombing and Navigation School at Mather Air Force Base, California, from March 1956 to January 1958.

He spent the next six years with Strategic Air Command units at Davis-Monthan Air Force Base, Arizona, flying B-47s, with frequent missions to Guam and Alaska. In June 1964 he was assigned to the Space Systems Division, Los Angeles, as the satellite range instrumentation support officer. He later served as commander of the Kodiak Satellite Tracking Station in Alaska and returned to Los Angeles in March 1969 as executive officer, Space and Missile Systems Organization (now the Air Force Space Division).

Following graduation from the University of Southern California, he was assigned to Da Nang Air Base, Vietnam, in January 1971 and flew EC-47s in Southeast Asia for a year. General Hall became chief avionics engineer for the B-1 strategic manned bomber at Headquarters, Aeronautical

Systems Division, Wright-Patterson Air Force Base, Ohio, in March 1972. Two years later, after the design and test of the B-1 avionics suite, he became systems program director of the division's Avionics Program Office. He was later designated the assistant deputy for the Reconnaissance/Strike/Electronic Warfare System Program Office.

In April 1975 he became vice commander, 2750th Air Base Wing, Wright-Patterson Air Force Base, and assumed command of the wing in January 1977. He was appointed director of materiel management, San Antonio Air Logistics Center, Kelly Air Force Base, Texas. He became deputy for systems (now reconnaissance and electronic warfare systems), Headquarters, Aeronautical Systems Division, Wright-Patterson Air Force Base, in July 1978. In May 1981 he became commander, Lowry Technical Training Center, Lowry Air Force Base, Colorado.

He was promoted to major general on July 1, 1981, with date of rank September 1, 1977. He was a master navigator with 4,000 flying hours in FB-111s, EF-111s, F-4G Wild Weasels, and United States Navy A-7Ds. His military decorations and awards include the Distinguished Service Medal, Legion of Merit, Distinguished Flying Cross, Bronze Star Medal, Meritorious Service Medal (one oak leaf cluster), Air Medal (two oak leaf clusters).

James Frank Hamlet

★★ ———————————————————— ★★

Major General

Born December 13, 1921, Alliance, Ohio. He received a B.S. degree in business administration from St. Benedict's College, Atchison, Kansas. His military education includes Infantry School, Basic and Advanced Courses; United States Army Command and General Staff College; and the United States Army War College.

He has held a wide variety of important command and staff positions. From August 1963 to May 1966, he served as project officer, later as doctrinal developments officer, United States Army Combat Developments Command Combined Arms Agency, Fort Leavenworth, Kansas. From May 1966 to July 1967, he served first as operations officer, 11th Aviation Group, 1st Cavalry Division; then officer, 227th Aviation Battalion; later executive officer, 11th Aviation Group, 1st Cavalry Division, United States Army, Vietnam.

He returned from overseas and was selected as a student at St. Benedict's College, Atchison, Kansas, from August 1967 to February 1968. From February 1968 to June 1969, he was chief, Airmobility Branch,

Maj. Gen. James Frank Hamlet

Doctrine and Systems Division, United States Army Combat Developments Command Combat Arms Group, Fort Leavenworth, Kansas. From August 1969 to June 1970, he was a student at the United States Army War College, Carlisle Barracks, Pennsylvania.

He returned to Vietnam from July 1970 to August 1972, where he first served as commanding officer, 11th Aviation Group, 1st Cavalry Division (Airmobile); next as assistant division commander, 101st Airborne Division (Airmobile); later as commanding general, 3rd Brigade, 1st Cavalry Division, United States Army, Vietnam.

In August 1972 he return to the United States and was assigned as commanding general, 4th Infantry Division and Fort Carson, Colorado. In 1974 he was assigned as inspector general, United States Army Headquarters, Washington, D.C.

He was appointed to major general on June 1, 1973, retired from the Army in 1981. His military awards and decorations include the Distinguished Service Medal, Legion of Merit (with two oak leaf clusters), Distinguished Flying Cross, Soldier's Medal, Bronze Star Medal (with oak leaf cluster), Air Medal (49 awards), Army Commendation Medal (with three oak leaf clusters), Combat Infantryman Badge, Parachutist Badge, Senior Army Aviator Badge, United States Army Aviation Hall of Fame, United States Infantry Hall of Fame.

Robert Alonzo Harleston

★ ———————————————————— ★

Brigadier General

Born January 28, 1936, in Hempstead, New York, he married the former Bernice Robinson. They have three children: Robert, Bernice, and Paul. He received a B.A. degree in business administration from Howard University in 1958, an M.S. in political science and public safety from Michigan State University in 1965, and a J.D. from Georgetown University Law Center, Washington, D.C., in 1984.

His military career began in 1958 when after graduating from Howard University he was commissioned a second lieutenant in the Military Police Corps. He entered the Military Police Officers Basic Course, Fort Gordon, Georgia; afterwards receiving an assignment as a leader of a Military Police security platoon at a nuclear weapons storage facility in Romulus, New York. General Harleston has held a wide variety of important command and staff positions, including commanding the corrections facility at Fort Dix, New Jersey (the Army's largest confinement facility) from 1972 to 1974; and corrections staff officer for the Department of the Army from 1974 to 1975, where he developed the Army's procedures for its corrections program.

From 1976 to 1978, he served as director of operations, United States Army Criminal Investigation Command. From 1978 to 1980, he was assigned as provost marshal (chief of police), Fort Hood, Texas. At Fort Hood, he ensured the safety and well-being of more than 65,000 people on a 339-square-mile post, one of the largest geographical installations and concentrations of troops in the free world—1,500 military police officers and enlisted members under his command.

From 1984 to 1986, he served as chief executive officer, Department of the Army Inspector General Agency. From 1986 to 1988, General Harleston was assigned as a national level assistant for the Department of Defense Inspector General. From 1988 to 1989, he served as deputy commanding general, United States Army Community and Family Support Center.

General Harleston retired from military service in 1989 but did not retire from criminal justice work. Shortly after leaving the Army, he became warden at the Eastern Correctional Institution, Maryland's newest prison. His military awards and decorations include the Legion of Merit, Bronze Star (with oak leaf cluster), Meritorious Service Medal, Air Medal, Army Commendation medal (with oak leaf cluster).

General Harleston has these words for men and women who are considering joining the Army: "Those who are going in with a commitment,

Brig. Gen. Robert Alonzo Harleston

remember that it's a matter of performance, how you do your job, rather than the type of job you are assigned. All jobs are important, and you should treat them as such."

Ernest James Harrell

★★ ——————————————————— ★★

Major General

Born October 30, 1936, Selma, Alabama. He received a bachelor of science degree in civil engineering–construction from Tuskegee Institute and a master of science degree in engineering from the University of Arizona. Military schools attended by Harrell: Engineer School, Officer Basic and Advanced Courses; United States Army Command and General Staff College; and United States Army War College.

He joined the United States Army in 1960, a student in the Engineer Officer Orientation Course, Fort Belvoir, Virginia. In April 1963 he was appointed commander of Company B, 94th Engineer Battalion, United States Army, Europe. From June 1965 to December 1967, he was a civil engineer with the 539th Detachment, 1st Special Forces Group (Airborne), 1st Special Forces, Okinawa. From December 1967 to July 1970, he served as an instructor, later assistant professor, of military science at Arizona State University, Tempe, Arizona.

From July 1970 to May 1971, he served as executive officer, 809th

Maj. Gen. Ernest James Harrell

Engineer Battalion (Construction), Thailand. From June 1974 to June 1976, he was appointed inspector general, Inspector General Office, Washington, D.C. From October 1977 to July 1979, he served as commander, 43rd Engineer Battalion (Combat) (Heavy), Fort Benning, Georgia. From July 1979 to July 1982, he served as a personnel assignments officer, Lieutenant Colonels Division and Colonels Division.

He was promoted in September 1981 to lieutenant colonel; in October 1982 to colonel while serving at the United States Army Military Personnel Center, Alexandria, Virginia.

From June 1984 to July 1986, he served as commander, 2nd Engineer Group, Eighth United States Army, Korea. On March 1, 1988, he was promoted to brigadier general and assigned as commanding general, United States Army Engineer Division on the Ohio River in Cincinnati, Ohio. In July 1988, he was assigned as commanding general, United States Army Engineer Division, Europe. On March 3, 1991, he became commander and division engineer, United States Army Corps of Engineers, North Pacific Division.

He was appointed major general on February 1, 1991. His military decorations and awards include the Legion of Merit, Bronze Star Medal, Meritorious Service Medal (three oak leaf clusters), Air Medal, Army Commendation Medal, National Defense Service Medal, Vietnam Service Medal (four oak leaf clusters), Combat Infantryman Badge, Parachutist Badge.

Marcelite J. Harris

★ ———————————————————— ★

Brigadier General

Born January 16, 1943, in Houston, Texas, she is the daughter of Cecil Oneal and Marcelite Elizabeth Terrell Jordan. She married Maurice A. Harris of Portsmouth, Virginia. They have a son, Steven, and a daughter, Tenecia. She was graduated from Kashmere Gardens Junior-Senior High School, Houston, in 1960. She earned a bachelor of arts degree in speech and drama from Spelman College in 1964 and a bachelor of science degree in business management from the University of Maryland, Asian Division, in 1989. The general completed Squadron Officer School in 1975; Air War College in 1983; Harvard University's Senior Officers National Security Course in 1989; and the CAPSTONE General and Flag Officer Course in 1990.

In September 1965 she entered the United States Air Force through Officer Training School, Lackland Air Force Base, Texas. Upon graduation in December 1965, she was assigned to the 60th Military Airlift Wing, Travis Air Force Base, California, as assistant director for administration. In January 1967 she became administrative officer for the 388th Tactical Missile Squadron, Bitburg Air Base, West Germany, and in May 1969 was reassigned as maintenance analysis officer, 388th Tactical Fighter Wing, Bitburg.

She completed her tour of duty in West Germany and upon graduation in May 1971 from the Aircraft Maintenance Officer Course at Chanute Air Force Base, Illinois, became the Air Force's first woman to be an aircraft maintenance officer. Three months later she became maintenance supervisor, 49th Tactical Fighter Squadron, Korat Royal Thai Air Force Base, Thailand. On return to the United States, she was assigned as job control officer, 916th Air Refueling Squadron, Travis Air Force Base, California; in September 1973 she became the maintenance supervisor. In September 1975 General Harris was assigned as a personnel staff officer, Headquarters, United States Air Force, Washington, D.C., where she served as a White House aide to President Jimmy Carter.

In May 1978 she became commander of Cadet Squadron 39, United States Air Force Academy, Colorado Springs, Colorado, an assignment that made her one of the first two women to be air officers commanding. The general returned to maintenance when she became maintenance control officer, the 384th Air Refueling Wing, McConnell Air Force Base, Kansas, in July 1980. In July 1981 she became Strategic Air Command's first woman maintenance squadron commander when she assumed command of the

Brig. Gen. Marcelite J. Harris

384th Avionics Maintenance Squadron at McConnell. Eight months later, she assumed command of McConnell's 384th Field Maintenance Squadron.

In November, 1982 she was assigned to the Pacific Air Forces Logistic Support Center, Kadena Air Base, Japan. She became the Air Force's first woman deputy commander for maintenance at Keesler Air Force Base, Mississippi, in March 1986 and the first woman wing commander in Air Training Command's 3300th Technical Training Wing, Keesler Technical Training Center, in December 1988. She assumed her present position in September 1990.

On September 8, 1990 she was appointed brigadier general, becoming the first black female general in the United States Air Force. General Harris's military awards and decorations include the Bronze Star Medal, Meritorious Service Medal (four oak leaf clusters), Air Force Commendation Medal (one oak leaf cluster), Presidential Unit Citation, Air Force Outstanding Unit Award (with "V" device and seven oak leaf clusters), Air Force Organizational Excellence Award (one oak leaf cluster), National Defense Service Medal, Vietnam Service Medal (with three service stars), Air Force Overseas Ribbon-Short, Air Force Overseas Ribbon-Long (one oak leaf cluster), Air Force Longevity Service Award Ribbon (four oak leaf clusters), Republic of Vietnam Gallantry Cross (with palm), Republic of Vietnam Campaign Medal.

Charles Alfonso Hines

★★ ——————————————————— ★★

Major General

Born September 4, 1935, Washington, D.C. He and his wife, Veronica, have seven children: Tracy, Charles, Kelley, Christina, Michael, Nicholas, and Timothy. Upon completion of the Reserve Officers Training Corps curriculum as a distinguished military graduate and the educational course of study at Howard University in 1942, he was commissioned a second lieutenant and awarded a bachelor of science degree in physical education. He also holds a master of science degree in police administration and public safety from Michigan State University. He received a master of military arts and science from the United States Army Command and General Staff College, and a Ph.D. in sociology from Johns Hopkins University. His military education includes completion of the Infantry Officer Basic Course, the Military Police Officer Advanced Course, the United States Army Command and General Staff College, and the Army War College.

He has held a wide variety of important command and staff positions, culminating in his last assignment as commanding general, United States Army Chemical and Military Police Centers and Fort McClellan, Fort McClellan, Alabama. From February 1954 to January 1957, he was assigned in the enlisted service, initial active duty training at Fort Jackson, South Carolina, later assignments to Battery A, 504th Field Artillery Battalion, Fort Kobbe, Canal Zone, and Company M, 20th Infantry Regiment, Fort Davis, Canal Zone. From March 1962 to April 1962, he was a student in the Infantry Officer Orientation Course (later Airborne Course), United States Army Infantry School, Fort Benning, Georgia.

Other key assignments include duty from December 1987 to August 1989 as director of manpower, Office of the Deputy Chief of Staff for Personnel, United States Army, Washington, D.C.; from August 1985 to December 1987 as director, Officer Personnel Management Directorate, United States Army Military Personnel Center, Alexandria, Virginia. From July 1983 through July 1985, he served as commander, 14th Military Police Brigade, and provost marshal, VII Corps, United States Army, Europe. From July 1981 to June 1983, he was chief, Force Management Issue Team, later deputy director and director, Women in the Army Policy Review Group, Office of the Deputy Chief of Staff for Personnel, United States Army, Washington, D.C.

From June 1980 to July 1981, he served as strategic research analyst, later director of evaluation and organization effectiveness, United States

Maj. Gen. Charles Alfonso Hines

Army War College Staff and Faculty, Carlisle Barracks, Pennsylvania. From October 1972 to January 1975, he served as chief, Criminal Intelligence Program, later operations officer and chief, Criminal Information Division, United States Army Criminal Investigation Command, Washington, D.C. From June 1971 to June 1972, he was chief, Plans and Operations Division, Office of the Provost Marshal, Eighth United States Army.

General Hines completed the Executive Development Course at the University of Maryland; the Executive Development Course at the John F. Kennedy School of Government, Harvard University; the Program for Senior Executives in National and International Security at the John F. Kennedy School of Government, Harvard University; and the Federal Bureau of Investigation National Academy.

He was appointed brigadier general on September 1, 1985; major general, September 1, 1988. His awards and decorations include the Legion of Merit (three oak leaf clusters), Bronze Star Medal, Meritorious Service Medal (six oak leaf clusters), Army Commendation Medal (two oak leaf clusters), Parachutist Badge, Army General Staff Identification Badge.

General Hines appears in *Who's Who in American Colleges and Universities* and was selected to the Outstanding Young Men of America Foundation, and serves as an adviser to the President's Committee on Employment of People with Disabilities.

Johnny J. Hobbs

★ ─────────────────────────── ★

Brigadier General

Born February 28, 1943, Newark, N.J. He was graduated from Barringer High School in Newark in 1960 and Rutgers University in 1964 where he earned a bachelor of arts degree in sociology. He also received a master's in social work administration from Rutgers University in 1972. He later attended law school at Loyola University, New Orleans, and received his law degree (J.D.) in 1983. His military education includes Squadron Officer School, 1981; Air Command and Staff College, 1982; and the National Security Management Course, Industrial College of the Armed Forces, 1985 (outstanding graduate).

He began his military career as an Air Force Reserve Officer Training Corps cadet at Rutgers University in 1960. Upon graduation in June 1964, he was commissioned a second lieutenant. He received his wings in June 1966 upon completion of undergraduate pilot training at Williams Air Force Base, Arizona. His first assignment was George Air Force Base, California, where he became an F-4C pilot in February 1967. He was then assigned to the 497th Tactical Fighter Squadron (Night Owls), Ubon Royal Thai Air Base, Thailand, for a combat tour flying F-4C aircraft. From 1968 to 1970, he was assigned to the 35th Tactical Fighter Squadron at Yokota Air Base, Japan.

He was released from active duty in June 1970. In 1974, he joined the Michigan Air National Guard in Battle Creek and served until 1976 as a squadron pilot in a forward air controller mission. He then transferred to the Louisiana Air National Guard where he served in numerous positions, ranging from squadron pilot to assistant operations officer to squadron commander, 122nd Tactical Fighter Squadron (TFS), until 1985. General Hobbs, as squadron commander, led the 122nd TFS through the conversion to the F-15. The 122nd became the first Air National Guard unit to fly the F-15. He transferred to the 113th Tactical Fighter Wing (parent wing of the 122th Tactical Fighter Squadron) in 1985 and assumed the position of vice wing commander in October 1985.

He was appointed deputy commanding general for air, District of Columbia National Guard, with command and control over all elements of the District of Columbia Air National Guard, in June 1988.

The general is a command pilot with more than 4,000 flying hours in the T-37, T-38, O-2, F-100, F-4C, and F-4D aircraft. His awards and decorations include the Distinguished Flying Cross, Air Medal, Meritorious Service Medal (one oak leaf cluster), Presidential Unit Citation,

Brig. Gen. Johnny J. Hobbs

National Defense Service Medal, Armed Forces Expeditionary Medal, Vietnam Service Medal, Air Force Longevity Service Award Ribbon, Armed Forces Reserve Medal, Small Arms Expert Marksmanship Ribbon, Air Force Training Ribbon, Republic of Vietnam Gallantry Cross, Republic of Vietnam Campaign Medal, District of Columbia Meritorious Service Medal.

Arthur Holmes, Jr.

★★ ——————————————————— ★★

Major General

Born May 12, 1931, in Decatur, Alabama, he married the former Wilma King. They have three children: Deborah, Sharon, and Arthur O. Holmes. He received a Reserve Officer Training Corps commission as second lieutenant in 1952 and has over 30 years of active commissioned service. General Holmes's civilian education includes a bachelor of science degree from Hampton Institute and a master of business administration degree from Kent State University. His military schooling includes the Field Artillery Officer Basic Course, the Ordnance Officer Advanced Course, the Command and General Staff College, and the United States Naval War College.

General Holmes career is characterized by a succession of demanding assignments in both staff and command positions. He commanded the 724th Maintenance Battalion, 24th Infantry, Fort Riley, Kansas, from 1968

Maj. Gen. Arthur Holmes, Jr.

to 1969. In 1979 he commanded the 62nd Maintenance Battalion, United States Army Qui Nhon Support Command, Vietnam. While assigned to the 1st Infantry Division, Fort Riley, Kansas, from 1975 to 1977, General Holmes served first as the commander of the Division Support Command and then as assistant division commander.

He was assigned as executive to the Secretary of the Army in Washington, D.C., from 1977 to 1979 and immediately thereafter served as deputy commanding general, United States Army Tank-Automotive Materiel Readiness Command, Warren, Michigan. In 1980 General Holmes became director of readiness, United States Army Materiel Development and Readiness Command, Alexandria, and in 1982, he moved to Headquarters, Department of the Army, Washington, D.C., where he was assigned as deputy inspector general for inspections. He served in that capacity until 1983 when he assumed duties as the assistant deputy chief of staff for logistics, United States Army, Washington, D.C.

In August 1984 he was named commanding general of the United States Army Tank-Automotive Command, Warren, Michigan. General Holmes has earned a number of awards and decorations: the Legion of Merit, Bronze Star Medal, Meritorious Service Medal (with oak leaf cluster), Joint Service Commendation Medal, Army Commendation Medal (with two oak leaf clusters).

Edward Honor

★★★ ——————————————————— ★★★

Lieutenant General

Born March 17, 1933, in Melville, Louisiana, he married the former Phyllis Whitehurst. Upon completion of the Reserve Officers Training Corps curriculum and the educational course of study at Southern University, A&M College, he was commissioned a second lieutenant and awarded a bachelor of arts degree in education. His military education includes completion of the Basic Armor Officer Course, the Basic and Advanced Courses of the Transportation School, the United States Army Command and General Staff College, and the United States Army War College.

He has held a wide variety of important command and staff positions. He served as commander, 36th Transportation Battalion, later commander, 24th Transportation Battalion, United States Army, Cam Ranh Bay Support Command, Vietnam, from 1969 to 1970. His staff assignments include director, Transportation, Energy, and Troop Support, Office of the Deputy Chief of Staff for Logistics, United States Army, Washington, D.C.; director, Plans, Doctrine, and Systems, United States Army Materiel Development and Readiness Command, Alexandria, Virginia; director, Personal Property, Military Traffic Management and Terminal Service, Washington, D.C.; chief, Transportation Service Branch, Transportation Division, Office of the Chief of Staff for Logistics, United States Continental Army Command, Fort Monroe, Virginia. He also served as passenger

Lt. Gen. Edward Honor

movements officer and as chief of Passenger Service Division with the Military Traffic Management and Terminal Service, Washington, D.C.

Other key assignments held include command assignments as commander, Military Traffic Management Command, Transportation Terminal Group, Europe, Rotterdam, Netherlands. He was assigned as commander of the 37th Transportation Group, 4th Transportation Brigade, United States Army, Europe. In 1979 he was assigned to the Joint Chiefs of Staff at the Pentagon as deputy director, Plans and Research.

His military awards and decorations include the Defense Superior Service Medal, four awards of the Legion of Merit, two awards of the Bronze Star Medal, two awards of the Meritorious Service Medal, Joint Service Commendation Medal, two awards of the Army Commendation Medal.

Charles E. Honore
★★ ———————————————— ★★
Major General

Born April 20, 1934, in Baton Rouge, Louisiana, he is married to Jane Auzenne Honore, and they have four children: Charles, Jr., Melinda, Marlene, and Myra. Upon completion of the Reserve Officers Training Corps curriculum and the education course of study at Southern University Agricultural and Mechanical College in 1956, he was commissioned a second lieutenant and awarded a bachelor of arts degree in geography. He also holds a master of science in administration from George Washington University. His military education includes completion of the Armor Basic and Advanced Officer courses, the United States Army Command and General Staff College, and the Industrial College of the Armed Forces.

He has held a wide variety of command and staff positions in Vietnam, Europe, and the United States. He served as deputy chief of staff, Support/Commander, United States Army Element, Central Army Group, Europe, and chief, United States Army Readiness Group, Los Angeles, California. In addition to duty with the Department of the Army Office of the Inspector General, where he served as an investigator and later as the inspector general, Investigations Division, General Honore has had tours of duty as commander, 1st Brigade, 5th Infantry Division (Mechanized); commander, Headquarters Command, Fort Polk, Louisiana; deputy commander, Schweinfurt Military Community, Federal Republic of Germany; commander, 2nd Battalion, 64th Armor, 3rd Infantry Division; executive officer, 1st Squadron, 7th Cavalry, 1st Cavalry Division; and assistant division commander, 3rd Infantry Division (Mechanized), United States Army, Europe.

General Honore retired on July 31, 1990. His military awards and

Maj. Gen. Charles E. Honore

decorations include the Legion of Merit, Bronze Star Medal, Meritorious Service Medal (with oak leaf cluster), Air Medal, Army Commendation Medal, Combat Infantryman Badge.

Chauncey M. Hooper

★ —————————————————— ★

Brigadier General

Born June 5, 1894, in New Jersey. He entered the Army July 15, 1917. Served in both World Wars. A former lawyer and politician, he held the rank of colonel in the army when he retired in 1946. He remained active in the 369th Anti-Aircraft Artillery Group of New York, which he commanded during World War II. He became the first black to achieve the rank of brigadier general in the New York National Guard. He was promoted to Brigadier General on June 30, 1954 and retired on June 5, 1958. He died December 31, 1966.

Benjamin L. Hunton

★ —————————————————— ★

Brigadier General

Married the former Jean Cooper, and they had a son, Benjamin. He is a graduate of Howard University, receiving a B.A. degree in 1940, and a

M.A. degree in history in 1942. He earned a Ph.D. degree from American University in 1954.

From 1942 to 1966, he was a teacher and administrator in the Washington, D.C. school system. From 1966 to 1970, he served both the Department of Interior and the Department of Health, Education, and Welfare. In 1970, he was appointed assistant director of education and training for the Bureau of Mines, U.S. Department of Interior, in Washington, D.C. He administered a nationwide health and safety training program for the mineral industries and supervised all education and training efforts assigned to the bureau under the Coal Mine Health and Safety Act of 1969.

He was promoted to brigadier general on June 10, 1971, and assumed his duties as commander of the 97th Army Reserve Command in Fort George G. Meade, Maryland, in November 1972. He was commissioned during World War II and is a graduate of the Army Command and General Staff College at Fort Leavenworth, Kansas. He has written two studies which were published by the public schools of Washington, D.C. — "Study of Selected School Dropouts, 1963-1966" in 1967, and "Basic Track in Junior High School" in 1962.

His awards include the Meritorious Service Award, the World War II Victory Medal, the American Theatre Service Medal and the Armed Forces Reserve Medal (with hourglass). He was a member of the White House Committee on Civil Rights and Minority Affairs and the District of Columbia Commission on Academic Facilities.

Talmadge Jeffries Jacobs

★ ————————————————————— ★

Brigadier General

Born in Pendleton, North Carolina. He received a B.S. degree from Morgan State University. He earned a D.O. degree from the Philadelphia College of Osteopathic Medicine. He has held a variety of both career building and command staff assignments.

Jacobs served in several capacities at the headquarters of the 79th Army Reserve Command. He served as the assistant to the commanding general. He was assigned as the deputy chief of staff for personnel and administration. He was appointed chief of staff for the commanding general. He served as the commander of the 157th Infantry Brigade. In the United States Army Reserves he was appointed to the one star rank of brigadier general.

Brig. Gen. Talmadge Jeffries Jacobs

Avon C. James

★ ──────────────────────── ★

Brigadier General

Born October 9, 1930, in Hampton, Virginia, he married the former Borma M. Upton of Ipswich, England. They have a son, Stephen, and a daughter, Sheryl. He was graduated from Frederick Douglass High School, Baltimore, in 1947 and earned a bachelor's degree from Morgan State University in 1951.

He enlisted in the Air Force in 1951, serving as a weather observer with the Air Weather Service prior to entering Officer Candidate School. Following commissioning as a second lieutenant in June 1953, he attended Personnel Officer School and was assigned to the 81st Fighter Wing, Royal Air Force Station, Bentwater, England, as a personnel officer. In July 1957 he returned to the United States and was assigned to the 1001st Air Base Wing, Andrews Air Force Base, Maryland. While serving with the wing, General James was assigned as a personnel officer with the Field Maintenance Squadron, Operations Group, Maintenance and Supply Group, and completed his tour of duty as chief of the Consolidated Base Personnel Office.

In June 1963 he returned to England with the 304th Munitions Maintenance Squadron, Royal Air Force Station, Alconbury, where he served as chief of personnel and administration. In September 1965 he was assigned

Brig. Gen. Avon C. James

to the 7232nd Munitions Maintenance Group at Ramstein Air Base, Germany, as chief, Personnel and Administration Division. He returned to the United States in March 1967, assigned to the Analysis and Programming Branch of the Air Force Command Post's Systems Division, Headquarters, United States Air Force, Washington, D.C. During this assignment he served in several positions, each involving the development of applications software in support of the United States Air Force command and control system.

In July 1972 General James was assigned as a computer systems staff officer with the Automatic Data Processing Equipment Selection Directorate at Hanscom Air Force Base, Massachusetts, until July 1973 when he was assigned as chief of staff, Electronic Systems Division, Air Force Systems Command, Hanscom Air Force Base. In June 1978 he was assigned as the first deputy commander for data automation, Headquarters, Air Force Communications Command, Scott Air Force Base, Illinois, responsible for the overall management and direction of eight data automation organizations that provided a broad range of services to the Office of the Secretary of Defense, Headquarters, United States Air Force, major commands, bases, and designated government agencies. In February 1980 he was assigned as director of computer resources, Office of the Comptroller of the Air Force, Headquarters, United States Air Force, Washington, D.C.

He was appointed brigadier general on June 1, 1980, with the same date of rank. His military decorations and awards include the Legion of Merit (one oak leaf cluster), Meritorious Service Medal, Air Force Commendation Medal (one oak leaf cluster), Air Force Organizational Excellence Award.

Daniel James, Jr.

★★★★ ───────────────────── ★★★★

General

Born on February 11, 1920, in Pensacola, Florida, where he was graduated from Washington High School in June 1937. From September 1937 to March 1942, he attended Tuskegee Institute, where he received a bachelor of science degree in physical education and completed civilian pilot training under the government-sponsored Civilian Pilot Training Program. He remained at Tuskegee as a civilian instructor pilot in the Army Air Corps Aviation Cadet Program until January 1943 when he entered the program as a cadet and received his commission as a second lieutenant, July 1943. He next completed fighter pilot combat training at Selfridge Field, Michigan, and was assigned to various units in the United States for the next six years.

In September 1949, James went to the Philippines as flight leader for the 12th Fighter-Bomber Squadron, 18th Fighter Wing, Clark Field. In July 1950, he left for Korea, where he flew 101 combat missions in F-15 and F-80 aircraft. He returned to the United States and in July 1951 went to Otis Air Force Base, Massachusetts, as an all-weather jet fighter pilot with the 58th Fighter-Interceptor Squadron (FIS) and later became operations officer.

In April 1953 he became commander of the 437th FIS, and in August 1955 he assumed command of the 60th FIS. He graduated from the Air Command and Staff College in June 1957. In December 1966 he went to Ubon Royal Thai Air Force Base, Thailand. He flew 78 combat missions into North Vietnam. He led a flight into the Bolo Mig Sweep in which seven communist Mig 21s were destroyed, the highest total kill of any mission during the Vietnam War. He became deputy assistant secretary of defense (public affairs) in March 1970, and during his tenure at the Pentagon, James was promoted to brigadier general on July 1, 1970.

He assumed duty as vice commander of the Military Airlift Command, Scott Air Force Base, Illinois, on September 1, 1975, and was promoted to four stars on September 1, 1975. James was the first black American to be a full general in the history of the United States military service. He was assigned as commander in chief, NORAD/ADCOM, North American Air Defense Command. General James had operational command of all United States and Canadian strategic aerospace defense forces. He was responsible for the surveillance and air defense of North American aerospace and for providing warning and assessment of hostile attack on the continent by bombers or missiles.

On February 1, 1978, Gen. Daniel "Chapple" James, Jr., ended a long military career at the top of the heap after beginning as a young black lieutenant who risked court-martial to fight racial segregation. The Air Force arranged full military honors for General James's retirement ceremony, which marked the close of his nearly 35 years of service, spanning three wars. At a farewell Pentagon news conference, he reflected with obvious satisfaction that he had made it to the top of the heap, a dream fulfilled.

The general was widely known for his speeches on Americanism and patriotism for which he was editorialized in numerous national and international publications. Excerpts from some of the speeches have been read into the Congressional Record. He was awarded the George Washington Freedom Foundation Medal in 1967 and again in 1968. He received the Arnold Air Society Eugene M. Zuckert Award in 1970 for outstanding contributions to Air Force professionalism: "fighter pilot with a magnificent record, public speaker, and eloquent spokesman for the American Dream we so rarely achieve." The F-4C Phantom warplane flown by James sits outside the Aerospace Science and Health Education Center named in his honor at Tuskegee University. General James died on February 25, 1978.

Nathaniel James
★★ —————————————————— ★★
Major General

Was born July 28, 1935, in Branchville, South Carolina. He received a B.A. degree from the University of New York. He was commissioned second lieutenant of artillery, in June 1959. General James, was promoted to the rank of brigadier general of the line, in the New York National Guard on September 28, 1988, and on March 3, 1992, he was promoted to major general of the line. He married the former Mary L. Kuykendall and they have four children: Roslyn, Nathaniel Jr., Darryl and Eric. The general picture hangs in a position of honor at the United States Field Artillery, ocs Hall of Fame at Fort Sill, Oklahoma.

Charles B. Jiggetts
★ —————————————————— ★
Brigadier General

Born in Henderson, North Carolina, he married the former Barbara Mosley of Frederica, Delaware. They have one daughter, Victoria Lynn. He was graduated from high school at Henderson Institute in 1943 and received a bachelor of arts degree in political science from Howard University in 1950. He graduated from Squadron Officer School at Maxwell Air Force

Brig. Gen. Charles B. Jiggetts

Base, Alabama, in 1957 and completed Air Command and Staff College in 1963. He completed the Air War College in 1970 and the Industrial College of the Armed Forces Associate program in 1972.

In 1944 he enlisted in the United States Army Air Forces and was honorably discharged in May 1946. He was commissioned a second lieutenant in August 1950 through the Reserve Officers Training Corps program. His initial assignment was as a group adjutant and supply officer with the Basic Military Training Center, Sampson Air Force Base, New York. He attended flying school at James Connally Air Force Base, Texas, in 1952 and later became an aircraft observer and rador intercept officer. He served in that capacity at Tyndall Air Force Base, Florida; McGuire Air Force Base, New Jersey; and Elmendorf Air Force Base, Alaska.

In July 1957 he joined the 98th Fighter-Interceptor Squadron, Dover Air Force Base, Delaware, as flight and later squadron radar officer. He attended the Communications Officer Course at Keesler Air Force Base, Mississippi, in 1959. Upon completion of the course in 1960, he was assigned to the 27th Communications Squadron, Anderson Air Force Base, Guam, as squadron operations officer. In June 1963, General Jiggetts was a maintenance officer, chief of maintenance, and wing communications-electronics officer with the 92nd Strategic Aerospace Wing, Fairchild Air Force Base, Washington. The wing had operational responsibility for Fairchild-based Atlas E intercontinental ballistic missiles, B-52s, and KC-135s.

Transferring to Headquarters, Seventh Air Force, Tan Son Nhut Air Base, Vietnam, in May 1966, the general served as a communications-electronics requirements officer. General Jiggetts returned to the United

Charles B. Jiggetts   135

States in May 1967 as a joint communications staff officer with the United States Strike Command, MacDill Air Force Base, Florida. In August 1969 he was assigned to Headquarters, United States Air Force, Washington, D.C., as technical assistant to the director for telecommunications policy, Office of the Assistant Secretary of Defense (Installations and Logistics). He next served at Headquarters Strategic Air Command, Offutt Air Force Base, Nebraska, as chief, Program Management Division for Communications-Electronics.

From September 1971 to July 1974, General Jiggetts served as military assistant to the director of the Office of Telecommunications Policy, Executive Office of the President of the United States, Washington, D.C. He then became vice commander of the Air Force Communications Command's Northern Communications Area, Griffiss Air Force Base, New York. He served as commander, Northern Communications Area, from July 1976 to June 1979. The general transferred to Pacific Command at Camp H. M. Smith, Hawaii, as director of communications and data processing (later reorganized as Directorate of Command, Control, and Communications System), J-6. In February, 1981 he was assigned to Scott Air Force Base as Air Force Communications Command's deputy commander for combat communications and reserve force matters. He assumed his present duties in July 1981.

He was appointed brigadier general on April 1, 1977, with date of rank March 29, 1977. His military decorations and awards include the distinguished Service Medal, Defense Superior Service Medal, Legion of Merit (one oak leaf cluster), Bronze Star Medal, Meritorious Service Medal, Joint Service Commendation Medal, Air Force Commendation Medal. He also wears the air traffic controller's badge.

Julius Frank Johnson

★ ──────────────────────── ★

Brigadier General

Born February 8, 1940, Fort Leavenworth, Kansas. He received a bachelor of science degree in social science from Lincoln University and an M.D. in counseling psychology. He received a ROTC commission to second lieutenant in February 1964.

From February 1964 to April 1964, he was a student in the United States Army Infantry Center and School, Fort Benning, Georgia. From June 1964 to July 1965, he served as a rifle platoon leader, later reconnaissance platoon leader, later assistant S-3 operations officer, Headquarters,

Brig. Gen. Julius Frank Johnson

3rd Battalion, 32nd Infantry, Eighth United States Army, Korea. From July 1965 to January 1967, he was assigned as a platoon leader, later commander, Company E (Honor Guard), 1st Battalion, 3rd Infantry (Old Guard), Fort Meyer, Virginia.

He was promoted to first lieutenant on August 1, 1965, and captain on November 1, 1966. From January 1967 to March 1967, he was a student in the Special Forces Officer Qualification Course, United States Army Special Warfare School, Fort Bragg, North Carolina. From July 1967 to June 1968, he served as adjutant, 1st Battalion, 327th Infantry; later commander, Company A, 1st Battalion, 327th Infantry; later S-4 logistics officer, 1st Battalion, 327th Infantry, 101st Airborne Division, United States Army, Vietnam.

From June 1968 to July 1969, he was a platoon adviser, 2nd Student Battalion, Student Brigade; later, a student at the United States Army Infantry Center and School, Fort Benning, Georgia. From July 1969 to July 1972, he served as assistant professor of military science at Lincoln University, Jefferson City, Missouri. From July 1972 to February 1973, he was the commander of the Mobile Security Training Team, then the S-3 (Operations) Officer, Field Training Command, United States Military Advisory Group, Military Assistance Command, Vietnam.

From April 1973 to June 1974, he was assigned as the operations officer, Department of Non-Resident Instruction, later a student at the United States Army Command and General Staff College, Fort Leavenworth, Kansas. From July 1974 to May 1976, he served first as operations officer, G-2 (intelligence), Staff, United States Army Element, I Corps Group, Eighth United States Army, Korea, later as the S-3 (operations) officer, 3rd Brigade, 2nd Infantry Division, United States Army, Korea. From June 1976 to April 1981, he was personnel management officer, Officer Personnel Management Division, United States Army Military Personnel Center, Alexandria, Virginia, then personnel staff officer, Officer Division, Office of the Deputy Chief of Staff for Personnel, United States Army, Washington, D.C.

He was promoted to major on June 9, 1976, and lieutenant colonel on July 14, 1979. From June 1981 to June 1983, he was commander of the 2nd Battalion, 36th Infantry, 3rd Armored Division, United States Army, Europe. From June 1983 to June 1984, he was a student at the United States Army War College, Carlisle Barracks, Pennsylvania. From June 1984 to March 1985, he was director of operations (J-3), Armed Forces Inaugural Committee, Fort Lesley J. McNair, Washington, D.C.

He was promoted to colonel on November 1, 1984. From February 1988 to July 1989, he served as director, Joint Staff, Armed Forces Inaugural Committee, Washington, D.C. From July 1989 to June 1990, he was assistant division commander, 1st Armored Division, United States Army, Europe, and the Seventh Army. He was promoted to brigadier general on September 1, 1989. In June 1990 he was assigned as commanding general, First Reserve Officer Training Corps Region, Fort Bragg, North Carolina. He has received numerous awards and decorations: the Silver Star, the Bronze Star Medal (with two oak leaf clusters), Defense Meritorious Service Medal, Defense Superior Service Medal, Meritorious Service Medal, Air Medal, Army Commendation Medal (with oak leaf cluster), Combat Infantryman Badge, Parachutist Badge, Air Assault Badge.

Walter Frank Johnson III

★ ———————————————— ★

Brigadier General

Born August 13, 1939, Charleston, South Carolina. He earned a B.S. degree in zoology from West Virginia State College, an M.A. degree in political science from the University of Missouri.

His military career began in July 1961 when he entered the United States Army as a doctor in the Medical Service Corps, Officer Orientation Course, Medical Field Service School, Fort Sam Houston, Texas. From September 1961 to July 1963, he was assigned as a platoon leader, Headquarters and Headquarters Company, 2nd Airborne Brigade, 504th Infantry, 82nd Airborne Division, Fort Bragg, North Carolina. From August 1963 to June 1966, he was assigned first as a platoon leader, Company D,

Brig. Gen. Walter Frank Johnson III

then commander, Company D, then platoon leader, Company B, later as commander, Company B and S-1 adjutant all with the 8th Medical Battalion, 8th Infantry Division, United States Army, Europe.

In June 1966 he returned to the United States, a student in the Medical Service Corps Officer advanced course, Fort Sam Houston, Texas. From December 1966 to January 1968, he was assigned as the assistant plans and operations officer, later plans officer, 44th Medical Brigade, United States Army, Vietnam. Returning to the United States in January 1968, he was assigned as an instructor at the Brooke Army Medical Center, Fort Sam Houston, Texas. From July 1970 to June 1971, he was a student at the United States Army Command and General Staff College, Fort Leavenworth, Kansas.

From June 1972 to May 1977, Johnson was assigned first as a plans officer, later chief, Force Structure Branch, Plans and Operations Division, Health Care Operations Directorate, Office of the Surgeon General, United States Army, Washington, D.C. From May 1977 to May 1978, he served as commander, 2nd Medical Battalion, 2nd Infantry Division, Korea. From May 1978 to June 1980, he was assigned as the assistant executive officer, Office of the Surgeon General, United States Army, Washington, D.C. From June 1980 to June 1981, he was a student at the Industrial College of the Armed Forces, Fort Lesley J. McNair, Washington, D.C.

From October 1981 to October 1985, he was assigned to the Surgeon General Office, Washington, D.C., serving first as the assistant to the chief, Medical Service Corps, deputy director, personnel; next as chief executive to the surgeon general.

On November 1, 1985, Johnson was promoted to brigadier general and assigned as chief (the youngest ever appointed), Medical Service Corps, director, Health Care Operations, United States Army, Falls Church, Virginia. Gen. Walter Frank Johnson III retired on October 31, 1988.

His military awards and decorations include the Distinguished Service Medal, Legion of Merit (with oak leaf cluster), Bronze Star Medal, Meritorious Service Medal (with oak leaf cluster), Army Commendation Medal (with oak leaf cluster), Senior Parachutist Badge, Expert Field Medical Badge.

Wendell Norman Johnson

★★ ——————————————————— ★★

Rear Admiral

Born in Boston, Massachusetts, he married the former Helen Underwood of Boston, Massachusetts. They have three children: Laura, Lois, and W. Norman, Jr. He graduated from the New England College of Pharmacy and holds a master of arts degree in international communications from American University.

He was commissioned an ensign in May 1957 and began his Navy career on the auxiliary ship USS *Lookout.* A graduate of the United States Naval Postgraduate School, Engineering Curriculum, and the Armed Forces Staff College, Johnson also attended the National War College where he was recognized for outstanding scholarship by the college

Rear Adm. Wendell Norman Johnson

commandant and the Chief of Naval Operations. Subsequent sea duty included fire control and gunnery officer on the aircraft carrier USS *Coral Sea* and weapons officer on the destroyer USS *Ingraham,* later serving as executive officer on the destroyer USS *Jonas Ingram.* Johnson served as commander of the Charleston Naval Base in February 1987, and in August 1987 he assumed command of Mine Warfare Command in an additional duty capacity. Johnson was promoted to rear admiral in 1983. Rear Admiral Johnson retired from the Navy on April 14, 1989. Johnson's outstanding civic contributions were recognized by his mayoral appointment to a Community Relations Commission serving Duval County and the city of Jacksonville, Florida.

Rear Admiral Johnson's decorations and awards include the Legion of Merit, Meritorious Service Medal (with gold star in lieu of second award), Navy Commendation Medal (with gold star in lieu of second award), Navy Achievement Medal, Navy Combat Action Ribbon, Republic of Vietnam Honor Medal First Class, Order of Sikatuna, Philippine Government.

Hazel W. Johnson-Brown

★ ——————————————— ★

Brigadier General

Born October 10, 1927, in West Chester, Pennsylvania, the daughter of Clarence L. and Garnett Johnson. She married David B. Brown. She earned a diploma in nursing from Harlem Hospital in New York City, a bachelor's degree in nursing from Villanova University, a master's degree in nursing education from Teacher's College, Columbia University, and a doctorate in educational administration from Catholic University. In addition, she holds honorary doctorates from Morgan State University, Villanova University, and the University of Maryland.

From 1950 to 1953, she worked as a staff nurse in the emergency ward of Harlem Hospital in New York. Her responsibilities included evening and night duty; initial admission work-up for all patients except obstetrics. From 1953 to 1955, she was a staff nurse in the medical cardiovascular ward at Veterans Administrative Hospital, Philadelphia, Pennsylvania. There she became head nurse on ward within three months of employment. Entering the Army Nurse Corps in 1955, she served for the next 12 years in a variety of positions at Walter Reed Army Medical Center, the 8169 Hospital in Japan, Madigan General Hospital, Letterman General Hospital, 45th Surgical Hospital at Fort Sam Houston, and Valley Forge General Hospital.

Brig. Gen. Hazel W. Johnson-Brown

From 1967 to 1973, she was assigned to the staff of the United States Army Medical Research and Development Command as a project director in the Army Medical Department field hospital system. Upon completion of her doctoral studies, she was appointed director of the Walter Reed Army Institute of Nursing. In 1978, she was transferred to Korea to assume the positions of assistant for nursing, Office of the Surgeon, Eighth Army Command; chief, Department of Nursing, United States Army Hospital, 121 Evacuation Hospital, Seoul, South Korea; and chief consultant for nursing matters to the senior medical officer, Eighth Army Command.

In 1979 she was selected to the position of chief, Army Nurse Corps, and was promoted to the rank of brigadier general. General Johnson-Brown became the sixteenth chief of the Army Nurse Corps, the first chief holding an earned doctorate, the fourth chief to hold the rank of brigadier general, and the first black woman general in the history of the United States military services.

Among General Johnson-Brown's significant recognitions are Army Nurse of the Year awards from Letterman General Hospital and the Daughters of the American Revolution, the Army Commendation Medal (with oak leaf cluster), the Meritorious Service Medal, and the Legion of Merit. Upon retirement from active duty in 1983, General Johnson-Brown received the Distinguished Service Medal.

Prior to joining the faculty at George Mason University, Dr. Johnson-Brown served as assistant professor in the Graduate Nursing Administration program at Georgetown University and director of governmental affairs for the Washington office of the American Nurses' Association.

From 1983 to the present, Dr. Johnson-Brown has endeavored to translate her leadership skill and concern for young people, especially black youth, to work in her civilian position. As director, Division of Governmental Affairs, she worked diligently to increase the minority participation in professional positions with her office and the professional organization. That work continues in her teaching in her present organization, George Mason University. Within the university, she served as chair of the Minority Affairs Committee, consultant to the George Mason University Alumni Association, member of the Cultural Diversity Committee of the School of Nursing, and mentor to three black nursing students—further indication of her interest in furthering the careers of young black men and women. In addition to these activities, she maintains her membership in Black Women United for Action of Northern Virginia and was appointed in 1986 a member of the Board of Military Affairs for the Commonwealth of Virginia by Douglas Wilder, governor of Virginia.

In 1984, she was one of 13 women to receive the Outstanding Women of Color Award and one of 12 women to receive the National Coalition of 100 Black Women's Candace Award. Dr. Hazel Johnson-Brown, professor and member of the graduate faculty, School of Nursing, George Mason University. Was named in August 1989 director, Center for Health Policy, a new center in the School of Nursing. Dr. Johnson-Brown teaches health-care public policy and health-care administration.

Richard L. Jones

★ ———————————————— ★

Brigadier General

Born on December 21, 1893, in Albany, Georgia. He received his B.S. degree from the University of Cincinnati, Ohio. Served in the all black Infantry National Guard Regiment, the 369th Infantry Regiment, which was called to duty during World War II. The name of the regiment was eventually changed to the 369th Coast Artillery (AA) Group. He remained in the Illinois Army National Guard after World War II. He held a wide variety of important command and staff positions culminating in an appointment to the one star rank of brigadier general in the Illinois Army National Guard. Chicago's Richard L. Jones National Guard Center was named in his honor. He died in 1977.

Kenneth U. Jordan

★ ─────────────────────────────── ★

Brigadier General

Born in South Pittsburg, Tennessee. He received a bachelor of science degree in public administration from the University of Tennessee in Knoxville, Tennessee, in 1966, a J.D. degree from Vanderbilt University School of Law, Nashville, Tennessee, in 1974.

He was commissioned a second lieutenant in the United States Air Force through the ROTC program, while at the University of Tennessee. From 1966 to 1968, he served as a squadron section commander at Minot Air Force Base, North Dakota. From 1968 to 1969, he was the executive support officer at Ubon Royal Thai Air Force Base, Thailand. From 1969 to 1970, he was commander, Headquarters Squadron, MacDill Air Force Base, Florida.

He joined the Tennessee Air National Guard in 1976. Jordan left active duty in 1970, and accepted a position as an employee relations specialist for General Foods Corporation in White Plains, New York. From 1974 to 1975, he was an associate director, Fair Employment Practices Clinic, and clinical instructor at Vanderbilt Law School. From 1975 to 1977, he was the assistant dean for administration at Vanderbilt Law School. From 1977 to 1981, he was the director of the Opportunity Development Center at Vanderbilt University. From 1981 to 1983, he served as executive assistant to the president, later as interim vice president for development and public relations, later vice president for administration and general counsel, at Meharry Medical College, Nashville, Tennessee.

From 1983 to 1984, he was a student at the Air Command and Staff College, at the Air University, Maxwell Air Force Base, Montgomery, Alabama. From January 1985 to October 1985, he served as an attorney-adviser, Director, Equal Employment Opportunity Staff, Department of Justice, Washington, D.C. From October 1985 to January 1987, he served first as executive assistant to the assistant attorney general for administration, then as chief of staff, in the Justice Management Division, Department of Justice, Washington, D.C. He also served on the board of directors for the Department of Justice Federal Credit Union.

From January 1987 to August 1988, he served as an executive assistant to the governor (cabinet-level appointment) in the state capital, Nashville, Tennessee. He also served as chairman of the Governor's Task Force on Housing.

In September 1988 he was promoted to brigadier general, becoming the first black to serve as the assistant adjutant general for the Tennessee Air

Brig. Gen. Kenneth U. Jordan

National Guard. He has served on numerous boards, both civic and community: Tennessee Task Force on the Supply of Minority Teachers (governor's representative); Statewide Area Health Education Centers (AHEC) Advisory Committee, Meharry Medical College; Boy Scouts' Inner-City Task Force Finance Committee; Chairman, Project Blueprint Committee, United Way of Middle Tennessee; National Committee for Employer Support of the Guard and Reserve (Tennessee committee), United States Department of Defense (term expires January 1994).

Larry Reginald Jordan

★ ———————————————— ★

Brigadier General

Born February 7, 1946, in Kansas City, Kansas, he married the former Nannette Pippen, and they have two sons, Larry, Jr., and Karl. He received a bachelor of science degree from the United States Military Academy in 1968, a master of arts degree from Indiana University in 1975. His military schooling includes the Armor School, Basic Course (1968); United States Marine Corps Amphibious Warfare School (1972); United States Army Command and General Staff College (1979); National War College (1987).

He received his commission as a second lieutenant in 1968 after he graduated from the United States Military Academy. From August 1968 to October 1968, he was a student at the Ranger Course, United States Army

Brig. Gen. Larry Reginald Jordan

Infantry School, Fort Benning, Georgia. His initial assignment was with the 2nd Battalion, 66th Armor, Fort Hood, Texas, as a tank platoon leader. From July 1969 to March 1970, he was assigned to Vietnam where he served with the 1st Infantry Division as an infantry platoon leader with Company B, 2nd Battalion, 2nd Infantry and 1st Infantry divisions, United States Army, Vietnam. From March 1970 to June 1970, he was executive officer, Troop A, 2nd Squadron, 1st Cavalry Division, United States Army, Vietnam.

He returned to the United States in July 1970 and was assigned as commander of Company C (later Headquarters Company), 1st Battalion, 63rd Armor, 1st Infantry Division (Mechanized), Fort Riley, Kansas. Subsequent assignments included tours with the Combat Arms Training Board, Headquarters, TRADOC, and the faculty of the United States Military Academy. In 1979 he was reassigned to USAREUR where he served as executive officer, 3rd Battalion, 33rd Armor, 3rd Armored Division, and later as war plans officer, Office of the Deputy Chief of Staff for Logistics, United States Army, Europe. In May 1982 he returned to the United States and was assigned as staff action officer, Office of the Deputy Chief of Staff for Operations and Plans, United States Army, Washington, D.C.

In November 1983 General Jordan assumed command of 1st Battalion, 67th Armor, 2nd Armored Division, and remained until May 1986. Following completion of studies at the National War College, he was assigned duties with the Directorate of Operational Plans and Interoperability, J-7, OJCS. Prior to assuming duties as assistant division commmander for support, 1st Armored Division, General Jordan served as the assistant division commander for support, 3rd Armored Division, Hanau, Germany; chief of staff, 1st Armored Division, Ansbach, Germany; and commander, 2nd Brigade, 3rd Infantry Division, Kitzingen, Germany. In November 1991 he was assigned as assistant division commander, 8th Infantry Division (Mechanized), United States Army, Europe, and Seventh Army.

He was appointed brigadier general in November 1991. His military decorations and awards include the Silver Star, Bronze Star Medal (with "V" device and one oak leaf cluster), Bronze Star Medal (two oak leaf clusters), Defense Meritorious Service Medal, Army Meritorious Service Medal (two oak leaf clusters), Army Commendation Medal (with "V" device), Army Commendation Medal (one oak leaf cluster), Army Achievement Medal (one oak leaf cluster), Combat Infantryman Badge, Parachutist Badge, Ranger Tab, Joint Chiefs of Staff Identification Badge, Army Staff Identification Badge.

John Q. Taylor King, Sr.
★★★ ——————————————— ★★★
Lieutenant General

Born September 25, 1921, in Memphis, Tennessee, he married the former Marcet Alice Hines of Chicago, Illinois. They have three sons, one daughter, and nine grandchildren. He was graduated from Anderson High School in Austin, Texas. He received a bachelor of arts degree from Fisk University, Nashville, Tennessee, in 1941; a bachelor of science degree from Huston-Tillotson College in Austin, Texas; a master's of science from DePaul University, Chicago, Illinois; and a Ph.D. from the University of Texas at Austin. He received an honorary doctor of laws from Southwestern University, Georgetown, Texas, and St. Edward's University, Austin, Texas; an honorary doctor of humane letters from Austin College, Sherman, Texas, and Fisk University; and an honorary doctor of science from Huston-Tillotson College.

He entered World War II as a private, served as a captain in the Pacific theater, and retired from the Army of the United States as a major general on August 22, 1983. Since World War II, he has served in Alaska, Japan, Korea, Okinawa, Germany, Hawaii, and many other United States Army and United States Air Force installations. He has completed courses at several senior service schools, including the Command and General Staff College, the Air War College, the Industrial College of the Armed Forces, the Logistics Executive Development Course, and the SROG at the Army War College. He has received many military awards and decorations.

Former Texas governor Mark White appointed him lieutenant general in the Texas State Guard in 1985. He joined the faculty of Huston-Tillotson

Lt. Gen. John Q. Taylor King, Sr.

College in 1947, was professor of mathematics for several years and dean of the college for five years, was appointed president in 1965 and chancellor in 1987. He retired on June 30, 1988, and served as director and chair of the Center for the Advancement of Science, Engineering, and Technology (CASET), a research component of the college.

Well known as a writer, collaborating with others on four textbooks in mathematics and contributing many articles to professional and religious journals, Dr. King is coauthor with his wife of two books, *Stories of Twenty-Three Famous Negro Americans* and *Famous Black Americans,* and a booklet on the life of Mrs. Mary McLeod Bethune. General King served as a member of the board of directors of several organizations including Texas Commerce Bank–Austin, Austin Chapter National Conference of Christians and Jews, the Capitol Area Council, and Boy Scouts of America, and as former chair of the Lone Star District. A former chairman of the Austin Civil Service Commission, he is a trustee of Austin College, a former trustee of Fisk University, and a member of the Philosophical Society of Texas. A licensed mortician, he served as president of King-Tears Mortuary, Inc.

He has received many awards and honors: the Roy Wilkins Meritorious Award, NAACP; the Arthur B. Dewitty Award; the Martin Luther King, Jr., Humanitarian Award; the Military/Education Award: the Whitney M. Young, Jr., Award; the Minority Advocate of the Year Award, Austin Chamber of Commerce.

James Richard Klugh

★★ ———————————————————— ★★

Major General

Born on June 22, 1931, in Greenwood, South Carolina, he married the former Theresa Minnis, and they have three children: Jerome, James, and Denise. He received an Army Reserve commission as a second lieutenant through the Reserve Officer Training Corps Program at South Carolina State University, where he also received a bachelor of science degree in public administration. His military education includes the Infantry School, the Chemical School, the United States Army Command and General Staff College, the Logistics Executive Development Course, and the United States Army War College.

He has held a wide variety of command and staff assignments, including a tour in Germany and staff assignment with the 101st Airborne Division in Vietnam. His significant assignments include commander, 502nd Supply and Transportation Battalion, 2nd Armored Division, Fort Hood, Texas; chief of staff, United States Army Tank-Automotive Command, Warren, Michigan; commander, Dugway Proving Ground, Utah; deputy director, Officer Personnel Management Division, United States Army Military Personnel Center, Alexandria, Virginia; and deputy commander for training development, United States Army Logistics Center, Fort Lee, Virginia.

He assumed his current duties at Aberdeen Proving Ground,

Maj. Gen. James Richard Klugh

Maryland, in February 1984 as deputy commanding general, Chemical Materiel, United States Army Armament, Munitions and Chemical Command, Commanding General, United States Army Chemical Research and Development Center.

His military awards and decorations include the Legion of Merit (with two oak leaf clusters), Meritorious Service Medal (with oak leaf cluster), several Air Medals, Army Commendation Medal (with two oak leaf clusters), Parachutist Badge.

In 1982 General Klugh was inducted into the South Carolina College Army Reserve Officer Training Corps Hall of Fame for outstanding contributions to the United States of America. He retired on March 31, 1990.

Fredric Homer Leigh

★ ──────────────────────────── ★

Brigadier General

Born March 29, 1940, in Ohio. He received a bachelor of arts degree in history from Central State University, a master of science degree in public relations from Syracuse University.

He entered the United States Army in 1963 with an ROTC commission as second lieutenant. From September 1963 to November 1963, he was a student in the Infantry Officer Basic Course at the United States Army Infantry Center and School, Fort Benning, Georgia. From December 1963 to February 1964, he was a student in the Ranger Course at the United States Army Infantry Center and School. From February 1964 to May 1964, he was a platoon leader in Company B, 1st Battalion, 2nd Infantry Brigade, Fort Devens, Massachusetts. From May 1964 to September 1964, he served as a member of the Infantry Committee, First United States Army Demonstration and Instruction Team, Camp Drum, New York.

He was promoted to first lieutenant on February 4, 1965, and in March 1965 assigned as an assistant operations officer in the 2nd Brigade, 5th Infantry Division (Mechanized), Fort Devens, Massachusetts. He was promoted to captain on August 25, 1966.

In July 1966 he was the commander of Company B, the 2nd Infantry Brigade, 1st Infantry Division, United States Army, Vietnam. From September 1966 to November 1968, he served as an assistant professor of military science at Tuskegee Institute, Tuskegee, Alabama. From December 1968 to December 1969, he served first as an assistant S-3 (operations), then as assistant G-3, plans officer, Headquarters and Headquarters

Brig. Gen. Fredric Homer Leigh

Company, 101st Airborne Division (Air Assault), United States Army, Vietnam. From January 1970 to September 1970, he was a student in the Infantry Officer Advanced Course at the United States Army Infantry Center and School, Fort Benning, Georgia.

He was promoted to major on January 20, 1970. From August 1972 to June 1973, he was a student at the United States Army Command and General Staff College, Fort Leavenworth, Kansas. From June 1973 to January 1976, he served as a plans, program, and budget officer in the Command Information Division, Office of the Chief of Information, United States Army, Washington, D.C. From January 1976 to May 1978, he served first as the executive officer of the 2nd Battalion, 503rd Infantry, then as executive officer of the 2nd Brigade, 101st Airborne Division (Air Assault), Fort Campbell, Kentucky.

He was promoted to lieutenant colonel on August 4, 1977. From July 1978 to July 1979, he was commander, 1st Battalion, 38th Infantry, 2nd Infantry Division, United States Army, Korea. From August 1979 to August 1981, he was a military assistant with the Assistant Secretary of the Army (Manpower and Reserve Affairs), United States Army, Washington, D.C. From August 1981 to June 1982, he was a student at the National War College, Fort McNair, Washington, D.C. From June 1982 to June 1983, he served as the senior military assistant, Office of the Secretary of the Army, United States Army, Washington, D.C.

From June 1983 to June 1985, he served as deputy director, Army Staff, Office of the Chief of Staff, United States Army, Washington, D.C. He was promoted to colonel on September 1, 1983. From July 1985 to May 1987, he was chief of staff, 19th Support Command, Eighth United States

Army, Korea. From August 1987 to August 1989, he served as commander, 1st Brigade, 101st Airborne Division (Air Assault), Fort Campbell, Kentucky. From August 1989 to March 1990, he served as director, Senior Leadership Research, United States Army War College, Carlisle Barracks, Pennsylvania. In March 1990 he was assigned as assistant division commander, 7th Infantry Division (Light), Fort Ord, California.

He was promoted to brigadier general on August 1, 1990. He has received numerous awards and decorations including the Legion of Merit (with two oak leaf clusters), Bronze Star Medal (with four oak leaf clusters), Bronze Star Medal (with "V" device), Meritorious Service Medal (with two oak leaf clusters), Air Medal, Army Commendation Medal (with oak leaf cluster), Combat Infantryman Badge, Parachutist Badge, Air Assault Badge, Ranger Tab.

Alfonso Emanual Lenhardt

★ ———————————————— ★

Brigadier General

Born October 29, 1943, New York, New York. He received a bachelor of science degree in criminal justice from the University of Nebraska at Omaha. He received a master's law administration from Central Michigan University.

He enlisted in the United States Army in November 1965. In October 1966 he entered the Tactical Officer, Infantry Officer Candidate School, 60th Company, of the 6th Student Battalion, Student Brigade, United States Army Infantry School, Fort Benning, Georgia. From October 1967 to September 1968, he was a platoon leader in Company C, 4th Battalion, 12th Infantry, 199th Infantry Brigade, United States Army, Vietnam. From October 1968 to June 1969, he served as commander, Company A, 10th Battalion, 4th Advanced Individual Training Brigade (Military Police), United States Army Training Center, Fort Gordon, Georgia.

He was promoted to captain on October 19, 1968. From June 1969 to December 1969, he served as chief, Military Police Subjects Committee, 4th Advanced Individual Training Center, Fort Gordon. From December 1969 to August 1970, he served as assistant S-2 (intelligence), S-3 (operations) officer, 4th Advanced Individual Training Brigade (Military Police), Fort Gordon.

From August 1970 to May 1971, he was a student at the Military Police Officer Advanced Course at Fort Gordon. From May 1972 to August 1972, he served as an action officer in the Special Activity Division, Operations

Brig. Gen. Alfonso Emanual Lenhardt

Directorate, United States Army Criminal Investigation Command, Washington, D.C. From August 1972 to February 1973, he served as chief, Operations Center, United States Army Criminal Investigation Command, Washington, D.C. From February 1973 to June 1973, he was chief of the Region Coordination Division, United States Army Criminal Investigation Command, Washington, D.C. From June 1973 to September 1973, he was a student at the Federal Bureau of Investigation National Academy, Quantico, Virginia. From September 1973 to August 1975, he was commander, Fort Eustis Field Office, 1st Regional United States Army Criminal Investigations Division Command, Fort Eustis, Virginia. From August 1975 to June 1976, he was a student at the United States Army Command and General Staff College, Fort Leavenworth, Kansas.

He was promoted to major on June 5, 1976. From June 1976 to December 1976, he was a student at Wichita State University, Wichita, Kansas. From December 1976 to June 1977, he served as operations officer in the Provost Marshal Office, Fort Dix, New Jersey. From June 1977 to June 1978, he was executive officer, 759th Military Police Battalion, Fort Dix, New Jersey. From June 1978 to June 1980, he served as company tactical officer, Staff and Faculty, United States Army Military Academy.

From June 1980 to May 1981, Lenhardt served as chief, Policy Branch, Office of the Provost Marshal, United States Army, Europe, and Seventh Army. He was promoted to lieutenant colonel on July 13, 1980. From June 1981 to May 1983, he served as 385th Military Battalion, VII Corps, United States Army, Europe. From May 1983 to June 1984, he was a student at the National War College, Fort Lesley J. McNair, Washington, D.C. From June 1984 to March 1985, he was deputy director, Research, and assistant to director, Strategic Defense Initiative Organization, Office of the Secretary of Defense, Washington, D.C.

He was promoted to colonel on November 1, 1984. From March 1985 to June 1986, he was executive officer and assistant to the director, Strategic Defense Initiative Organization, Office of the Secretary of Defense, Washington, D.C. From June 1986 to June 1988, he was the commander of the 18th Military Police Brigade, V Corps, United States Army, Europe. From July 1988 to August 1989, he served as deputy provost marshal, Office of the Provost Marshal, United States Army, Europe, and Seventh Army.

In September 1989 he was promoted to brigadier general and assigned as deputy commanding general, East, United States Army Recruiting Command, Fort Sheridan, Illinois. He has received numerous awards and decorations: the Defense Superior Service Medal, Bronze Star Medal, Purple Heart, Meritorious Service Medal (with two oak leaf clusters), Air Medal, Joint Service Commendation Medal, Army Commendation Medal (with two oak leaf clusters), Army Achievement Medal, Humanitarian Service Medal, Combat Infantryman Badge, Parachutist Badge.

Lester L. Lyles

★ ———————————————————— ★

Brigadier General

Born April 20, 1946, in Washington, D.C., he married the former Mina McGraw of Washington, D.C. They have four children: Renee, Phillip, Leslie, and Lauren. He was graduated from McKinley Technical High School in 1963. He earned a bachelor of science degree in mechanical engineering from Howard University in 1968 and a master of science degree in mechanical and nuclear engineering, through the Air Force Institute of Technology program, from New Mexico State University in 1969. He completed the Defense Systems Management College in 1980, Armed Forces Staff College in 1981, and National War College in 1985. He attended the National and International Security Management Course at the John F. Kennedy School of Government, Harvard University, in 1991.

A distinguished graduate of the Air Force Reserve Officer Training Corps program, he was commissioned as a second lieutenant in 1968. Upon completion of graduate school in February 1969, General Lyles was assigned as a propulsion and structures engineer in the Standard Space Launch Vehicles Program Office, Headquarters, Space and Missiles Systems Organization, Los Angeles Air Force Station, in California. In November 1971 he became a propulsion engineer in the Headquarters, Aeronautical

Brig. Gen. Lester L. Lyles

Systems Division, Wright-Patterson AFB, Ohio, located in the Short-Range Attack Missile Program Office. In July 1974 the general was assigned to Headquarters, United States Air Force, Washington, D.C., as program element monitor for the SRAM strategic missile and was subsequently reassigned as executive officer to the deputy chief of staff for research and development.

In March 1978 General Lyles was selected as aide-de-camp and special assistant to the commander of Air Force Systems Command. He later attended the Defense Systems Management College from January to June 1980. Upon graduation from the Armed Forces Staff College in January 1981, the general returned to Wright-Patterson AFB as avionics division chief in the F-16 System Program Office. He later became the deputy director for special and advanced projects. He completed National War College in June 1985, then became director of tactical aircraft systems under the deputy chief of staff for systems, AFSC headquarters. The general was reassigned to Los Angeles AFS in June 1987 as director, Medium Launch Vehicles Program Office. In April 1988 he became assistant deputy commander for launch systems at Headquarters, Space Systems Division, Los Angeles. He was reassigned as the assistant deputy chief of staff for requirements, AFSC headquarters, in August 1989.

He was appointed brigadier general on May 1, 1991, with same date of rank. His military awards and decorations include the Legion of Merit, Meritorious Service Medal (three oak leaf clusters), Air Force Commendation Medal, Senior Missileman Badge, Space Badge.

James Franklin McCall

★★★ ──────────────────────────── ★★★

Lieutenant General

Born June 25, 1934, Philadelphia, Pennsylvania. He received a bachelor of science degree in economics from the University of Pennsylvania and a master's of business administration in comptrollership from Syracuse University.

He entered the United States Army in March 1958 and became a platoon leader in Company A, 12th Battalion, 4th Training Regiment, United States Army Training Center, Fort Knox, Kentucky. From December 1958 to August 1959, he was the commander of Company A, 12th Battalion, 4th Training Regiment, United States Army Training Center. From August 1959 to March 1960, he was an instructor in the 12th Battalion, 4th Training Regiment.

On September 4, 1959, he was promoted to first lieutenant. From March 1960 to June 1961, he was a platoon leader, Combat Support Company, 1st Battle Group, 7th Cavalry, United States Army, Europe. From June 1962 to January 1963, he served as assistant S-2 with the 1st Battle Group, 3rd Infantry, Fort Myer, Virginia. He was promoted to captain on September 4, 1962. From January 1963 to June 1963, he was commander, Company C, 1st Battle Group, 3rd Infantry, Fort Myer, Virginia. From August 1963 to July 1964, he was a student in the Infantry officer Advanced Course (later Ranger Course) at the United States Infantry School, Fort Benning, Georgia. From July 1964 to October 1965, he served as the S-2, 2nd Battalion, 6th Infantry, Berlin Brigade, United States Army, Europe. From November 1965 to April 1966, he was secretary of the general staff, Headquarters, Berlin Brigade, United States Army, Europe. From June 1966 to November 1966, he was the commander of Company M, 4th Battalion, 2nd Basic Training Brigade, Fort Dix, New Jersey.

He was promoted to the rank of major on November 23, 1966. From April 1967 to May 1968, he served as an adviser on Advisory Team 96, United States Military Assistance Command, Vietnam. From May 1968 to May 1969, he was a student at the United States Command and General Staff College, Fort Leavenworth, Kansas. From August 1970 to July 1973, he served as a military assistant, Office of the Assistant Secretary of the Army (Financial Management), Washington, D.C.

He was promoted to lieutenant colonel on November 9, 1971. From August 1973 to August 1974, he was commander, 1st Battalion, 31st Infantry, 2nd Infantry Division, Korea. From September 1974 to August 1975, he served as a staff officer with the Army Materiel Acquisition Review

Lt. Gen. James Franklin McCall

Committee-Armament, United States Materiel Command, Alexandria, Virginia. From August 1975 to June 1976, he was a student at the Industrial College of the Armed Forces, Fort Lesley J. McNair, Washington, D.C.

On February 1, 1976, he was promoted to colonel. From June 1976 to June 1977, he served as executive, Office of the Director of the Army Budget, Comptroller of the Army, Washington, D.C. From July 1977 to April 1979, he was the commander of the 4th Training Brigade, United States Army Armor School, Fort Knox, Kentucky; from June 1979 to July 1980, chief, Procurement Programs and Budget Division, Materiel Plans and Programs Directorate, Office of the Deputy Chief of Staff for Research, Development, and Acquisition, United States Army, Washington, D.C.

He was promoted to brigadier general on March 1, 1980. From July 1980 to June 1984, he served as comptroller, United States Army Materiel Development and Readiness Command, Alexandria, Virginia. He was promoted to major general on September 1, 1983. From June 1984 to July 1988, he served as the director of the Army budget, Office of the Comptroller, United States Army, Washington, D.C.

On July 1, 1988, he was promoted to lieutenant general. In July 1988, he was assigned as comptroller of the Army, Office of the Secretary of the Army, Washington, D.C. He has received numerous awards, decorations and badges, including the Parachutist Badge, Distinguished Service Medal, Legion of Merit (with oak leaf cluster), Meritorious Service Medal, Air Medal, Army Commendation Medal (with oak leaf cluster), Combat Infantryman Badge.

Raymond V. McMillan

★ ———————————————————— ★

Brigadier General

Born August 15, 1933, in Fairmont, North Carolina, he married the former Maxine Tyler of Hillside, New Jersey. They have two children: Raymond and Debra. He earned bachelor and master of science degrees in electrical engineering from the University of Wyoming in 1970 and 1971, respectively. The general was graduated from Squadron Officer School, Maxwell Air Force Base, Alabama, in 1962; Armed Forces Staff College of the Armed Forces, Fort Lesley J. McNair, Washington, D.C., in 1977. He completed the Senior Executive Course at the Massachusetts Institute of Technology in 1983.

After enlisting in the United States Air Force in August 1950 and completing basic training at Lackland Air Force Base, Texas, he was assigned to Highland Air Force Station in New Jersey as a radar maintenance technician. Upon attaining the rank of technical sergeant, General McMillan attended Officer Candidate School at Lackland Air Force Base and was commissioned a second lieutenant in December 1958. He was then assigned as a student in the Armament Officers Course Lowry Air Force Base, Colorado, and remained there as a technical instructor in the Avionics Officer Course. During this period he attended Squadron Officer School at Maxwell Air Force Base.

In June 1964 the general was assigned to Francis E. Warren Air Force Base, Wyoming, as a Minuteman missile launch officer. After completing this assignment in 1968, he attended the University of Wyoming under the Air Force Institute of Technology Program. He was assigned to Hanscom Air Force Base, Massachusetts, in January 1971 as a radar engineer in the Airborne Warning and Control System Program Office for E-3As.

General McMillan was a radar engineer on the first flight of one of the radar test aircraft and has more than 200 flying hours as a test engineer in the Airborne Warning and Control System Program. He attended the Armed Forces Staff College from January to July 1973. He was then assigned to Andrews Air Force Base, Maryland, and served as chief, the Airborne Warning and Control System Division, Air Force Systems Command, later as executive officer for the deputy chief of staff, systems. He then attended the Industrial College of the Armed Forces.

Returning to Hanscom Air Force Base in June 1977, the general served as program director of the SEEK IGLOO Program, the program to replace all surveillance radars in Alaska. While at Hanscom, he also served as program director of the Joint Surveillance System, the replacement program

Brig. Gen. Raymond V. McMillan

for the Semi-Automatic Ground Environment System, and as assistant deputy chief of staff for surveillance and control system.

In March 1980 General McMillan was given the task of forming an Air Force Systems Command detachment in Colorado Springs, Colorado. The detachment assists the commander in chief, North American Air Defense, and the commander, Space Command, in resolving system acquisition problems. When the Space Command System Integration Office was formed in 1981, he became the deputy chief of the organization and served in both positions until May 1983. The general then returned to Andrews Air Force Systems Command. General McMillan returned to Headquarters, North American Aerospace Defense Command and Space Command, in April 1984 as deputy chief of staff, systems integration, and chief, Systems Integration Office, Space Command.

In September, 1985 Brigadier General McMillan served as chief, System Integration Office, and assistant deputy chief of staff, Systems Integration, Logistics and Support, at the United States Air Force Space Command, Peterson Air Force Base, Colorado.

He was appointed brigadier general on September 1, 1984, with the same date of rank. His military decorations and awards include the Defense Superior Service Medal, Legion of Merit, Meritorious Service Medal (one oak leaf cluster), Air Force Commendation Medal, Air Force Outstanding Unit Award, Air Force Organizational Excellence Award, Army Good Conduct Medal (with two bronze loops). He wears the Space Badge and the Senior Missile Badge.

Marion Mann

★ ——————————————————————— ★

Brigadier General

Born March 29, 1920, in Atlanta, Georgia. He and his wife, Ruth, have two children—Marion, Jr., and Judith R. He received a B.S. degree from Tuskegee Institute in 1940 and an M.D. degree from Howard University College of Medicine in 1954. In 1961 he earned a Ph.D. from Georgetown University.

General Mann began his military career in 1942 during World War II. He remained on in the active Army until 1950 when he transferred to the United States Army Reserves. He has held a wide variety of important command and staff positions, culminating in his final assignment, from 1975 to 1980, as a brigadier general in the United States Army Reserves. He retired from the United States Army Reserves in 1980. He also served as dean of the College of Medicine of Howard University from 1970 to 1979. He served in positions from assistant to full professor in the Department of Pathology, and in 1988 he was appointed associate vice president for research at Howard University.

He holds membership in numerous organizations, including the National Medical Association, and the National Academy of Sciences. He has received numerous honors and awards, civic and military.

Brig. Gen. Marion Mann

Frank Lee Miller, Jr.

★★ ──────────────────── ★★

Major General

Born January 27, 1944, in Atchison, Kansas, he married the former Paulette C. Duncan of Tacoma, Washington. They have three children: Frank III, Michael, and Toni. He received a bachelor of arts degree in business administration from the University of Washington in 1973, a master of science degree from Troy State University in 1979.

He entered the Army in October 1965 as a private and attended the Field Artillery Officer Candidate School immediately after basic training. He was commissioned on September 13, 1966, and assigned to Fort Lewis, Washington, as a basic training company training officer. From June 1967 to September 1968, he served as a forward observer, with Battery B, 1st Battalion, 5th Artillery, 1st Infantry Division, United States Army, Vietnam.

He returned to the United States in September 1968, then attended Field Artillery Officer Advanced Course, United States Army Field Artillery School, Fort Sill, Oklahoma. Upon graduation, he returned to Fort Lewis and was assigned to the 212th Field Artillery Group where he commanded A Battery, 2nd Battalion, 34th Field Artillery. After Fort Lewis, General Miller served a tour in Korea at battalion and division levels.

Returning from Korea in 1971, he attended the University of Washington, Seattle. In August 1973 he was assigned as motor officer, 1st Infantry Division, Fort Riley, Kansas. While in the 1st Division Artillery, General Miller commanded his second battery, served as a battalion S-3, participated in four REFORGER exercises. In June 1977, after he graduated from the United States Army Command and General Staff College at Fort Leavenworth, Kansas, he was assigned as operations and intelligence officer, Silk Purse Control Group, United States European Command, Mildenhall, England. Returning to the United States in July 1908, he was promoted to lieutenant colonel and selected to command the 1st Battalion, 35th Field Artillery, Fort Stewart, in Georgia.

After 30 months of that command, he was selected for promotion to colonel and attended the Naval War College in Newport, Rhode Island, where he graduated with distinction in June 1984. General Miller served as chief of staff, United States Army National Training Center, from July 1984 to July 1986. In August 1986 he was assigned to Athens, Greece, where he assumed command of the 558th United States Army Artillery Group. He returned to Fort Sill, Oklahoma, as chief of staff. In June 1989 he assumed command of III Corps Artillery.

Maj. Gen. Frank Lee Miller, Jr.

He was appointed brigadier general on June 1, 1990. His decorations and awards include the Legion of Merit (one oak leaf cluster), Distinguished Flying Cross, Bronze Star Medal (with "V" and two oak leaf clusters), Meritorious Service Medal, Air Medal (with "V" and 19 oak leaf clusters), Joint Service Commendation Medal, Army Commendation Medal (four oak leaf clusters), State of Georgia Meritorious Service Medal, Vietnamese Cross of Gallantry (with silver star), Aircraft Crew Member Badge.

James W. Monroe

★ ———————————————————— ★

Brigadier General

Born March 12, 1942, in North Carolina. He received a bachelor of science degree in electrical engineering from West Virginia State College in 1963, a master of arts degree in political science from the University of Cincinnati in 1973. He received an ROTC Commission to second lieutenant on October 5, 1963.

From October 1963 to December 1963, he was a student in the Ordnance Officer Basic Course, United States Army Ordnance Center and School, Aberdeen Proving Ground, Maryland. From February 1964 to April 1964, he was a student in the Armor Officer Basic Course, United States Army Armor School, Fort Knox, Kentucky. From August 1964 to February 1966, he served as platoon leader, Armored Cavalry, B Troop;

Brig. Gen. James W. Monroe

later platoon leader, Troop A, 2nd Squadron, 9th Cavalry, 24th Infantry Division, United States Army, Europe.

He was promoted to first lieutenant on April 5, 1965. From February 1966 to June 1967, he was commander, 621st General Supply Company, United States Army, Europe. Promoted to captain on September 20, 1966, from June 1967 to June 1968, he was a student in the Defense Language Institute, East Coast Branch, United States Naval Station, Anacostia, Washington, D.C. From June 1968 to June 1969, he was assigned as ordnance adviser, United States Military Training Mission, Saudi Arabia. From July 1969 to June 1970, he was a student in the Ordnance Officer Advanced Course, United States Army Ordnance Center and School, Aberdeen Proving Ground, Maryland.

From June 1970 to June 1972, he served as assistant professor of military science, First United States Army, Fort Meade, Maryland, with duty at the University of Cincinnati, Ohio. From August 1973 to July 1976, he was assigned as strategic intelligence officer in the Office of the Assistant Chief of Staff for Intelligence, United States Army, Washington, D.C. From August 1976 to June 1977, he was a student in the United States Army General and Command Staff College, Fort Leavenworth, Kansas.

From June 1977 to July 1978, he was commander, 61st Maintenance Company, Eighth United States Army, Korea. From July 1978 to October 1979, he was assigned as executive officer of the 709th Maintenance Battalion, 9th Infantry Division, Fort Lewis, Washington; from November 1979 to June 1982, deputy commander, later commander, Division Materiel and Management Center, and executive officer of Division Support Command, 9th Infantry Division, Fort Lewis, Washington.

He was promoted to lieutenant colonel on November 7, 1979. From June 1982 to March 1985, he was the commander of the 71st Maintenance Battalion, VII Corps, United States Army, Europe. From June 1985 to June 1986, he was a student in the Industrial College of the Armed Forces, Fort Lesley J. McNair, Washington, D.C. He was promoted to colonel on February 1, 1986. From June 1986 to June 1987, he served as a member of the faculty of the Senior Service College, National Defense University, Fort Lesley, J. McNair, Washington, D.C. From July 1987 to July 1989, he was the commander of the Division Support Command, 24th Infantry Division (Mechanized), Fort Stewart, Georgia.

From July 1989 to July 1990, he was assigned as assistant chief of staff, G-4 (logistics), Third United States Army, Fort McPherson, Georgia. From August 1990 to April 1991, he served in Saudi Arabia, where he was assigned the duties of logistics officer on the "Patton's Third Army" staff and designated the deputy chief of staff for logistics and host nation support, ARCENT. In this position, he was a close logistics planner and adviser to the in-country United States Army commander.

General Monroe initiated the logistics planning and arrangements to support United States Army forces and certain Marine and Air Force units in Desert Shield and Desert Storm. He coordinated host-nation support requirements and acquisitions from Saudi Arabia, which aided the United States ground forces in prosecuting a quick victory over enormous distances and against a larger enemy force. He returned from his duties in Desert Shield and Desert Storm to assume his assignment as deputy commanding general for procurement and readiness, United States Army Tank-Automotive Command, Warren, Michigan.

His decorations and awards include the Legion of Merit, Defense Meritorious Service Medal, Meritorious Service Medal (three oak leaf clusters), Army Commendation Medal, Bronze Star Medal.

Ernest R. Morgan

★ —————————————— ★

Brigadier General

Born in Petersburg, Virginia. General Morgan is a graduate of Virginia State College and the University of Maryland. He has held a wide variety of important command and staff positions. He was the staff officer in the Office of the Chief of Staff for Forces Development at the Pentagon in Washington, D.C. He served as the director of the national security seminars at United States Army War College. He also served as professor of military science at Prairie View A&M College.

Brig. Gen. Ernest R. Morgan

He was appointed to the rank of brigadier general and assigned as the adjutant general for the District of Columbia National Guard. He was appointed to the two star rank of major general and assigned as the adjutant general of the Virgin Islands.

Norris W. Overton

★ ——————————————————— ★

Brigadier General

Born January 6, 1926, in Clarksville, Tennessee, he married the former Patricia Cole of Waukegan, Illinois. He was graduated from Crispus Attucks High School in Indianapolis in 1946. He received his bachelor of science degree in accounting in 1951 from Indiana University and was designated as a distinguished military graduate from the Air Force Reserve Officers Training Corps program and commissioned a second lieutenant. He received a master's in business administration from the Air Force Institute of Technology in 1959 and was graduated from the advanced management program at the Harvard University School of Business Administration in 1972. General Overton completed the Air Command and Staff College and the Industrial College of the Armed Forces by correspondence and the Air War College by seminar.

After completing the accounting and disbursing officer course at Fort Benjamin Harrison, Indiana, General Overton was assigned as finance

Brig. Gen. Norris W. Overton

officer with the 18th Fighter Bomber Wing, Chinhai, Korea, in February 1952. Assignments followed as deputy finance officer, Forbes Air Force Base, Kansas; finance officer, Grenier Air Force Base, New Hampshire; finance officer, Bordeaux Air Base, France; and deputy accounting and finance officer, Lindsey Air Base, Germany.

In 1959, he became chief, Comptroller Services Division, Air Force Plant Representative Office, Curtiss-Wright Corporation, Woodridge, New Jersey. A similar assignment followed in 1960 to the Milwaukee Contract Management District, Milwaukee. In January 1963 General Overton assumed duties as the staff accounting and finance officer, Karamursel Common Defense Installation, Turkey.

He was an associate professor of aerospace studies at the University of Iowa from 1964 to September 1968, then reassigned as base comptroller, Tan Son Nhut Air Base, Vietnam. He was transferred to Headquarters, United States Air Force, Washington, D.C., in October 1969 as executive officer to the deputy assistant comptroller for accounting and finance and later assigned as the assistant deputy assistant comptroller for accounting and finance. In November 1972 General Overton became deputy chief of staff, comptroller, United States Air Force Academy. He was assigned as deputy chief of staff, comptroller, Headquarters, Pacific Air Forces, in February 1976. In June 1979 he became assigned vice commander, Army and Air Force Exchange Services, Dallas.

He was appointed brigadier general on May 1, 1979, with date of rank April 24, 1979. His military decorations and awards include the Legion of Merit (one oak leaf cluster), Bronze Star Medal (one oak leaf cluster), Air Force Commendation Medal, Air Force Outstanding Unit Award Ribbon,

Republic of Korea Presidential Unit Citation, Republic of Vietnam Gallantry Cross (with palm).

Emmett Paige, Jr.

★★★ ———————————————————— ★★★

Lieutenant General

Born February 20, 1931, Jacksonville, Florida, the son of Emmett and Elizabeth Core Paige. He married the former Gloria McClary, and they have three children: Michael, Sandra, and Anthony. General Paige dropped out of high school at age 16 not to hang out in the streets but to fulfill his lifelong dreams of a military career.

After leaving Stanton High School at that early age, he enlisted as a private in the United States Army. He began his army career in August 1947. He held a host of important assignments in the United States and abroad, including Japan, Germany, Korea, the Philippines, and Vietnam. Earlier in his 39-year military career, the general was with the 25th Infantry Division in Nara, Japan, as a Morse code radio operator in the late 1940s. A short while after enlisting in the Army, Paige had earned his GED high school diploma and later received a bachelor's degree in general arts from the University of Maryland before receiving a master's in public administration from Penn State University. He entered Officer Candidate School at Fort Monmouth, New Jersey, graduating in July 1952.

When asked why he chose the Army, he said, "The Army and Air Force were all one and the same back then, and they sent me down to Mac-Dill airbase in Tampa. I took a battery of tests and the Sergeant said, 'Well, you qualified for the ground forces or the Air Corps,' and I said, 'Where does the Air Corps give basic training?' He said, 'Sheppard Field in Texas.' When I found out the temperature there was 110 degrees, I told him I'd go with the ground forces — they trained at Fort Dix in New Jersey."

Asked if race made a difference in his career, he said, "Officer Candidate School comes to mind. I've never forgotten who I am, having been born and raised in the South. When I went to Officer Candidate School in Fort Gordon, Georgia, I was the first and only black in the leadership course you had to finish to get into OCS. The commandant of the school, a West Pointer, said at the end of the course, 'Student Paige, I guess you think that we've been very unfair and given you a harder time than necessary,' and I said, with a smile on my face, 'As a matter of fact, sir, I do.' Then he said, 'You're right. You have set the standard for the Negroes who are going to have to be just as good as your white contemporaries. You're

Lt. Gen. Emmett Paige, Jr.

going to have to be twice as good. I'm not saying that that's fair or that's right, but those are the facts.' As he went on talking, I could see he was about to come to tears. Inside, the tears were there, but I didn't let them come out because I was pissed that I had to go through this. But I knew he was right. I had seen it as an enlisted man—black lieutenants sitting at a separate table in the officers' mess, in a black field artillery battalion where the bulk of the officer corps was white. And then, at OCS in Fort Monmouth, it was the same thing. But I was determined not to let the bastards kick me out. So yes, race has made a difference, but if anything, I think it's made me a better person."

After OCS, tours followed at Fort Bliss, Texas (1952–53), Karlsruhe, Germany (1954–1956), and still later at Fort Devens, Massachusetts, and Fort Carson, Colorado. He was in Korea in 1959–1960 and in the Philippines with the Defense Communications Agency at Clark Air Force Base in 1962–1965. In 1969 he commanded the 361st Signal Battalion in Vietnam as a lieutenant colonel with the famed 1st Signal Brigade, returning to the Defense Communications Agency, Arlington, Virginia, in 1970.

University and War College Training followed. In April 1976 he made history when he was promoted to brigadier general, the first black to reach general rank in the United States Army Signal Corps. The second star came in 1979, the third in 1984 when he came to historic Fort Huachuca (black "buffalo soldiers" were stationed there in 1913) to command the ISC and direct about 40,000 civilian and military personnel.

In November 1986 he was honored for his outstanding accomplishments with the Information Systems Command when he received the Distinguished Service Medal from the Army's chief of staff at a special ceremony in the Pentagon. Included among the general's other decorations are three Legions of Merit, the Bronze Star, Meritorious Service Medals, and the Joint Service Commendation Medal. He retired from the Army in 1987.

Julius Parker, Jr.

★★ ——————————————— ★★

Major General

Born April 14, 1934, in New Braunfels, Texas, he married the former Dorothy June Henry, and they have three children: Julian R., Jules G., and Dorvita J. Upon completion of the Reserve Officers Training Corps curriculum and the educational course of study at Prairie View A&M University in 1955, he was commissioned a second lieutenant and awarded a bachelor of science degree in biology and chemistry. He also holds a master of science degree in public administration from Shippensburg State College. His military education includes completion of the Infantry Officer Basic and Advanced Courses, the United States Army Command and General Staff College, and the United States Army War College.

He has held a wide variety of important command and staff positions. He was assigned as executive to the assistant chief of staff for intelligence, United States Army, Washington, D.C.; deputy chief, Staff for Intelligence, United States Army Forces Command, Fort McPherson, Georgia; deputy chief, Staff for Intelligence, United States Army, Europe, and the Seventh Army; and deputy director, Management and Operations, Defense Intelligence Agency, Washington, D.C.

General Parker served in Vietnam as a senior district adviser. Returning to the United States, he performed duties as combat intelligence staff officer, ground surveillance officer, and branch chief, Office of the Assistant Chief for Intelligence, United States Army, Washington, D.C. from 1969 to 1972. He commanded the Military Intelligence Battalion, 66th Military Intelligence Group, United States Army, Europe, from July 1972 to December 1973. Upon completion of that assignment, he served as the assistant chief of staff, G-2 (intelligence), 3rd Armored Division, Europe, followed by attendance at the United States Army War College, Carlisle Barracks, Pennsylvania. Upon graduation, General Parker was retained at Carlisle Barracks as a faculty member and strategic analyst in the Strategic Studies Institute until May 1977.

Assigned to colonel-level command in Korea from July 1977 to July 1979, he successfully organized and integrated four independent intelligence

Maj. Gen. Julius Parker, Jr.

units to form the Army's first multidisciplined brigade-level intelligence organization, the 501st Military Intelligence Group. He remained in this position until he was assigned as commanding general, United States Army Intelligence Center/Commandant, United States Army Intelligence School. His military awards and decoration include the Legion of Merit, the Bronze Star Medal (with "V" device and oak leaf cluster), Purple Heart, Meritorious Service Medal (with three oak leaf clusters), Combat Infantryman's Badge, Parachutist Badge.

Jude Wilmot Paul Patin

★ ———————————————————— ★

Brigadier General

Born January 25, 1940, Baton Rouge, Louisiana. He received a bachelor of science degree in architectural engineering from Southern University in 1962, a master of science in industrial engineering from Arizona State University in 1971.

He received an ROTC commission to second lieutenant in 1962, and from September 1962 to November 1962, he was a student in the Field Artillery Officer Basic Course, United States Army Field Artillery School, Fort Sill, Oklahoma. From December 1962 to October 1963, he was a reconnaissance survey officer, Service Battery, 1st Missile Battalion, 42nd Artillery, United States Army, Europe. From October 1963 to January 1964,

Brig. Gen. Jude Wilmot Paul Patin

he was a survey officer with the 3rd Missile Battalion, 32nd Artillery, 214th Artillery Group, Fort Sill, Oklahoma.

On March 4, 1964, he was promoted to the rank of first lieutenant. From January 1964 to February 1965, he was the commander of Headquarters Battery, 3rd Missile Battalion, 32nd Artillery, 214th Artillery Group, Fort Sill, Oklahoma. From March 1965 to June 1966, he served as an architectural engineer in the Installation Section, 593rd Engineer Company, Fort Sill, Oklahoma.

He was promoted to captain on April 16, 1966. From July 1966 to May 1967, he served as commander, 697th Engineer Company (Pipeline); then commander, 561st Engineer Company (Construction), 44th Engineer Group (Construction), United States Army, Thailand.

From June 1967 to March 1968, he was a student in the Army Engineer Officer Advanced Course at the United States Army Engineer School, Fort Belvoir, Virginia. From March 1968 to December 1968, he was chief, Structures and Utilities Section, General Engineering Branch, Department of Engineering and Military Science, United States Army Engineer School, Fort Belvoir, Virginia. From January 1969 to March 1969, he served as assistant division engineer, 65th Engineer Battalion, 25th Infantry Division, United States Army, Vietnam. From April 1969 to December 1969, he was the operations officer of the Operations Division, United States Army Engineer Construction Agency, Vietnam.

He was promoted to the rank of major on July 11, 1969. From January 1970 to June 1971, he was a student at Arizona State University, Tempe, Arizona. From June 1971 to June 1974, he served as technical operations officer, then chief, Plans and Program Branch, Management Analysis

Office, United States Army Logistics Doctrine, Systems and Readiness Agency, then as the program analysis officer, Administration and Management Office, United States Army Logistics Evaluation Agency, Deputy Chief of Staff for Logistics, United States Army, New Cumberland, Pennsylvania.

From June 1974 to May 1976, he served as the S-3 (operations officer) then as executive officer of the 84th Engineer Battalion, 25th Infantry Division, Schofield Barracks, Hawaii. From June 1976 to June 1977, he was a student at the United States Army Command and General Staff College, Fort Leavenworth, Kansas. From June 1977 to May 1980, he served as an advisor to the 1138th Engineer Battalion (Combat) (Reserve Component), United States Army Readiness Region V, Fort Sheridan, Illinois.

He was promoted to lieutenant colonel on December 9, 1978. From May 1980 to May 1983, he was the commander of the 293rd Engineer Battalion, 18th Engineer Brigade, United States Army, Europe. From May 1983 to April 1985, he was a student, later director, of Insurgency Operations, United States Army War College, Carlisle Barracks, Pennsylvania. He was promoted to colonel on October 1, 1984. From May 1985 to July 1987, he was commander, 1st Training Support Brigade; later commander, 136th Engineer Brigade, United States Army Training and Engineer Center, Fort Leonard Wood, Missouri.

From August 1987 to September 1989, he served as the assistant chief of staff for engineering and housing, 21st Support Command, United States Army, Europe, and the Seventh Army. He was promoted to brigadier general on November 1, 1989. In October 1989 he was appointed commanding general, United States Army Engineer Division, North Central, Chicago, Illinois.

He has received numerous awards and decorations, including the Legion of Merit, the Bronze Star Medal, Meritorious Service Medal with two oak leaf clusters, Air Medal, Army Commendation Medal with oak leaf cluster, Parachutist Badge.

Frank E. Petersen

★★★ ——————————————— ★★★

Lieutenant General

Born March 2, 1932, Topeka, Kansas. He earned both a bachelor's degree and a master's degree from George Washington University in Washington, D.C. Virginia Union University awarded him an honorary doctor of law degree. He attended many service schools.

Lt. Gen. Frank E. Petersen

In June 1950 he joined the United States Navy as an apprentice seaman, serving as an electronic technician. On October 1, 1952, Frank E. Petersen was commissioned second lieutenant in the Marine Corps after completing the Naval Aviation Cadet Program. He had considerable flight activity in Korea where he served as the commander of a Marine fighter squadron, a Marine aircraft group, a Marine amphibious brigade, and a Marine aircraft wing.

During his two tours of duty in Korea and Vietnam, General Petersen flew 350 combat missions with over 4,000 hours in various fighter and attack aircraft, and he earned the Distinguished Flying Cross, America's highest aviation medal, and six Air Medals. General Petersen was the first black in the naval services to command a tactical air squadron. In 1968 he commanded the Marine Fighter Attack Squadron 314 in Vietnam. Under his command, this squadron received the Hanson Award for Aviation as the best fighter squadron in the Marine Corps.

In 1979, while General Petersen was serving as chief of staff of the 9th Marine Amphibious Brigade on Okinawa, President Jimmy Carter nominated Frank E. Petersen, Jr., for advancement to brigadier general. With the Senate confirmation, Petersen, the Marine Corps's first black aviator, became the first black marine to attain general rank.

When he retired from the Marine Corps on August 1, 1988, he was serving as commanding general, Marine Corps Development and Educational, Quantico, Virginia. When he left the service, he was the senior ranking aviator in the United States Marine Corps and the United States Navy, with respective titles of "Silver Hawk" and "Grey Eagle." In this regard, the date of his designation as an aviator preceded all other aviators in the

United States Air Force and the United States Army. His numerous decorations include the Defense Superior Service Medal, Legion of Merit (with combat "V"), Distinguished Flying Cross, Purple Heart, Meritorious Service Medal, Air Medal, Navy Commendation Medal (with combat "V"), Air Force Commendation Medal.

John F. Phillips

★★ ———————————————————— ★★

Major General

Born on September 3, 1942, in Neches, Texas, and was graduated from Climons High School there in 1959. He received a bachelor of science degree in biology and chemistry (with honors) from Jarvis Christian College in 1963, a master of science degree in logistics management from the Air Force Institute of Technology in 1975. He pursued additional studies at North Texas State University and Texas Southern University. He is an honor graduate of the Institute of Aerospace Safety Engineering (graduate and undergraduate school), University of Southern California. He completed Squadron Officer School in 1971, Industrial College of the Armed Forces in 1976, and the National War College in 1983.

He was commissioned as a second lieutenant through Officer Training School at Lackland Air Force Base, Texas, in December 1963 and earned his navigator wings at James Connally Air Force Base, Texas. After completing KC-135 combat crew training at Castle Air Force Base, California, in February 1967, he was assigned to Travis Air Force Base, California, where he flew as an instructor navigator. During this time he flew regular combat missions in Vietnam, accumulating more than 300 combat flying hours.

He entered pilot training at Williams Air Force Base, Arizona, and graduated with top honors in July 1970. He was then assigned to the 1st German Air Force Squadron, Sheppard Air Force Base, Texas, as a T-37 instructor pilot and was awarded German pilot's wings. From December 1973 to August 1975, he served as an inspector and flight examiner with the Air Training Command inspector general's staff at Randolph Air Force Base, Texas. He then attended the Air Force Institute of Technology, Wright-Patterson Air Force Base. Upon graduation in September 1976, he became system manager for the F-100 and J-85 engines at Kelly Air Force Base, Texas.

In December 1978, he was assigned as a logistics systems analyst at Doshan Tappeh Air Base, Iran, until the fall of the Shah. Phillips remained

Maj. Gen. John F. Phillips

in Iran under the Khomeini regime until his expulsion in February 1979. He transferred to Wright-Patterson and served as deputy program manager for logistics, KC-10 Joint Program Office. In January 1982 he was appointed system program director for the TR-1 and later become director of all airlift and trainer systems.

Phillips attended the National War College from August 1982 to September 1983 and distinguished himself in both academics and athletics. He was then assigned to the Weapons System Program Division, Directorate of Logistics Plans and Programs, Headquarters, United States Air Force, Washington, D.C. He first served as deputy division chief, then chief, and later as deputy director of logistics plans and programs. From July 1985 to July 1986, he was military assistant to the assistant secretary of the Air Force for research development and logistics. After this assignment, he served as vice commander, Logistics Management Systems Center, Wright-Patterson.

He assumed his current position in October 1988. He was promoted to brigadier general on October 1, 1988. He is a senior pilot with more than 3,000 flying hours. His military awards and decorations include the Legion of Merit, Meritorious Service Medal (with two oak leaf clusters), Air Medal, Air Force Commendation Medal (with oak leaf cluster), Combat Readiness Medal, Republic of Vietnam Gallantry Cross (with palm).

Colin L. Powell

★★★★ ——————————————————— ★★★★

General

Born April 5, 1937, in New York City, he married the former Alma Vivian Johnson, and they have three children: Michael, Linda, and Annemarie. Around 1940 the family, which Powell recalls as having been "strong and close," moved to the South Bronx, where he was graduated from Morris High School in 1954. At the City College of New York he majored in geology and got his first taste of military life as a cadet in the ROTC.

He has explained that he enrolled in ROTC because as an ambitious young black man in the 1950s, he had learned to take advantage of what few attractive opportunities existed and found his temperament well suited to military discipline. Former classmates remember that he displayed rare leadership ability on campus, motivating many other students to succeed. General Powell was appointed commander of the Pershing Rifles, the ROTC class of 1958, with the rank of cadet colonel.

As one of the more than 16,000 American military advisers sent to South Vietnam by President John F. Kennedy, Powell was assigned from 1962 to 1963 to a South Vietnamese infantry battalion patrolling the border with Laos. While marching through a rice paddy one day in 1963, he stepped into a Punji-stick trap, impaling his foot on one of the sharpened stakes concealed just below the water's surface. He was given a Purple Heart, and in that same year he was awarded the Bronze Star.

In 1968, Powell returned for a second Vietnam tour of duty with infantry as a battalion executive officer and division operations officer. He was injured a second time in a helicopter crash landing.

In 1971 he earned an M.B.A. degree from George Washington University. In 1972 he was selected to be a White House Fellow and served his fellowship year as special assistant to the deputy director, Office of the President. In 1973 he assumed command of the 1st Battalion, 32nd Infantry, Korea. Upon completion of the National War College in 1976, he assumed command of the 2nd Brigade, 101st Airborne Division (Air Assault), Fort Campbell, Kentucky.

In 1977, General Powell went to Washington to serve in the office of the secretary of defense. Over the next three years, he served as senior military assistant to the secretary of energy. In 1981 he became the assistant division commander for operations and training, 4th Infantry Division commander for operations and training, 4th Infantry Division (Mechanized), Fort Carson, Colorado. In 1983, he returned to Washington to serve as senior military assistant to Secretary of Defense Caspar Weinberger.

Gen. Colin L. Powell

In July 1986 he assumed command of the V United States Army Corps, Frankfurt, Germany. In January 1987 Powell returned to the White House to serve as deputy assistant to National Security Adviser Frank Carlucci. A military man at heart, he had to be persuaded to accept the job by his commander in chief, President Reagan.

After the Iran-Contra scandal, Powell distinguished himself by reorganizing the National Security Council according to the recommendations of the Tower Commission. He also proved invaluable as the chairman of the interagency review group that coordinated the activities of the CIA, the State Department, the Defense Department, and other agencies. When Carlucci took over as secretary of defense in 1989, Powell became assistant to President Reagan on national affairs (military matters), the first black to hold this position.

In April 1989 General Powell assumed command of the United States Army Forces Command (FORSCOM), which directs operations and training for all active and Reserve troop units in the continental United States as well as all Army National Guard units in the 48 continental states, Alaska, Puerto Rico, and the Virgin Islands. Powell became the first black general to command FORSCOM, his first four-star assignment. (The FORSCOM functions as the Army component of the Atlantic Command, responsible for command and control of assigned forces in the Atlantic-Caribbean area.)

In August 1989 he was nominated as Chairman of the Joint Chiefs, the first black general nominated for the top post in the armed forces, passing over 30 other four-star generals, most of them more senior. In October 1989 General Powell was confirmed by the United States Senate as chairman of the Joint Chiefs of Staff. As chairman of the Joint Chiefs, General Powell serves as the principal military adviser to the president, the National Security Council, and the secretary of defense, and as a member of the Pentagon executive committee established by Defense Secretary Dick Cheney.

Since taking over this post, he has been more willing to use military force than any of his predecessors since the 1960s. Other Joint Chiefs chairmen, fearing another Vietnam-type disaster, have been reluctant to commit United States troops. But General Powell tells the President: "If you want to use force, we can do it."

His military career is impressive by its content and the unprecedented rise he has made to chairman of the Joint Chiefs of Staff. Being the nation's senior military leader is an accomplishment distinguished by its very importance and influence. General Powell was selected as the recipient of the NAACP's 1991 Spingarn Award, the highest honor bestowed by the nation's oldest and largest civil rights organization. The announcement of his selection was made by Dr. Benjamin L. Hooks, the NAACP executive director.

His military awards and decorations include the Defense Distinguished Service Medal (with two oak leaf clusters), Purple Heart, Distinguished Service Medal, Legion of Merit (with oak leaf cluster), Soldier's Medal, Bronze Star Medal, Air Medal, Joint Service Commendation Medal, Army Commendation Medal, Expert Infantryman Badge, Combat Infantryman Badge, Parachutist Badge, Pathfinder Badge, Ranger Tab, Presidential Service Badge, Secretary of Defense Identification Badge, Army Staff Identification Badge, Joint Chiefs of Staff Identification Badge.

William E. Powell

★★ ——————————————————— ★★

Rear Admiral

Born April 12, 1936, in Indianapolis, Indiana, he married Loretta Braxton Mitchell of Norfolk, Virginia. They have two sons: William Clinton Powell III and David Anthony Powell. He received a bachelor of science (naval science) degree from the United States Naval Academy in 1959, a master's in business administration from George Washington University in 1969.

Powell's first duty after Supply Corps School in Athens, Georgia, was as the supply officer aboard the USS *Nicholas* (DDE-449). In 1962 he was assigned as the planning officer at the Naval Air Station, Point Mugu, California. This assignment was followed by two years at the Naval Supply Depot, Subic Bay, Philippines, where he obtained experience in inventory management and assisted in special support projects in Vietnam.

Rear Adm. William E. Powell

From July 1966 until 1968, Powell served as ship design and fleet support coordinator for the Naval Supply Systems Command in Washington, D.C. In May 1969 he was assigned as the financial management and planning officer, Staff Commander Cruiser Destroyer Force Atlantic. Reporting to USS *Intrepid* (CV-11) in August 1971, Powell assumed duties as the supply officer and participated in deployments to northern Europe and the Mediterranean.

In April 1974 he reported to the Aviation Supply Office and was initially assigned as industrial support officer, later as Stock Control Branch head for power plants. Powell attended the Industrial College of the Armed Forces in 1977, and upon completion in 1978 he reported to the Naval Supply Center, Oakland, California, as director of the Planning Department. In July 1980, he returned to Washington, D.C., and served as the assistant for supply policy to the director, Aviation Programs Division, Office of the Chief of Naval Operations. From 1982 through 1984, he served as commanding officer, Naval Supply Depot, Subic. He was then assigned to Naval Supply Systems Command as director, Supply Corps Personnel, until May 24, 1985, when he assumed command of the Naval Supply Center, Norfolk, Virginia.

Rear Admiral Powell's dates of rank are as follows:
     June 27, 1955: midshipman
     June 3, 1959: ensign
     December 3, 1960: lieutenant (junior grade)
     June 1, 1963: lieutenant
     May 1, 1968: lieutenant commander
     November 1, 1971: commander

July 1, 1979: captain
October 17, 1985: rear admiral
November 1, 1988: (retired)

Winston D. Powers

★★★ ———————————————————— ★★★

Lieutenant General

Born December 19, 1930, in New York City, he married the former Jeanette Wyche. They have two children: Diane and David. He receivd a bachelor of arts degree from McKendree College, Lebanon, Illinois, in 1961. He also attended graduate school at the George Washington University, Washington, D.C., and completed the Industrial College of the Armed Forces, Fort Lesley J. McNair, Washington, D.C.

He began his military career by enlisting in the United States Air Force in November 1950. After basic training he was assigned to the Air Defense Command, Hancock Field, New York. He volunteered for navigator training at Ellington Air Force Base, Texas, in September 1952 and graduated the following year. He then had combat crew training at Randolph Air Force Base in Texas and upon completion was assigned as a navigator instructor at Ellington Air Force Base in August 1953.

In May 1957 he entered the Tactical Communications Officer Training School at Scott Air Force Base, Illinois. After graduation in June 1958, he was assigned as commander, Detachment 2, 6123rd Air Control and Warning Squadron, Cheju-Do Auxiliary Air Field, South Korea. He returned to Scott Air Force Base in June 1959 for duty with the 1918th Communication Squadron. From August 1961 to July 1963, General Powers was assigned to the Air Force Command Post at the Pentagon as a communications officer. He was then selected to attend the communications system engineering program of American Telephone and Telegraph Company in New York. In August 1964 he completed the education-with-industry program and became a communications engineer for the Defense Communications Agency–United Kingdom, Royal Air Force Station, Croughton, England.

The general transferred to the Tactical Communications Area at Langley Air Force Base, Virginia, in August 1967 as director of tactical communications operations and then as director of fixed communications operations. He returned to a flying assignment in July 1970 with the 460th Reconnaissance Wing, Tan Son Nhut Air Base, Vietnam, flying 75 combat missions in EC-47s.

From July 1971 to October 1973, he was assigned to the Organization

Lt. Gen. Winston D. Powers

of the Joint Chiefs of Staff as the Air Force member of the Plans and Policy Division, J-6. General Powers then moved to Headquarters, United States Air Force, Washington, D.C., as special assistant for joint matters in the Directorate of Command, Control, and Communications, Office of the Deputy Chief of Staff, Programs and Resources.

When he returned to South Korea in February 1974, General Powers served as commander of the 2146th Communications Group and director of communications-electronics for the 314th Air Division at Osan Air Base. Upon his return to the United States in November 1974, he was again assigned to Air Force headquarters as chief, Plans and Programs Division, Directorate of Command, Control, and Communications, where he also served as chairman, Command, Control, and Communications, Panel, later as a member of the Program Review Committee, Air Staff Board. The general became deputy director of telecommunications, and command and control resources, Office of the Assistant Chief of Staff, Communications and Computer Resources at Air Force headquarters in September 1975, director in June 1978.

In July 1978 he was appointed deputy director of command, control, and communications at Headquarters, United States Air Force. He transferred to Peterson Air Force Base, Colorado, in October 1978 and served initially as the deputy chief of staff for communications, electronics, and computer resources, North American Aerospace Defense Command and Aerospace Defense Command. He became chief, Systems Integration Office, Headquarters, Aerospace Defense Center, in January 1981 and took command of the Space Communications Division at Peterson Air Force Base in January 1981, command of the Space Communications Division,

Peterson Air Force Base, in January 1983. He was assigned as director, Defense Communications Agency, Washington, D.C., in September 1983.

He was appointed lieutenant general on October 1, 1983. General Powers is a master navigator with more than 4,000 flying hours. His military decorations and awards include the Distinguished Service Medal, Legion of Merit, Meritorious Service Medal (two oak leaf clusters), Air Medal (one oak leaf cluster), Air Force Commendation Medal, Presidential Unit Citation Emblem, Air Force Outstanding Unit Award Ribbon (with "V" device).

Thomas Levi Prather, Jr.

★★ ──────────────────── ★★

Major General

Born June 25, 1940, Washington, D.C. He received a bachelor of science degree in music from Morgan State University, a master of science degree in contracting and procurement management from Florida Institute of Technology.

He received an ROTC commission as second lieutenant, on July 19, 1962. From July 1962 to October 1962, he was a student in the Army Ordnance Officer Basic Course, United States Army Ordnance School, Aberdeen Proving Ground, Maryland. From October 1962 to May 1964, he was assigned as a platoon leader in the Service, Supply, and Recovery Platoon of the 546th Ordnance Company, later ordnance supply officer of the 84th Ordnance Battalion, United States Army, Europe.

He was promoted to first lieutenant, on January 19, 1964. From May 1964 to August 1965, he was assigned as ordnance supply officer, 66th Ordnance Battalion, Europe. From August 1965 to October 1965, he was a student in the Armor Officer Basic Course, United States Army Armor School, Fort Knox, Kentucky. From October 1965 to April 1966, he served as the executive officer of Headquarters Company, 1st Battalion, 66th Armor, 2nd Armored Division, Fort Hood, Texas.

He was promoted to captain on April 1, 1966. From April 1966 to May 1967, he served as the commander, battalion maintenance officer, S-4 (logistics), Headquarters Company, 1st Battalion, 66th Armor, 2nd Armored Division, Fort Hood, Texas. From June 1967 to September 1968, he was assistant brigade supply officer, later supply officer, 9th Support Battalion, 198th Infantry Brigade, United States Army, Vietnam. From September 1968 to September 1969, he was a student in the Ordnance Officer Advanced Course, United States Ordnance School, Aberdeen Proving Ground, Maryland.

Maj. Gen. Thomas Levi Prather, Jr.

He was promoted to major on May 23, 1969. From September 1969 to July 1970, he was assigned as chief, Consolidated Equipment Maintenance Division, Mobility Training Department, School Brigade, United States Army Ordnance School, Aberdeen Proving Ground, Maryland. From July 1970 to June 1971, he was a student in the United States Army Command and General Staff College, Fort Leavenworth, Kansas. From June 1971 to August 1973, he served as a personnel management officer in the Assignment Section, Ordnance Branch, Officer Personnel Management Directorate, United States Army Military Personnel Center, Alexandria, Virginia. From September 1973 to September 1974, he was a student at the Florida Institute of Technology, Melbourne, Florida. From September 1974 to June 1975, he served as a project officer in the Industrial Planning Branch, Industrial Management Division, United States Army Materiel Command, Alexandria, Virginia.

From June 1975 to June 1977, Prather was assigned as a military assistant, Office of the Assistant Secretary of the Army (Installations and Logistics), Washington, D.C. From June 1977 to January 1979, he was commander, Division Materiel Management Center, 8th Infantry Division, United States Army, Europe. He was promoted to lieutenant colonel on July 11, 1977. From August 1981 to June 1982, he was a student at the United States Army War College, Carlisle Barracks, Pennsylvania. From July 1982 to December 1984, he was assigned as director, Materiel Management Directorate, United States Army Communications-Electronics Command, Fort Monmouth, New Jersey.

He was promoted to colonel on August 1, 1983. From December 1984 to July 1987, he was commander, Tobyhanna Army Depot, Depot Systems

Command, United States Army Materiel Command, Tobyhanna, Pennsylvania. From July 1987 to July 1989, he served as deputy commander, 2nd Support Command, VII Corps, United States Army, Europe, and Seventh Army. From July 1989 to August 1990, he was assigned as deputy commanding general, United States Army Armament, Munitions and Chemical Command, Rock Island, Illinois.

He was promoted to brigadier general on September 2, 1989. In August 1990 he was assigned as commanding general, United States Army Troop Support Command, St. Louis, Missouri. He was promoted to major general in this assignment. He has received numerous awards and decorations: the Legion of Merit, Bronze Star, Meritorious Service Medal (with three oak leaf clusters), Army Commendation Medal (with two oak leaf clusters).

George Baker Price

★ ———————————————— ★

Brigadier General

Born August 28, 1929, in Laurel, Mississippi, he married the former Georgianna Hunter, and they have two children: Katherine James and William Robert. He received a B.S. degree from South Carolina State College in 1951, an M.S. degree from Shippensburg State College. His military education includes the United States Army Command and General Staff College and the United States Army War College.

General Price began his military career in 1951 when he served as a

Brig. Gen. George Baker Price

platoon leader. He has held a wide variety of important command and staff positions: operations officer, 1957 to 1961; personnel manager, 1961 to 1962; adviser with the 1st Vietnamese Infantry Division, 1964 to 1965. He returned to the United States and was assigned as a staff officer with the Department of the Army in Washington, D.C. from 1965 to 1968. His midlevel assignments include a tour as a battalion commander, 1968 to 1970; brigade commander, 1971 to 1973; chief of staff, 1973 to 1974; assistant division commander, 1974 to 1976.

He served as chief of staff from 1976 to 1978, retired in 1978. General Price's military awards include the Legion of Merit, Bronze Star, Purple Heart, Meritorious Service Medal, Army Commendation Medal, Infantryman Badge, Airborne Ranger Tab.

Bernard P. Randolph

★★★★ ———————————————— ★★★★

General

Born July 10, 1933, in New Orleans to Philip J. Randolph (deceased) and Claudia Randolph, he married Lucille Robinson Randolph in 1956, and they have six children: Michelle, Julie, Michael, John, Liane, and Mark. General Randolph received a bachelor of science degree in chemistry at Xavier University of Louisiana, New Orleans, bachelor (magna cum laude) and master of science degrees in electrical engineering from the University of North Dakota, Grand Forks, through the Air Force Institute of Technology in 1964 and 1965, respectively. He completed Squadron Officer School in 1959, Air Command and Staff College as a distinguished graduate, concurrently earning a master's in business administration from Auburn University in 1969; and was a distinguished graduate of the Air War College in 1974, all at Maxwell Air Force Base, Alabama.

His first assignment after completing aviation cadet training at Ellington Air Force Base, Texas, and Mather Air Force Base, California, was with the Strategic Air Command at Lincoln Air Force Base, Nebraska, from June 1956 to June 1962. He instructed and evaluated KC-97 and B-47 flight crews. While there, he was a member of a select crew. General Randolph attended the University of North Dakota until July 1965 and was then assigned to Los Angeles Air Force Station, as chief, on-orbit operations, Space Systems Division. He was next assigned as assistant deputy program director for launch and orbital operations and was responsible for all payload operations.

From August 1968 to October 1969, General Randolph attended Air

Gen. Bernard P. Randolph

Command and Staff College at Auburn University. He was then assigned Vietnam as an airlift operations officer at Chu Lai and airlift coordinator at Tan Son Nhut Air Base. He was responsible for the operation of about 50 C-7 and C-123 airlift sorties daily from Chu Lai and later coordinated the operations of all airlift control elements throughout Vietnam.

Upon his return to the United States in November 1970, General Randolph was assigned to Air Force Systems Command headquarters as chief of command plans in test evaluation and then as the executive officer to the deputy chief of staff, Operations, Headquarters, Air Force Systems Command, Andrews Air Force Base, Maryland. From August 1973 to June 1974, he was a student at the Air War College, at Maxwell Air Force Base, Alabama. From June 1974 to June 1980, General Randolph received sequential assignments at Los Angeles Air Force Station, California. First he served as director, Space Systems Planning, Space and Missile Systems, then as deputy system program director, Air Force Satellite Communications System; then as system program director, Air Force Satellite Communications System; later as program director, Space Defense Systems, Space Division.

From July 1980 to September 1981, he served as vice commander of the Warner Robins Air Logistics Center, Robins Air Force Base, Georgia. From September 1981 to May 1983, he was director, Space Systems and Command, Control and Communications, Office of the Deputy Chief of Staff, Research, Development, and Acquisition, Headquarters, United States Air Force, Washington, D.C. From May 1983 to June 1984, he was vice commander and deputy commander, Space Systems Acquisition, Space Division, Los Angeles Air Force Station.

From June 1984 to May 1985, he served as vice commander, Air Force Systems Command, Andrews Air Force Base, Maryland. From May 1985 to July 1987, he was deputy chief of staff, Research, Development, and Acquisition, Headquarters, United States Air Force, Washington, D.C. From July 1987 to April 1990, he served as commander, Air Force Systems Command, Andrews Air Force Base. During this assignment, he directed the research, development, testing, evaluation, and acquisition of aerospace systems for Air Force operational and support commands. As the commanding general, he was responsible for over 60,000 men and women, and a $35 billion annual budget, one-third of the Air Force's budget. He managed some 24,000 active contracts worth some $151 billion. He was also responsible for developing and directing the development and purchasing of all new weapons systems for the Air Force, including the F-15-E, the MX missile, the B-1 bomber, and the C-17 transport aircraft.

He was appointed to the four-star rank of general on August 1, 1992, the second African American to obtain this grade. General Randolph's military awards and decorations include the Distinguished Service Medal, Legion of Merit (with one oak leaf cluster), Bronze Star Medal, Meritorious Service Medal, Air Force Commendation Medal, Presidential Unit Citation, Air Force Organizational Excellence Award, Vietnam Service Medal (with four service stars), Republic of Vietnam Gallantry Cross (with palm), Vietnam Campaign Medal.

Joseph Paul Reason

★★★ ───────────────────────────── ★★★

Vice Admiral

Born March 22, 1941, in Washington, D.C., he married the former Dianne Lillian Fowler of Washington, D.C., and they have two children: Rebecca L. and Joseph P. Reason, Jr. He was graduated from the United States Naval Academy in 1965 with a bachelor of science degree (naval science).

Prior to being trained in nuclear propulsion engineering, he served as operations officer on the USS *J. D. Blackwood* (DE-219). Upon completion of training, he was assigned duties on the USS *Truxtun* (DLGN-35) and participated in her first deployment to Southeast Asia in 1968. In 1970 he earned a master of science degree in the management of computer systems from the U.S. Naval Postgraduate School, Monterey, California.

Joining the USS *Enterprise* (CVN-65) as electrical officer in 1971, he deployed twice to Southeast Asia and the Indian Ocean. After service as combat systems officer, again on USS *Truxtun,* Admiral Reason began a

Vice Adm. Joseph Paul Reason

tour as surface nuclear assignment officer at the Bureau of Naval Personnel. In late 1976 he was assigned as naval aide to the president of the United States. He served as aide to President Carter until mid-1979.

Subsequent duties included executive officer, USS *Mississippi* (CGN-40); commanding officer, USS *Coontz* (DDG-40); and commanding officer, USS *Bainbridge* (CGN-25). Prior to assuming his duties as commander, Naval Surface Force, Atlantic Fleet, Reason commanded Cruiser-Destroyer Group One. He led Battle Group ROMEO through operations in the northern and western Pacific and Indian Ocean regions and the Persian Gulf. As commander, Naval Base Seattle, from 1986 through 1988, he was responsible for all naval activities in Washington, Oregon, and Alaska.

Reason's awards include the Legion of Merit, Navy Commendation Medal, and Republic of Vietnam Honor Medal. He also wears the Navy Unit Commendation, Navy Meritorious Unit Commendation, and numerous other medals. The vice admiral's dates of rank were as follows:

June 28, 1961: midshipman
June 9, 1965: ensign
December 9, 1966: lieutenant (junior grade)
July 1, 1968: lieutenant
July 1, 1973: lieutenant commander
September 1, 1978: commander
October 1, 1983: captain
October 1, 1987: rear admiral (lower half)
April 21, 1989: rear admiral
January 1991: vice admiral

Hugh Granville Robinson

★★ ——————————————————————— ★★

Major General

Born on August 4, 1932, in Washington, D.C., he is the son of Colonel and Mrs. James H. Robinson. He married the former Matilda Turner. They have three children: Hugh G. Robinson, Jr., Susan Robinson, and Mia Turner Robinson.

He was commissioned in the United States Army Corps of Engineers in June 1954 after graduation from West Point. He has held a wide variety of important command and staff positions. From 1963 to 1965, he served as chief, Combat Branch, Engineer Strategic Studies Group, Washington, D.C. From 1965 to 1969, he was Army aide to President Lyndon Johnson, White House Detachment, Washington, D.C. In 1969 he subsequently served as executive officer, 45th Engineer Group, then as battalion commander, 39th Engineer Battalion (Combat), Vietnam.

General Robinson served in a variety of important career-building assignments preparatory to his most recent duties. In Vietnam he served from 1970 to 1972 as chief, Regional Capabilities Branch, Office of Deputy Chief of Staff for Operations, War Plans Divisions, at the Pentagon, Washington, D.C. From 1972 to 1974, he served subsequently executive officer, 3rd Regiment, USCC, West Point, New York, then as commanding officer, 3rd Regiment, USCC, West Point. From 1974 to 1976, he was commanding officer of the United States Army Engineer School Brigade, Fort Belvoir, Virginia; from 1976 to 1978, district engineer, United States Army Engineer District, Los Angeles, California. From 1978 to 1980, General Robinson served as deputy director, Civil Works, Office of the Chief of Engineers, United States Army, Washington, D.C. From 1980 to 1983, he was division engineer for the Southwestern Division, United States Army Corps of Engineers, Dallas, Texas.

In 1983 General Robinson retired. After retirement, General Robinson joined the Southland Corporation as vice president after election by the board of directors. Cityplace Development Corporation, a wholly owned subsidiary of Southland Corporation, was formed in January 1984, and General Robinson was appointed as president. Responsibilities included organizing and establishing the team of Cityplace Development Corporation, securing zoning on the first phase of development, and following through with all activities to zone, develop, construct, and manage the entire 160-acre development. Prior to leaving Cityplace, General Robinson completed the planning, design, and construction of a 42-story office building and 228 multifamily residential units.

Maj. Gen. Hugh Granville Robinson

In March 1989 he joined the Tetra Group as chairman and CEO. The Tetra Group is a consulting firm providing construction management and business development services. General Robinson also manages the southwest office of Grigsby Brandford & Co., Inc., a black-owned investment banking firm specializing in municipal securities.

His awards and decorations include the Distinguished Service Medal, Legion of Merit (with oak leaf cluster), Bronze Star (with oak leaf cluster), Meritorious Service Medal, Air Medal (with two oak leaf clusters), Joint Service Commendation Medal, Army Commendation Medal (with oak leaf cluster), Vietnamese Cross of Gallantry (gold star), Vietnamese Service Medal, Vietnam Campaign Medal, American Defense (with oak leaf cluster), Presidential Service Badge, Army Service Ribbon, Overseas Service Ribbon, Meritorious Unit Citation, Henry O. Flipper Award (1985), Vietnam Veteran of the Year Award (1985). General Robinson received a master's degree in civil engineering from Massachusetts Institute of Technology. He also completed the Armed Forces Staff College and the National War College. In 1983 he received an honorary doctor of laws from Williams College.

Roscoe Robinson, Jr.

★★★★ ———————————————————— ★★★★

General

Born October 28, 1928, in St. Louis, Missouri, where he received his elementary and secondary education. After graduation from Charles

Gen. Roscoe Robinson, Jr.

Sumner High School, he was appointed to the United States Military Academy, West Point. He was graduated in 1951 with a bachelor of science degree in military engineering and commissioned a second lieutenant.

After graduation, Robinson attended the Associate Infantry Officer Course and the Basic Airborne Course at Fort Benning, Georgia. He then joined the 11th Airborne Division at Fort Campbell, Kentucky, where he served as a platoon leader in the 188th Airborne Infantry Regiment until he went to Korea in October 1952. In Korea he served in the 31st Infantry Regiment, 7th Infantry Division, as a rifle company commander and battalion S-2. He was awarded the Bronze Star for his service in Korea.

Upon returning to the United States, he served in a variety of school and airborne unit assignments, highlighted by a tour with the United States Military Mission to Liberia in the late 1950s and the receipt of a master's in international affairs from the University of Pittsburgh in the early 1960s. As a lieutenant colonel, he served in Vietnam, first on the staff of the 1st Air Cavalry Division, then as the first black to command the 2nd Battalion, 7th Cavalry. For his Vietnam service, he was decorated with the Silver Star for valor.

Upon completion of the National War College in 1969, he served in Hawaii until his promotion to colonel when he assumed command of the 2nd Brigade, 82nd Airborne Division, in 1972. Among other assignments, he served as the commanding general, United States Army Garrison, Okinawa; commanding general, 82nd Airborne Division; and commanding general, United States Army, Japan/IX Corps.

In August 1982 he became the first black to become a four-star general in the Army (the second black in the armed forces, after Gen. Daniel

"Chappie" James). He also served as the United States representative to the North Atlantic Treaty Organization (NATO) Military Committee.

Charles Calvin Rogers

★★ ———————————————— ★★

Major General

Born on September 6, 1929, in Claremont, West Virginia, he married the former Margarete Schaefer, and they have two children: Jackie Linda and Barbara. He received a bachelor of science degree in mathematics from West Virginia State College, a masters of science degree in vocational education from Shippensburg State College, and master of science degree in theology from the University of Munich, West Germany. His military education included the Field Artillery School, Basic Course; the United States Army Artillery and Missile School, Advanced Course; the United States Army Command and General Staff College; United States Army War College.

He has held a wide variety of important command and staff positions. From June 1966 to November 1967, he was the commanding officer of the 1st Battalion, 2nd Brigade, Fort Lewis, Washington. From November 1967 to February 1968, he served as commander, 1st Infantry Division Artillery, United States Army, Pacific-Vietnam. From February 1968 to November 1968, he was commanding officer of the 1st Battalion, 5th Artillery, 1st Infantry Division, United States Army, Pacific-Vietnam.

On November 1, 1968, Lieutenant Colonel Rogers distinguished himself in action while serving as commanding officer with the 1st Battalion during the defense of a forward fire support base, Fishhook, near the Cambodian border in Vietnam. In the early morning, the fire support base was subjected to a concentrated bombardment of heavy mortar, rocket, and rocket-propelled grenade fire. Simultaneously the position was struck by a human ground assault wave led by sappers who breached the defensive barriers with bangalore torpedoes and penetrated the defensive perimenter.

General Rogers, with complete disregard for his safety, moved through the hail of fragments from bursting enemy rounds to the embattled area. He aggressively rallied the dazed artillery crewmen to man their howitzers, and he directed their fire on the assaulting enemy. Although knocked to the ground and wounded by an exploding round, General Rogers sprang to his feet and led a small counterattack force against an enemy element that had penetrated the howitzer positions. Although painfully wounded a second time during the assault, General Rogers pressed the

Maj. Gen. Charles Calvin Rogers

attack, killing several of the enemy and driving the remainder from the positions.

Refusing medical treatment, General Rogers reestablished and reinforced the defensive positions. As a second human wave attack was launched against another sector of the perimeter, he directed artillery fire on the assaulting enemy and led a second counterattack against the charging forces. His valorous example rallied the beleaguered defenders to repulse and defeat the enemy onslaught.

General Rogers moved from position to position through the heavy enemy fire, giving encouragement and direction to his men. At dawn the determined enemy launched a third assault against the fire base in an attempt to overrun the position. General Rogers moved to the threatened area and directed lethal fire on the enemy forces. Seeing a howitzer inoperative due to casualties, General Rogers joined the surviving members of the crew to return the howitzer to action and was seriously wounded by fragments from a heavy mortar round which exploded on the parapet of the gun position. Although too severely wounded to lead the defenders, General Rogers continued to give encouragement and direction to his men in defeating and repelling the enemy attack.

General Rogers's dauntless courage and heroism inspired the defenders of the fire support base to the heights of valor to defeat a determined and numerically superior enemy force. His relentless spirit of aggressiveness in action was in the highest traditions of the military service and reflected great credit upon himself, his unit, and the United States Army. For his bravery, he received the Medal of Honor, the highest military award for bravery that can be given to any individual in the United States.

From January 1969 to July 1969, he served as operations chief, J-3, United States Military Assistance Command, Vietnam. From August 1969 to May 1970, he served as a staff officer with the Readiness Division (later redesignated Troop Operations and Readiness Division), Operations, Directorate, Office, Office of Deputy Chief of Staff for Military Operations, United States Army, Washington, D.C. In June 1970 he was selected to attend the United States Army War College, Carlisle Barracks, Pennsylvania.

After completion of the War College, his assignment from September 1971 to January 1972 was assistant deputy commander, later deputy commander, V Corps Artillery, United States Army, Europe. From January 1972 to June 1973, he served as commanding officer of the 42nd Field Artillery Group, United States Army, Europe.

On July 1, 1973, he was appointed brigadier general. From 1973 to 1975, he served as the commanding general of the VII Corps Artillery, United States Army, Europe. In 1975 he was appointed major general. From 1975 to 1978, he served as deputy chief of staff, ROTC Headquarters, Training and Doctrine Command, Fort Monroe, Virginia. He returned to Europe in 1978, where he served first as deputy commanding general, V Corps; from 1980 to 1983 commanding general, VII Corps Artillery, Europe.

He retired in October 1983. General Rogers's military awards and decorations include the Medal of Honor, Legion of Merit (with oak leaf cluster), Distinguished Flying Cross, Bronze Star Medal (with "V" device and three oak leaf clusters), Air Medal (10 awards), Joint Service Commendation Medal, Army Commendation Medal (with three oak leaf clusters), Purple Heart, Parachutist Badge.

Jackson Evander Rozier, Jr.

★★ ———————————————— ★★

Major General

Born March 21, 1936, Richmond, Virginia. He received a B.S. in educational administration from Morgan State University, an M.A. in educational administration from Howard University.

He entered the United States Army on January 11, 1960, as a second lieutenant. From January 1960 to May 1960, he was a student in the signal officer basic course, Fort Monmouth, New Jersey. From May 1960 to July 1962, he was assigned first as executive officer, later commander, Headquarters Company, Combat Surveillance and Target Acquisition Training

Maj. Gen. Jackson Evander Rozier, Jr.

Command, Fort Huachuca, Arizona. His first overseas assignment was from July 1962 to November 1962 when he served as a radio officer for the 51st Signal Battalion, Europe. He was then assigned from December 1962 to October 1963 as a special services officer with I Corps, Special Troops, Korea.

Rozier returned to the United States as a student in the Air Defense Career course, Fort Bliss, Texas. From March 1964 to December 1965, he was assigned as an electronic warfare officer with the 24th Artillery Group, Coventry, Rhode Island. From December 1965 to December 1967, he was assigned first as a materiel officer, later executive officer, with the 71st Maintenance Battalion; then secretary, General Staff, 3rd Support Brigade, Europe.

He left Europe in December 1967 for Vietnam, where he served first as a supply officer with the United States Army Support Command. Then in June 1968 he was assigned as the deputy director general for supply.

Returning to the United States in January 1969, Rozier was a student in the Army Logistics Management Course at Fort Lee, Virginia. From June 1969 to October 1970, he served as an international logistics staff officer with the United States Army's Materiel Command, Washington, D.C. From December 1970 to June 1971, he was a student at the Armed Forces Staff College, Norfolk, Virginia. From August 1972 to March 1975, he was personnel management officer, United States Army Military Personnel Center, Alexandria, Virginia. From March 1975 to October 1976, Rozier served as commander, 801st Maintenance Battalion, 101st Airborne Division (Air Assault), Fort Campbell, Kentucky.

From November 1976 to July 1977, he was executive officer, Division

Support Command, 101st Airborne Division (Air Assault), Fort Campbell, Kentucky. From August 1977 to June 1978 he was a student in the Industrial College of the Armed Forces, Fort Lesley J. McNair, Washington, D.C. From September 1978 to December 1978, he was a student in the Defense Language Institute, Presidio of Monterey, California.

From December 1978 to March 1981, he was commander, Division Support Command, 8th Infantry Division (Mechanized), United States Army, Europe. From March 1981 to October 1983, he served as commanding general of the United States Army Ordnance Center and School, Aberdeen Proving Ground, Maryland.

Rozier was promoted to brigadier general on November 1, 1981. From November 1983 to June 1986, General Rozier served as the Director, Plans and Operations, Office of the Deputy Chief of Staff for Logistics, Washington, D.C. In June 1986 he returned to Europe as deputy chief, Staff for Logistics, United States Seventh Army. On July 1, 1987, he was promoted to major general. He returned to the United States in October 1989 to his last assignment, director, supply and maintenance, Office of the Deputy Chief of Staff for Logistics, United States Army, Washington, D.C.

Major General Jackson Evander Rozier, Jr., retired from the Army on June 30, 1990. His military decorations and awards include the Legion of Merit, Bronze Star Medal, Meritorious Service Medal (with two oak leaf clusters), Parachutist Badge, Army Staff Identification Badge.

Horace L. Russell

★ ——————————————————— ★

Brigadier General

Born February 26, 1937, in Jamaica, New York, he married the former Catherine Allen of Oxford, North Carolina. He was graduated from Highland High School in Gastonia, North Carolina, in 1954. He received a bachelor of science degree in mechanical engineering from Bradley University in 1958, in 1965 a master of science degree in aerospace engineering from the Air Force Institute of Technology, and a Ph.D. in engineering from Purdue University in 1971.

As a 1976 Air Force research associate, he attended the National Security Program at Mershon Center, Ohio State University, and was recognized as a Mershon Fellow. The general completed Squadron Officer School in 1963, Air Command and Staff College in 1972, the Industrial College of the Armed Forces in 1979.

After completing the Air Force Reserve Officer Training Corps program

Brig. Gen. Horace L. Russell

as a distinguished graduate, he was commissioned a second lieutenant in June 1958 and assigned to the University of Wisconsin for training in meteorology. In July 1959 he was assigned to Seymour Johnson Air Force Base, North Carolina, as a base operations weather officer. In June 1960 he became a weather officer at Headquarters, 19th Air Force, Seymour Johnson. From July 1962 to December 1965, he was assigned to the 341st Strategic Missile Wing, Malmstrom Air Force Base, serving as an instructor and deputy Minuteman combat crew commander, then as a crew commander.

He transferred to the Air Force Aero-Propulsion Laboratory at Wright-Patterson Air Force Base, Ohio, in December 1965 as a project engineer for advanced development of aircraft jet engines. From September 1967 to June 1970, he attended Purdue University, then returned to Wright-Patterson as chief of the Aerospace Dynamics Branch, Air Force Flight Dynamics Laboratory. In June 1973 the general was assigned to Headquarters, Air Force Systems Command, Andrews Air Force Base, Maryland, as program manager for energy conversion and mechanics, then chief, Physical and Engineering Sciences Division.

He was assigned to the Air Force Office of Scientific Research, Bolling Air Force Base, Washington, D.C., as deputy director for plans and operations from July 1975 to September 1976. In June 1977 he was assigned as study director for tactical command, control, and communications, Office of the Assistant to the Chief of Staff for Studies and Analyses, Headquarters, United States Air Force, Washington, D.C. In July 1978 he transferred to the Industrial College of the Armed Forces, Fort Lesley J. McNair, Washington, D.C., as a faculty member and student.

He served as chief, Programming Division, Office of the Deputy Chief of Staff for Research, Development, and Acquisition, Air Force headquarters, from June 1979 until July 1980. He then became director of defense programs, National Security Council Staff, in the White House. In August 1984 he became director for Joint Chiefs of Staff in Washington, D.C. In September 1986 he was assigned as deputy director for the national strategic target list, Joint Strategic Target Planning Staff, Offutt Air Force Base, Nebraska.

He was appointed brigadier general on June 1, 1984, with date of rank October 1, 1983. His military decorations and awards include the Defense Superior Service Medal (one oak leaf cluster), Meritorious Service Medal (three oak leaf clusters), Air Force Commendation Medal, Air Force Outstanding Unit Award (one oak leaf cluster), Combat Readiness Medal.

Richard Saxton

★ —————————————————— ★

Brigadier General

Served for over 30 years in both active service and in the Army National Guard. The source for this fact was *Black Americans in Defense of Our Nation* (1985) published by the Department of Defense, Office of Deputy Assistant Secretary of Defense for Equal Opportunity and Safety Policy. No other information could be obtained.

Donald Laverne Scott

★ —————————————————— ★

Brigadier General

Born February 8, 1938, Hunnewell, Missouri. He received a bachelor of science in art from Lincoln University, master of science, Human Relations from Troy State University.

He received an ROTC commission to second lieutenant in 1960, and from September 1960 to November 1960, he was a student in the Infantry Officer Orientation Course, United States Army Infantry School, Fort Benning, Georgia. From November 1960 to December 1961, he was a platoon leader for Company E, 2nd Battalion, 2nd Training Regiment, United States Army Training Center, Fort Leonard Wood, Missouri.

Brig. Gen. Donald Laverne Scott

He was promoted to first lieutenant on March 24, 1962, and from December 1961 to July 1962 was the commander of Company E, 2nd Battalion, 2nd Training Regiment, Fort Leonard Wood, Missouri. From July 1962 to November 1962, he was a student in the Intelligence Research Course, United States Army Intelligence School, Fort Holabird, Baltimore. From November 1962 to December 1964, he was assigned as intelligence research officer, Region I, 113th Intelligence Corps Group, duty station Chicago, Illinois.

He was promoted to captain on July 9, 1964. From December 1964 to December 1965, he was a student in the Vietnamese language, Defense Language Institute, West Coast Branch, Presidio of Monterey, California. From December 1965 to September 1967, he served as an intelligence research officer, later chief, of Counterintelligence Section, 441st Military Intelligence Detachment, 1st Special Forces Group (Airborne), 1st Special Forces, United States Army, Okinawa.

From September 1967 to May 1968, he served as a staff officer with the 97th Civil Affairs Group, 1st Special Forces, United States Army, Okinawa. From May 1968 to June 1969, he was a student in the Infantry Officer Advanced Course, United States Army Infantry School, Fort Benning, Georgia. From June 1969 to November 1969, he served as psychological operations officer, Office of the Assistant Chief of Staff, G-5, 4th Infantry Division, United States Army, Vietnam. From November 1969 to March 1970, he served as executive officer, 1st Battalion, 35th Infantry, 4th Infantry Division, Vietnam.

From March 1970 to June 1970, he served as S-3 of the 1st Battalion, 14th Infantry, 4th Infantry Division, United States Army, Vietnam. From

June 1970 to May 1972, he was an assistant professor of military science at Tuskegee Institute, Tuskegee, Alabama. From August 1972 to February 1973, he was the senior adviser, Office of the Territorial Forces, United States Military Assistance Command, Vietnam. From February 1973 to July 1974, he served as project officer, Threats Branch, War Games Division, Combat Operations Analysis Directorate; later project officer (combat developments), Program Management Integration Office, United States Army Combined Arms Development Activity, Fort Leavenworth, Kansas.

From August 1974 to June 1975, he was a student at the United States Army Command and General Staff College, Fort Leavenworth, Kansas. From June 1975 to May 1977, he served as chief, Training Division, United States Army Garrison, Fort Lewis, Washington. He was promoted to lieutenant colonel on September 9, 1976. From May 1977 to October 1978, he served as executive officer, 1st Infantry Brigade, 9th Infantry Division, Fort Lewis, Washington. From October 1978 to June 1980, he was commander, 3rd Battalion, 47th Infantry, 9th Infantry Division, Fort Lewis, Washington.

From June 1980 to June 1981, he served as professor of military science at Tuskegee Institute, Tuskegee, Alabama. From June 1981 to May 1982, he was a student at the Air War College, Maxwell Air Force Base, Alabama. From May 1982 to May 1983, he served as deputy inspector general, Office of the Inspector General, United States Army, Europe, and the Seventh Army.

He was promoted to colonel on October 1, 1982. From March 1985 to October 1986, he was the inspector general of VII Corps, United States Army, Europe. From October 1986 to August 1988, he served as assistant division commander, 1st Cavalry Division, Fort Hood, Texas.

On March 1, 1988, he was promoted to brigadier general. In September 1988 he was appointed chief of staff of the Second United States Army, Fort Gillem, Georgia. He has received numerous awards and decorations, including the Legion of Merit, Bronze Star Medal (with five oak leaf clusters), Meritorious Service Medal, Air Medal, Army Commendation Medal, Combat Infantryman Badge, Parachutist Badge.

Fred C. Sheffey, Jr.

★★ ———————————————————— ★★

Major General

Born August 27, 1928, McKeesport, Pennsylvania. He is married to the former Jane Hughes of Providence, Kentucky, and they have two sons,

Maj. Gen. Fred C. Sheffey, Jr.

Alan and Steven, and a daughter, Patricia. He was graduated from the ROTC program at Central State College, Wilberforce, Ohio, in June 1950 as a distinguished military graduate and was commissioned a second lieutenant of infantry and awarded a bachelor of science degree in economics.

In October 1950, he joined the 25th Infantry Division, fighting in Korea, as an infantry platoon leader. He was wounded and medically evacuated to the United States in April 1951, several weeks after promotion to first lieutenant. After hospitalization, he was assigned as a weapons instructor with the 5th Infantry Division Faculty at Indiantown Gap Military Reservation, Pennsylvania. He was detailed to the Quartermaster Corps in 1953 and attended the Quartermaster Officer Basic and Advanced Courses at Fort Lee, Virginia.

From August 1953 to June 1962, in addition to attending these schools, he had a series of logistical assignments in inventory management, supply, and maintenance at the Nahbollenback Depot in Europe and the Columbus General Depot in Columbus, Ohio. He was promoted to captain, on July 9, 1954, to major on November 28, 1961. While at Columbus General Depot, he engaged in business studies at Ohio State University and received the M.B.A. degree in June 1962.

From June 1962 to December 1964, he served on the staff of the United States Army Communications Zone, Europe. Following this assignment, he attended the Command and General Staff College, graduating in May 1965. He was then assigned to the 4th Infantry Division, Fort Lewis, Washington, where he served as division supply officer, later executive officer, 4th Division Supply and Transport Battalion.

On January 11, 1966, he was promoted to lieutenant colonel and assigned as commander, 266th QM Battalion, Fort Lewis, Washington. He deployed with this unit to Vietnam in June 1966. On his return to the United States, he was assigned to the Office of the Deputy Chief of Staff for Logistics, Department of the Army, as chief, Base Operations Branch, in financial management.

He graduated from the National War College in June 1969 and continued studies in International Affairs at George Washington University. For the latter, he was awarded a master of science degree in September 1969. He was promoted to colonel on November 20, 1970, and in May 1971 took command of the 54th General Support Group in Vietnam. In July 1972, he was again assigned to the Office of the Deputy Chief of Staff for Logistics, Department of the Army, where he served as the director of financial resources in the Pentagon until his promotion to brigadier general on July 1, 1973. On July 2, 1973, he became director Operation and Maintenance Resources (Provisional), and served in this capacity until May 20, 1974, when he was assigned as deputy director, supply and maintenance.

He joined the United States Army Materiel Development and Readiness Command, Alexandria, Virginia, in August 1975 as the director of materiel management. In March 1976, he was nominated by the president for promotion to major general and was promoted on August 2, 1976. On September 29, 1977, he assumed command of the United States Army Quartermaster Center, Fort Lee, Virginia. In this capacity, he also served as commandant of the United States Army Quartermaster School.

His medals and awards include the Legion of Merit (with two oak leaf clusters), Bronze Star Medal, Meritorious Service Medal, Army Commendation Medal (with two oak leaf clusters), Purple Heart, Combat Infantryman Badge.

Alonzo E. Short, Jr.

★★★ ————————————————————— ★★★

Lieutenant General

Born January 27, 1939, in Greenville, North Carolina, he married the former Rosalin Reid of Orange, New Jersey. He and his wife have one son, Stanley, and one daughter, Daniele. He holds a bachelor of science in education from Virginia State College and a master's in business management from the New York Institute of Technology, Long Island, New York. His military education includes the United States Army Signal School Officer Basic and Advanced Courses, the Military Advisor and Technical

Lt. Gen. Alonzo Earl Short, Jr.

Assistance School, the Armed Forces Staff College, the Communications/Electronics Systems Engineer Course, and the Army War College.

Since entering the Army in June 1962, General Short has held a variety of assignments with increasing responsibility throughout his career. He was a platoon leader and staff officer at Fort Riley, Kansas. From 1965 to 1967, he had assignments as a staff officer, company commander, and executive officer of a signal battalion in Europe. In 1967 he was assigned as a staff planning and engineering officer in Vietnam, followed by an assignment to Okinawa, first as battalion S-3, then executive officer, and finally, battalion commander in the Strategic Communications Command–Okinawa Signal Group. He served his second tour in Vietnam in 1972–1973 as an adviser.

In 1975, Short was assigned as a staff officer in the Defense Communications Agency. Following that assignment, he was a battalion commander in the 101st Airborne (Air Assault) Division, Fort Campbell, Kentucky. In 1979, Short began a tour as a staff planner with the Army Communications Command, Fort Huachuca. He then served as commander of the 3rd Signal Brigade at Fort Hood, Texas. He was assigned as deputy commander (ERADCOM), Adelphi, Maryland, from July to October 1984.

Short was promoted to brigadier general on June 1, 1986, assuming command as deputy commanding general, deputy program manager, Army Information Systems, United States Army Information Systems Engineering Command, Fort Belvoir, Virginia. On September 7, 1988, Short was promoted to major general concurrent with becoming deputy commanding general, Information Systems Engineering Command (ISEC), then commanding general. He was promoted to lieutenant colonel before he retired in 1990.

George Macon Shuffer, Jr.

★ ──────────────────────────── ★

Brigadier General

Born September 27, 1923, in Palestine, Texas, he married the former Maria Cecilia Rose. They have 11 children and 12 grandchildren. He received an associate of arts degree from Monterey Peninsula College, bachelor of science degree from the University of Maryland. In 1959, he completed requirements for a master of arts in history at the University of Maryland.

He enlisted in the Army on August 16, 1940, at Fort Huachuca, Arizona. After basic training, he was promoted to corporal and assigned as a training instructor at Camp Wolters, Texas. He attained the rank of sergeant before selection to attend the Infantry Officer Candidate School at Fort Benning, Georgia, in October 1942.

In World War II, he served as an intelligence and reconnaissance platoon leader with the 93rd Infantry Division in the Pacific theater. He participated in campaigns in the northern Solomons, the Bismark Archipelago, New Guinea, and the southern Philippines. He served as an infantry company commander in the 25th Infantry Division during the Korean War. He participated in the first UN offensive, Communist Chinese forces intervention, the first UN counteroffensive, and the Communist Chinese forces spring offensive.

On April 16, 1951, he suffered a serious head wound while making an assault crossing of the Han-Tan River. He recovered fully after 15 months of hospitalization at Walter Reed Army Medical Center, in Washington, D.C. From 1962 to 1964, he served as a military adviser to the Republic of China Army in Taiwan. In 1964 he returned to the United States and took command of the 2nd Battalion, 2nd Infantry, Fort Devens, Massachusetts.

When United States military forces were committed to combat in South Vietnam a year later, General Shuffer took his battalion into battle. He returned to the United States in 1966 at the United States Army War College, Carlisle Barracks, Pennsylvania. Upon graduation from the War College in 1967, he was assigned to staff duty in the Office of the Deputy Chief of Staff for Military Operations at the Pentagon. He became a military assistant in the Office of the Secretary of Defense in 1968.

From April 1970 to October 1971, he commanded the 193rd Infantry Brigade, Panama Canal Zone. Returning to the Pentagon in October 1971, he served as assistant director, Individual Training, Office of the Deputy Chief of Staff for Personnel. He became assistant division commander, 3rd Infantry Division, Germany, in 1973, and served in that position until 1974

Brig. Gen. George Macon Shuffer, Jr.

when he was hospitalized at Walter Reed Army Medical Center for an arthritic disease.

On July 1, 1975, he was medically retired from the Army in the rank of brigadier general, completing 35 years of active service. His decorations and awards include the Distinguished Service Medal, three Silver Stars, Purple Heart Medal, three Bronze Stars, six Air Medals, Parachutist Badge, three Combat Infantryman Badges, Army Commendation Medal, Legion of Merit (three oak leaf clusters), Secretary of Defense Identification Badge, Presidential Unit Citation, General Staff Identification Badge, Meritorious Service Medal.

Isaac D. Smith

★★ ——————————————————— ★★

Major General

Born May 2, 1932, in Wakefield, Louisiana, he married the former Mildred L. Pierre, and they have two children, Debra J. and Ronald L.

Upon completion of the Reserve Officers Training Corps curriculum and the educational course of study at Southern University A&M College, he was commissioned a second lieutenant and awarded a bachelor of science in agriculture. He also holds a master's in public administration from Shippensburg State College. His military education includes completion of the Field Artillery School, basic and advanced courses; United

Maj. Gen. Isaac D. Smith

States Army Command and General Staff College; and the United States Army War College.

He has held a wide variety of important command and staff positions. He was chief, Doctrine and Systems Integration Division, Requirements Directorate, Office of the Deputy Chief of Staff for Operations and Plans, United States Army, Washington, D.C.; commanding general, United States Army Second Reserve Officer Training Corps Region, Fort Knox, Kentucky; and assistant division commander, 1st Armored Division, United States Army, Europe.

General Smith served as deputy chief of staff, Operations and Intelligence, Allied Forces Central, Europe. In Vietnam, he was commander of the 8th Battalion, 4th Artillery, XXIV Corps Artillery, United States Army, Vietnam, and later served as operations officer, 23rd Army of the Republic of Vietnam Infantry Division, United States Military Assistance Command, Vietnam.

He followed this assignment with a tour in Europe as commander, 2nd Battalion, 75th Field Artillery, 36th Field Artillery Group, V Corps Artillery, United States Army, Europe. He returned to the United States as a staff officer in the Unit Training and Readiness Division, Office of the Assistant Chief of Staff for Force Development, later Office of the Deputy Chief of Staff for Military Operations, Washington, D.C.

After attendance at the United States Army War College, Carlisle Barracks, Pennsylvania, he became deputy director, Army Equal Opportunity Programs, Human Resources Directorate, Office of the Deputy Chief of Staff for Personnel, United States Army, Washington, D.C. He was commander of Division Artillery, 1st Infantry Division (Mechanized), Fort

Riley, Kansas, then became special assistant to the commander, Third Reserve Officer Training Corps Region, Fort Riley. He then served as chief of staff, 1st Infantry Division (Mechanized), Fort Riley, Kansas.

His military awards and decorations include the Silver Star, the Legion of Merit (with oak leaf cluster), Bronze Star Medal, Meritorious Service Medal (with oak leaf cluster), Army Commendation Medal (with two oak leaf clusters), Army General Staff Identification Badge.

Nathaniel Smith

★ ——————————————————— ★

Brigadier General

Appointed to the one star rank in the Army National Guard. The source for this fact was *Black Americans in Defense of Our Nation* (1985) published by the Department of Defense, Office of Deputy Assistant Secretary of Defense for Equal Opportunity and Safety Policy. No other information could be obtained.

Billy King Solomon

★ ——————————————————— ★

Brigadier General

Born November 16, 1944, in Oakwood, Texas. He received a B.S. degree in agriculture from Prairie View A&M University in 1966. He earned a M.S. degree in procurement/contract management from Florida Institute of Technology in 1982. He began his military career in October 1966 as a second lieutenant in the Quartermaster Officer Basic Course at Fort Lee, Virginia.

In December 1966, he was assigned as first officer in charge, and later as platoon leader of Company A, 502nd Supply and Transportation Battalion with the 2nd Armored Division at Fort Hood, Texas. In October 1967, he was assigned as the stock control officer of the 624th Supply and Service Company, 226th Supply and Service Battalion, with the United States Army in Vietnam. In January 1968, he served as a Platoon Leader with the 506th Supply and Service Company, and later as S-3 (operations) officer with the 266th Supply and Service Battalion.

In October 1968, he returned to the United States and was assigned G-4

Brig. Gen. Billy King Solomon

(logistics) with the 2nd Armored Division again at Fort Hood. He became a student in the Quartermaster Officer Advanced Course (October 1970 to August 1971). From August 1971 to March 1972, he served as commander of Headquarters Company with the 88th Supply and Service Battalion in Vietnam. From March 1972 to September 1972, he was assigned as the S-3 officer (operations), Logistical Support Activity in Vietnam. In the fall of 1972, he was assigned as a supply and logistics officer with the 109th Military Intelligence Group in Fort Meade, Maryland. Beginning in May 1974 he served for a year as a civil affairs officer for the 902nd Military Intelligence Group at Fort Meade, Maryland. From May 1975 to December 1977, he served as the chief logistics officer with the United States Army Communications Command Agency in the Canal Zone at Fort Clayton, Panama.

From December 1977 to July 1978, he was a student at the Armed Forces Staff College at Norfolk, Virginia. From July 1978 to June 1982, he was assigned as a personnel management officer with the Military Personnel Center at Alexandria, Virginia. From June 1982 to June 1983, he served as protocol officer in the Office of the Chief of Staff, Army, in Washington, D.C. From June 1983 to June 1985, Solomon served as the commander of the 498th Support Battalion, with the 2nd Armored Division, United States Army in Europe and Seventh Army.

He then became a student in the Industrial College of the Armed Forces. From June 1986 to May 1989, he served as chief of quartermaster, Chemical Branch; later chief of Combat Service Support Division, Enlisted Personnel Management Directorate, United States Army Personnel Command at Alexandria, Virginia. In May 1989, he was assigned as the commander of the Division Support Command with the 5th Infantry Division (Mechanized) at Fort Polk, Louisiana.

Billy King Solomon was promoted to the one star rank of brigadier general on October 1, 1992. His awards and decorations include the following: Legion of Merit (with oak leaf cluster), Bronze Star Medal (with oak leaf cluster), Meritorious Service Medal (with three oak leaf clusters), Army Commendation Medal (with oak leaf cluster), Army Achievement Medal.

John Henry Stanford

★★ ──────────────── ★★

Major General

Born September 14, 1938, Darby, Pennsylvania. He received a bachelor of arts in political science from Pennsylvania State University, a master's personnel management/administration from Central Michigan University.

He received an ROTC commission to second lieutenant on June 10, 1961. From August 1961 to January 1962, he was a student at the Infantry Officer Basic Course and the Ranger Course, United States Army Infantry School, Fort Benning, Georgia. From January 1962 to May 1962, he was platoon leader, Company D, 2nd Air Reconnaissance Battalion, 36th Infantry, 3rd Armored Division, United States Army, Europe.

He was promoted to first lieutenant on December 10, 1962. In June of 1963, he was appointed commander, 40th Transportation Company, 15th Quartermaster Battalion, 6th Quartermaster Group, United States Army, Europe. From June 1963 to November 1964, he was a student in the Officer Fixed Wing Aviator Course, United States Army Aviation School, Fort Rucker, Alabama. He was promoted to captain on January 6, 1965.

From August 1965 to October 1965, he was the assistant S-1, Headquarters, Troop Brigade, Fort Rucker, Alabama. From January 1966 to April 1966, he served as a fixed wing Army aviator, 55th Aviation Company, Eighth United States Army, Korea. From August 1966 to July 1967, he was a fixed wing aviator, 73rd Aviation Company (Aerial Surveillance), 222nd Aviation Battalion, United States Army, Vietnam. From July 1967 to February 1968, he was a student in the Aircraft Maintenance Officer Course, United States Army Transportation School, Fort Eustis, Virginia.

From February 1968 to June 1968, he was assigned as chief, Electrical Section, United States Army Transportation School, Fort Eustis, Virginia. He was promoted to major on June 10, 1968. From June 1968 to February

Maj. Gen. John Henry Stanford

1969, he was a student in the Transportation Officer Advanced Course, United States Army Transportation School, Fort Eustis. From February 1969 to September 1969, he was a platoon commander with the 73rd Aviation Company, 210th Aviation Battalion (Combat), United States Army, Vietnam.

From September 1969 to May 1970, he was commander, 56th Transportation Company, 765th Transportation Battalion, 34th General Support Group, United States Army, Vietnam. From May 1970 to July 1971, he served as personnel staff officer, Directorate of Personnel and Community Activities, United States Army Transportation Center, Fort Eustis, Virginia.

From July 1971 to June 1972, he was a student in the United States Army Command and General Staff College, Fort Leavenworth, Kansas. From June 1972 to November 1972, he was a personnel management officer in the Office of Personnel Operations, Washington, D.C. From November 1972 to September 1975, he served as aviation assignments officer, later personnel management officer, Transportation Branch Office, Personnel Directorate, United States Army Military Personnel Center, Alexandria, Virginia.

He was promoted to lieutenant colonel on June 1, 1975. From June 1975 to May 1977, he was the commander of the 34th Support Battalion, 6th Cavalry Brigade (Air Combat), III Corps, Fort Hood, Texas. From June 1977 to May 1979, he served as a military assistant to the Under Secretary of the Army, Office of the Secretary of the Army, Washington, D.C. From June 1979 to June 1980, he was a student at the Industrial College of Armed Forces, Fort Lesley J. McNair, Washington, D.C.

He was promoted to colonel on August 1, 1979. From July 1980 to June 1981, he was commander, Division Support Command, 2nd Infantry Division, United States Army, Korea. From June 1981 to June 1984, he was first executive assistant to the special assistant to the Secretary of Defense; later serving as executive secretary for the Department of Defense, Office of the Secretary of Defense, in Washington, D.C.

From June 1984 to September 1986, he was commander, Military Traffic Management Command, Western Area, Oakland Army Base, Oakland, California. He was promoted to brigadier general on September 1, 1984. From September 1986 to June 1987, he was the deputy commander, Research and Development, United States Army Aviation Systems Command, St. Louis, Missouri. From June 1987 to August 1989, he was commanding general of the Military Traffic Management Command, Washington, D.C.

He was promoted to major general on May 1, 1988. In September 1989 he was appointed director of plans, J-5, United States Transportation Command, Scott Air Force Base, Illinois. He has received numerous awards and decorations, including the Master Army Aviator Badge, Distinguished Service Medal, Ranger Tab.

Robert Louis Stephens, Jr.

★ ———————————————————— ★

Brigadier General

Born September 21, 1940, Welch, West Virginia. He received a bachelor of science in education from West Virginia State College, a master of science in vocational education guidance from Alfred University.

He received an ROTC commission and entered the Army as a student in the Infantry Officer Basic Course, United States Army Infantry School, Fort Benning, Georgia. From November 1962 to April 1964, he served as a platoon leader for Company C, later S-4 (logistics), 1st Airborne Battle Group, 327th Infantry, 101st Airborne Division, Fort Campbell, Kentucky. From June 1964 to December 1964, he was a student at the Defense Language Institute, Presidio of Monterey, California. From January 1965 to April 1965, he was a student in the Special Forces Officer course, United States Army Special Warfare School, Fort Bragg, North Carolina.

From April 1965 to June 1967, he served as executive officer, later commander, Company B, 8th Special Forces Group (Airborne), 1st Special Forces, Fort Gulick, Panama. He was promoted to captain on April 11, 1966. From June 1967 to July 1968, he was assistant G-5 (civil affairs,

Brig. Gen. Robert Louis Stephens, Jr.

civic action), later commander, Company B, 1st Battalion, 7th Cavalry; later, commander, Headquarters Company, 3rd Brigade, 1st Cavalry Division (Airmobile), United States Army, Vietnam. From July 1968 to July 1969, he served as senior platoon advisor. Later he was a student in the Infantry Officer Advanced Course, United States Army Infantry School, Fort Benning, Georgia. On June 27, 1969, he was promoted to major.

From July 1969 to May 1971, he served as assistant professor of military science, Alfred University, New York. From August 1971 to June 1972, he was a student at the United States Army Command and Staff College, Fort Leavenworth, Kansas. From June 1972 to March 1973, he was assigned as the S-3 (operations) adviser, Delta Region Assistance Command, United States Military Assistance Command, Vietnam. From March 1973 to June 1976, he served as division race relations officer, later headquarters commandant, later executive officer, 3rd Battalion, 187th Infantry, later Adjutant, 3rd Brigade; then assistant G-1 (personnel), 101st Airborne Division (Airmobile), Fort Campbell, Kentucky.

From June 1976 to April 1978, he served as personnel staff officer, Alcohol and Drug Policy Branch, Leadership Division, Office of Deputy Chief of Staff for Personnel, United States Army, Washington, D.C. From April 1978 to April 1979, he served as military secretary, J-3 (operations), Organization of the Joint Chiefs of Staff, Washington, D.C.

He was promoted to lieutenant colonel on September 12, 1978. From May 1979 to June 1981, he was commander, the 2nd Battalion, 39th Infantry, 9th Infantry Division, Fort Lewis, Washington. From June 1981 to June 1982, he served as personnel staff officer, Leadership Division, Office of the Deputy Chief of Staff for Personnel, United States Army,

Washington, D.C. From June 1982 to June 1983, he was a student at the National War College, Fort McNair, Washington, D.C. From June 1983 to April 1985, he was assigned as inspector general, Military District of Washington, Fort McNair, Washington, D.C.

He was promoted to colonel on October 1, 1983. From April 1985 to June 1987, he was commander, Task Force Bayonet (later designated 193rd Infantry Brigade), United States Army South, Panama. From June 1987 to September 1988, he was deputy director for readiness, mobilization, and exercises, Office of the Deputy Chief of Staff for Operations and Plans, United States Army, Washington, D.C. From September 1988 to February 1990, he was assigned as assistant division commander, 9th Infantry Division (Motorized), Fort Lewis, Washington.

He was promoted to brigadier general on July 1, 1989. In February 1990 he was appointed chief, Joint United States Military Assistance Group, Thailand. He has received numerous awards and decorations, including the Legion of Merit, Bronze Star Medal (with "V" device and two oak leaf clusters), Purple Heart, Meritorious Service Medal (with five oak leaf clusters), Air Medal (with "V" device and three oak leaf clusters), Joint Service Commendation Medal (with oak leaf cluster), Combat Infantryman Badge, Air Assault Badge, Master Parachutist Badge.

Preston M. Taylor, Jr.

★ ——————————————————— ★

Brigadier General

Born October 11, 1933, Mobile, Alabama. He and his wife, Audrey, have a son, Christopher, and a daughter, Cinthia. He attended LaSalle University, Philadelphia, Pennsylvania, and earned a bachelor of arts degree in personnel management from Pepperdine University, California, a master of arts in personnel management from Central Michigan University. His military education includes completion of numerous aircraft communication and avionics courses and graduation from the Industrial College of the Armed Forces, Air Command and Staff College, and the Air Force Squadron Officer's School. While at Lakehurst, he completed the Naval Air Systems Command Five-Year Senior Executive Management Development Program and the Naval Air Engineering Center's Six-Month Executive Development Courses.

His military assignments include an active duty tour with the Air Force from 1954 to 1960, service as a communications electronics staff officer, state inspector general, and chairman of the minority officer recruiting

Brig. Gen. Preston M. Taylor, Jr.

committee for the New Jersey Air National Guard. In 1992 he served as the deputy adjutant general of New Jersey.

General Taylor is retired from civilian federal employment, having served as a supervisor in the Naval Aircraft Engine and Avionics Logistics Section, Naval Air Engineering Center, Lakehurst, New Jersey. His military awards and decorations include the Meritorious Service Medal, Air Force Commendation Medal, Air Force Organizational Excellence Award, Armed Forces Reserve Medal (with one hourglass device).

Lucius Theus

★★ ———————————————————— ★★

Major General

Born October 11, 1922, in Madison County, Tennessee, he married the former Gladys Marie Davis of Chicago, Illinois. He graduated from Community High School in Blue Island, Illinois. He has a bachelor of science degree from the University of Maryland in 1956, a master's in business administration from George Washington University in 1957, and is a graduate of the Harvard Advanced Management Program, Harvard University Graduate School of Business Administration, 1969.

During his Air Force career, General Theus attended the Statistical Control Officers School at Lowry Air Force Base, Colorado, in 1948, and in 1966 he was graduated with distinction from the Air War College at Maxwell Air Force Base, Alabama.

Maj. Gen. Lucius Theus

During World War II, he entered the Army Air Corps as a private in December 1942. After basic training, he attended the Army Administration School at Atlanta University. For the remainder of World War II, he served as an administrative clerk, chief clerk, and first sergeant of preaviation cadet and basic training squadrons at Keesler Field, Mississippi. He entered Officer Candidate School, graduating second in his class with a commission as second lieutenant in January 1946.

Following a one-year tour of duty as squadron adjutant at Tuskegee Army Air Field, Alabama, Theus went to Lockbourne Air Force Base, Ohio, as base statistical control officer. In August 1949 he was transferred to Erding Air Depot, Germany, where he served as the analysis and presentation officer, later commander, Statistical Control Flight, and depot statistical control officer. Theus was assigned in August 1952 to the Office of the Deputy Chief of Staff, Comptroller, Headquarters, United States Air Force, Washington, D.C., where he was chief, Materiel Logistics Statistics Branch. In October 1957, Theus was assigned to Headquarters, Central Air Materiel Forces, Europe, Chateauroux Air Base, France, as a statistical advisor to the comptroller, Headquarters, Air Materiel Forces, Europe.

In January 1959, Theus was assigned as chief, Management Services Office, Eastern Air Logistics Office, Athens, Greece. In February 1961 he was appointed chief, Management Analysis, Headquarters, Spokane Air Defense Sector, Larson Air Force Base, Washington. In December 1962 Theus was assigned as base comptroller at Kingsley Field, Oregon. His next assignment was base comptroller, Cam Ranh Bay Air Base, Vietnam. For more than five months of this assignment, he also was acting deputy base commander of Cam Ranh Bay Air Base.

Upon his return to the United States in July 1967, Theus was reassigned to Headquarters, United States Air Force, Office of the Comptroller of the Air Force, as a data automation staff officer in the Directorate of Data Automation. He served initially as chief, Technology and Standards Branch; then chief, Plans, Policy, and Technology Division; later chief, Program Management Division. During that assignment, he also performed additional duty as chairman of the Inter-Service Task Force on Education in Race Relations, Office of the Secretary of Defense. The recommendations of the task force led to establishment of the Defense Race Relations Institute and the Department of Defense education program in race relations.

In 1968 he attended the Department of Defense Computer Institute. In July 1971, he was assigned as director of management analysis, Office of the Comptroller of the Air Force. In June 1972, he was appointed special assistant for social actions, Directorate of Personnel Plans, Deputy Chief of Staff, Personnel, Headquarters, United States Air Force. On June 10, 1974, he was appointed director of accounting and finance, Office of the Comptroller of the Air Force, Headquarters, United States Air Force, and commander of the Air Force Accounting and Finance Center, Denver, Colorado.

General Theus was promoted to major general effective May 1, 1975, with date of rank July 1, 1972. His military decorations and awards include the Distinguished Service Medal, Legion of Merit, Bronze Star Medal, Air Force Commendation Medal (with one oak leaf cluster), Air Force Outstanding Unit Award Ribbon.

Gerald Eustis Thomas

★★ ———————————————————— ★★

Rear Admiral

Born June 23, 1929, in Natick, Massachusetts, he is the son of Walter W. Thomas and Leila L. (Jacobs) Thomas. He married the former Rhoda Holmes Henderson and they have three children: Kenneth A., Steven E., and Lisa D. Admiral Thomas received his undergraduate degree, a B.A. from Harvard, in 1951, a master's from George Washington University in 1966, and a Ph.D. in diplomatic history from Yale in 1973.

He began his Navy career in 1951, and for over thirty years he held a wide variety of important command and staff positions. From 1962 to 1963 he was the commanding officer of the USS *Impervious*. From 1963 to 1965 he served as the commander of the College Training Programs, Bureau of

Rear Adm. Gerald Eustis Thomas

the Naval Personnel. From 1966 to 1968 he served as the commanding officer of the USS *Bausell*. From 1968 to 1970 he served as the commanding officer and professor of naval science at Prairie View A&M College Naval ROTC Unit. After his promotion to the flag rank of admiral, he was assigned to the U.S. Navy, commander of Destroyer Squadron 5, from 1973 to 1975. He was assigned as the acting deputy assistant secretary of defense, for international security affairs and director of the Near East, South Asia and Africa Region, at the U.S. Dept. of Defense, from 1976 to 1978. Then his last military assignment, from 1978 to 1981, when he served as the senior rear admiral of the United States Pacific Fleet.

He retired in 1981 and from 1981 to 1983 was U.S. ambassador to Guyana; and was U.S. Ambassador to Kenya from 1983 to 1986. Navy to Guyana. From 1986 to 1991 he served as a Yale University lecturer, in the African-American studies program and history department. In May 1991 Dr. Thomas was named the new master of Davenport College in Grand Rapids, Michigan. For a man who has commanded squadrons of ships as an admiral in the U.S. Navy and who has supervised hundreds of diplomats as ambassador to Kenya, becoming master of a residential college might seem insignificant. But Dr. Thomas took the role very seriously. His experience as teacher, scholar and leader in the highest echelons of government brought knowledge that proved to be invaluable to Davenport and the entire Yale community. Davenport College Pres. Benno Schmidt, Jr., appointed Dr. Thomas to a five-year term, selecting him from a list of candidates compiled by a student and faculty search committee.

Robert L. Toney

★★ ——————————————————— ★★

Rear Admiral

Born August 30, 1934, in Monroe, Louisiana, he married the former Flora J. Wallace of San Diego, California. They have two daughters and one son. Admiral Toney attended Youngstown University, Youngstown, Ohio, from 1952 to 1954, and in 1957 was graduated from California State University, Chico, with a bachelor of arts degree.

Admiral Toney was commissioned an ensign in the United States Navy Reserve on October 31, 1957. He completed the NATO Defense College in 1977. He is the director, Logistics and Security Assistance, United States Pacific Command, Camp H. M. Smith, Hawaii. He advises the commander in chief, United States Pacific Command, on all matters dealing with the defense of the United States through bilateral logistics agreements, cooperative funds, logistics planning, transportation, civil engineering, and security assistance.

Admiral Toney's early Navy tours included duty as the assistant communications officer aboard the USS *Bennington* (CVA-20); staff officer, Commander, Training Command, United States Pacific Fleet; operations officer, USS *Guadalupe* (A-32); combat information officer, USS *Topeka* (CLG-8); senior projects officer, Destroyer Development Group, Pacific Fleet; special projects officer, Commander, Cruiser-Destroyer Group, Pacific; executive officer, USS *Cowell* (DD-547); special assistant, Chief of Naval Personnel, Washington, D.C.; commander, Navy Recruiting Command for Minority Affairs (Recruiting); executive officer, USS *Wichita* (AOR-1); command of USS *Kiska* (AE-35). Admiral Toney also served on the staff of the Commander, Allied Forces, Southern Europe, from August 1977 to April 1979, and as chief of staff officer, Commander, Service Group One, from April 1979 to March 1983.

In August 1983 he became commanding officer of the USS *Roanoke* (AOR-7). Upon promotion to flag rank in August 1984, Admiral Toney assumed duties as deputy commander, Naval Surface Force, United States, Pacific, in September 1984. In October 1985 he also assumed the additional duties as commander, Naval Surface Group, Long Beach. He assumed command of Naval Base, San Francisco, and Combat Logistic Group One in January 1986.

In May 1988, Rear Admiral Toney was selected for promotion to rear admiral (upper half). He assumed his present position in February 1989. Rear Admiral Toney's awards and decorations include the Legion of Merit, Defense Meritorious Service Medal, Navy Meritorious Service Medal

Rear Adm. Robert L. Toney

(second award), Navy Commendation Medal, Meritorious Unit Commendation, Armed Forces Expeditionary Medal, Vietnam Service Medal (fifth award), Republic of Vietnam Campaign Medal, National Defense Service Medal.

Guthrie Lewis Turner, Jr.

★ ──────────────────────── ★

Brigadier General

Born May 26, 1930, in Chicago, Illinois. He received a B.S. degree in biology from Shaw University in 1949. He earned a doctor of medicine degree from Howard University in 1953. He earned a master's degree in public health from Harvard University in 1966. Military schools attended include the Medical Service School, advanced course; the United States Army Command and General Staff College; and the United States Army War College.

He has held a wide variety of important command and staff positions, to include the following key assignments. From January 1965 to August 1965, he served as assistant chief of the Department of Aviation Medicine, at Lyster Army Hospital in Fort Rucker, Alabama. From June 1968 to June 1969, he served as the commander of the 15th Medical Battalion and surgeon, 1st Cavalry Division (Airmobile) in Vietnam. From August 1969 to July 1972, he served as the commander of Beach Army Hospital and

Brig. Gen. Guthrie Lewis Turner, Jr.

surgeon (later chief), Medical Activities Division, United States Army Primary Helicopter Center and School, Fort Wolters, Texas.

From August 1972 to July 1974, he was assigned as a surgeon with the VII Corps in Europe. From July 1974 to July 1976, he was assigned as the commander of the 130th General Hospital in Europe. He served as a consultant for aviation medicine in the Office of the Surgeon General in Washington, D.C. from July 1976 to March 1978. Then he was assigned as the commander of the United States Army Medical Command in Korea; and Surgeon for the United Nations Command and United States Forces Korea and Eighth United States Army.

On May 9, 1980, he was promoted the one star rank of brigadier general. He then became the commanding general of the Madigan Army Medical Center in Tacoma, Washington. He retired on July 31, 1983. His numerous military awards and decorations include: the Distinguished Service Medal, the Legion of Merit, the Air Medals, Army Commendation Medal, Master Parachutist Badge, and the Senior Flight Surgeon Badge.

Joseph Ellis Turner

★★ ——————————————— ★★

Major General

Born September 2, 1939, Charleston, West Virginia. He is the son of Joseph Turner and Annetta Frances Malone. He and his wife, Norma Jean, have three children: Dr. Alan T., Brian D., and Joseph E., Jr. Upon completion of high school, Turner attended West Virginia State College where he graduated and received his ROTC commission in 1961.

Upon entering the Army, he attended the Signal Officer's Basic Course. Later he was graduated from the Aviation Fixed and Rotary Wing Courses, the Signal Officer's Advanced Course, Army Aviation Safety Course, the Command and General Staff College, the Industrial College of the Armed Forces (National Security Management Course), and the Air War College of the Armed Forces (National Security Management Course).

He has completed the Federal Aviation Administration's Air Traffic Indoctrination Course, the University of Southern California's Aviation Safety and Management Course, and advanced studies in Human Resources Management at the University of Utah.

His active duty assignments include two tours in Vietnam, where he served as a fixed wing aviator in the 17th Aviation Company, 1st Air Cavalry Division; signal officer, 17th Aviation Group; and commander, Headquarters Company, 210th Combat Aviation Battalion. He also served as a fixed wing aviator for the Third United States Army, aviator and communications officer with the 187th Airplane Company, and signal platoon leader, 1st Battle Group, 29th Infantry.

Turner began his military career as a Reserve officer in January 1961 and was appointed a Regular Army Officer in April 1966. His principal Reserve assignments have included commander, 335th Signal Group and 3283rd United States Army Reserve Forces School. In the 81st United States Army Reserve Command, he served as deputy chief of staff for logistics, deputy chief of staff for resources management, operations/

Maj. Gen. Joseph Ellis Turner

training officers, aviation safety officer, and communication/electronics officer.

In March 1988 he was promoted to brigadier general and assigned as deputy commander, 335th Signal Command, East Point, Georgia. He became the first black Georgia reservist and the first black in the 81st United States Army Reserve Command to be promoted to general officer rank. In 1988 he was inducted into the Georgia Hall of Fame.

In September 1991, he was assigned as the commander of the 335th Signal Command. On May 21, 1992, General Turner was promoted to major general.

He is employed by Delta Airlines, where he serves as the first officer on the L1011 aircraft. He is a member of the Reserve Officers Association, the Signal Corps Association, the Armed Forces Communications/Electronics Association, the Air Line Pilot's Association, and the organization of Black Air Line Pilots.

John H. Voorhees

★★ ———————————————— ★★

Major General

Born August 12, 1936, in New Brunswick, New Jersey, he married the former Jeanine Carter, and they have two children: Melanie Shemyne and John Carter. He was graduated from New Brunswick High School in 1954. He received a bachelor of science degree in chemistry from Rutgers University in 1958 and a master's in management from the University of Southern California in 1967. He was designated a senior executive fellow of Harvard University in 1981. The general completed Squadron Officer School in 1962 and the National War College in 1973.

He received his commission in 1958 as a distinguished military graduate of the Air Force Reserve Officer Training Corps program at Rutgers. He then completed navigator training at James Connally Air Force Base, Texas, and Mather Air Force Base, California. From April 1960 to June 1966, he was a B-52 navigator with the 668th Bombardment Squadron, Griffiss Air Force Base, New York. He then entered the Air Force Institute of Technology program and completed his master's degree at the University of Southern California.

In June 1968 the general joined the 14th Tactical Fighter Squadron at Ubon Royal Thai Air Force Base, Thailand, as an F-4 navigator systems operator. During this assignment, he flew 176 combat missions, including

Maj. Gen. John H. Voorhees

100 over North Vietnam. Upon returning to the United States in May 1969, he was assigned to the Space and Missile Systems Organization headquarters at Los Angeles Air Force Station as chief of the Systems Effectiveness Branch and later as chief of the Test Support Division.

After graduation from the National War College in June 1973, he remained in Washington, D.C., as a research and development planner in the Organization of the Joint Chiefs of Staff. Moving to Wright-Patterson Air Force Base in July 1976, Voorhees was initially assigned as chief, Strategic Plans Division, then as director of plans at Air Force Logistic Command headquarters.

From July 1979 to May 1981 he was chief, B-52 and Missile Systems Management Division, Oklahoma City Air Logistics Center, Tinker Air Force Base, Oklahoma. He then became director of materiel management for the Sacramento Air Logistics Center, McClellan Air Force Base, California. In August 1982 he took command of the Defense Contract Administration Services Region in Los Angeles. He was assigned as deputy director, Logistics and Security Assistance, J4/7, Headquarters, European Command, Vaihingen, West Germany, in June 1984. In August 1986 he assumed command of the Defense Personnel Support Center, Defense Logistics Agency, Philadelphia.

He was promoted to major general on June 1, 1986. In January 1990, he became deputy chief of staff for contracting and manufacturing, Headquarters, Air Force Logistics Command, Wright-Patterson Air Force Base, Ohio. His duties include management of an $11 billion contracting program in support of the command's logistics mission. Air Force Logistics Command annually completes almost 450,000 contracting actions that support the United States Air Force as well as more than 70 friendly foreign air forces under the foreign military sales program. He is a master navigator with 3,800 flying hours in the B-52 and F-4C.

Calvin Agustine Hoffman Waller

★★★ ——————————————————————— ★★★

Lieutenant General

Born December 17, 1937, Baton Rouge, Louisiana. He received a bachelor of science in agriculture from Prairie View A&M University and a master of science in public administration from Shippensburg State University.

He entered the United States Army in August 1959 as a student in the Infantry Officer Basic Course, United States Infantry School, Fort Benning, Georgia. In June 1961 he was assigned as commander, 247th Chemical Platoon, Fort Lewis, Washington. On July 30, 1962, he was promoted to first lieutenant. From August 1963 to June 1963, he was a student at the United States Army Chemical Center and School, Fort McClellan, Alabama. He was promoted to captain on July 29, 1963. From December 1963 to June 1964, he served as the chief, Chemical, Biological, Radiological Center, Office of the Assistant Chief of Staff G-2/G-3, 7th Logistics Command, Eighth United States Army, Korea.

From February 1965 to April 1967, he served as an chemical officer, Headquarters, Headquarters Company; later brigade chemical officer, 2nd Brigade, 82nd Airborne Division, Fort Bragg, North Carolina. He was promoted to major on September 5, 1967. From July 1968 to May 1969, he was a student at the United States Army Command and General Staff College, Fort Leavenworth, Kansas. From April 1971 to July 1972, he served as a training staff officer, Policy and Programs Branch, Office of the Deputy Chief of Staff for Personnel, United States Army, Washington, D.C.

On June 1, 1975, he was promoted to lieutenant colonel. From August 1975 to May 1977, he was commander, 1st Battalion, 77th Armor, 4th Infantry Division (Mechanized), Fort Carson, Colorado. From August 1977 to June 1978, he was a student at the United States Army War College, Carlisle Barracks, Pennsylvania. From July 1980 to June 1981, he was senior military assistant, Office of Assistant Secretary of Defense (Manpower, Reserve Affairs and Logistics), Washington, D.C.

On August 1, 1980, he was promoted to colonel. From August 1983 to December 1983, he served as chief of staff for the 24th Infantry Division

Lt. Gen. Calvin Agustine Hoffman Waller

(Mechanized), Fort Stewart, Georgia. From December 1983 to June 1984, he was chief of staff, XVIII Airborne Corps, Fort Bragg, North Carolina. From June 1984 to July 1986, he served as assistant division commander, 82nd Airborne Division, Fort Bragg, North Carolina.

He was promoted to brigadier general on November 1, 1984. From July 1986 to July 1987, he served as deputy commanding general, I Corps and Fort Lewis, Fort Lewis, Washington. From July 1987 to July 1989, he was the commanding general of the 8th Infantry Division (Mechanized), V Corps, United States Army, Europe, and Seventh Army.

On November 1, 1987, he was promoted to major general. From August 1989 to November 1990, he was the commanding general of I Corps and Fort Lewis, Fort Lewis, Washington. He was promoted to lieutenant general on August 3, 1989. In November 1990 he was named deputy commander in chief, Central Command, Saudi Arabia (Desert Storm).

George Hilton Walls, Jr.

★ ———————————————————— ★

Brigadier General

Born November 30, 1942, in Parkesburg, Pennsylvania, he married the former Portia Diane Hall of Ahoskie, North Carolina. They have three sons: George III, Steven, and Kevin. He was graduated from West Chester State College in 1964 with a bachelor of science degree in education and was commissioned in 1965 upon completion of Officer Candidate School, Quantico, Virginia. He earned a master's in education from North Carolina Central University, Durham in 1975.

Following completion of the Basic School at Quantico and the Combat Engineer Officers Course, Camp Lejeune, North Carolina, he reported to the 3rd Engineer Battalion, 3rd Marine Division, Vietnam, in 1966. Assignments included platoon commander and assistant operations officer for the battalion.

He was promoted to first lieutenant in October 1966. Returning to the United States in 1967, he served as a platoon commander and company executive officer with the 2nd Engineer Battalion, 2nd Marine Division, Camp Lejeune, North Carolina. During this assignment, he was promoted to captain in July 1967. He was later reassigned to duty as senior instructor, Combat Engineer Instruction Unit, Marine Corps Engineer School.

He was transferred to Headquarters, 4th Marine Corps District, Philadelphia, Pennsylvania, where he served as an officer selection officer and assistant head, Personnel Procurement Branch. He next served aboard the USS *Franklin D. Roosevelt* (CVA-42) as commanding officer of a Marine detachment. In 1972 General Walls was assigned duty as Marine officer instructor, of the NROTC Unit at the North Carolina Central University. He also served for two years as the unit's executive officer.

He was promoted to major in August 1974 and while in this assignment completed his requirements for a master of art degree. From 1975 to 1976, he was a student at the Command and Staff College, Quantico. Upon completion of school, he reported to the Marine Corps Engineer School at Camp Lejeune where his assignments included, assistant school director, director of instruction, and commanding officer, Engineer Equipment Instruction Company. He was assigned as the Marine Corps representative at the United States Army Engineer School, Fort Belvoir, from 1980 to 1982, and was promoted to lieutenant colonel in August 1980.

General Walls graduated from the National War College in Washington, D.C., class of 1983. He was transferred overseas in July 1983, where he commanded Wing Engineer Squadron-17 until June 1984. Returning from overseas, he served as special assistant and Marine aide, Office of the Assistant Secretary of the Navy (Manpower and Reserve Affairs) from July 1984 until June 1987, and promoted to colonel in July 1986.

Reporting to Headquarters Marine Corps, Washington, D.C., he served from July 1987 until July 1989 as head, Engineer, Motor Transport, General Supply Branch, then as program manager for Engineer Systems, Marine Corps Research, Development, and Acquisition Command. General Walls was next assigned duty as the commanding officer and professor of naval science, NROTC, University of North Carolina. While serving in this capacity, he was selected for promotion to brigadier general on

Brig. Gen. George Hilton Walls, Jr.

March 13, 1991. He was assigned as commanding general, 2nd Force Service Support Group, FMF, Atlantic, Camp Lejeune, North Carolina, and commander, Joint Task Force, Guantanamo Bay, Cuba, since July 12, 1991.

His military awards and decorations include the Legion of Merit, Meritorious Service Medal, Navy Commendation Medal (with combat "V"), Navy Achievement Medal, Combat Action Ribbon. He is a past eastern regional vice president of the National Naval Officers Association and a member of the Legion of Honor, Chapel of the Four Chaplains.

John Marcella Watkins, Jr.

★ ——————————————————— ★

Brigadier General

Born July 2, 1942, in Evergreen, Alabama, he married the former Doris Bryant. They have two children, Monica and Daphne. He received a bachelor of science degree in industrial management from Tuskegee University in 1966, master's of business administration from the New York Institute of Technology in 1976. His military schooling included the Signal School, Basic (1966) and Advanced Course (1969); United States Army Command and General Staff College (1975); Defense Systems Management College (1979); and the Industrial College of the Armed Forces (1984).

General Watkins's major duty assignments include: December 1966 to September 1967, radio platoon leader, Company B, 50th Signal Battalion (Airborne), Fort Bragg, North Carolina; April 1968, commander, Company C, 523 Signal Battalion, United States Army, Vietnam.

He returned to the United States in November 1969 and in January 1970 he was a student in the Signal Officer Advanced Course, Fort Gordon, Georgia. From January 1970 to December 1970 he was a student in the Communications Systems Engineer Course, Fort Monmouth, New Jersey. In July 1973 he was assigned as radio officer, Headquarters, Eighth United States Army, Korea. He returned to the United States in June 1974 and in August 1974 he was selected to attend the United States Army Command and General Staff College, Fort Leavenworth, Kansas. From June 1975 to April 1978, he served as a personnel management officer at the United States Army Military Personnel Center, Alexandria, Virginia. In April 1978 he returned to Korea where he served as the executive officer of the 122nd Signal Battalion, 2nd Infantry Division, United States Army. In July 1979 he was selected to attend the Program Management Course at the Defense Systems Management College, Fort Belvoir, Virginia.

In December 1979 he was assigned as assistant corps communications-electronics officer, Headquarters Company, 3rd Signal Brigade, then in July 1980 assigned as commander, 16th Signal Battalion. From November 1982 to July 1983, General Watkins served as the deputy brigade commander, 3rd Signal Brigade, Fort Hood, Texas. In July 1983 he was selected to attend the Industrial College of the Armed Forces, Fort McNair, Washington, D.C. From June 1984 to February 1985 he was assigned as deputy director of communications, Armed Forces Inaugural Committee, Fort McNair, Washington, D.C.

Brig. Gen. John Marcella Watkins, Jr.

From February 1985 to July 1986, he served as chief, Plans Division, Office of the Assistant Chief of Staff for Information Management, United States Army, Washington, D.C. From July 1986 to November 1988, he served commander, 11th Signal Brigade, United States Army Information Systems Command, Fort Huachuca, Arizona. From November 1988 to November 1990, he was secretary of the Military Communications Electronics Board, J-6, Joint Staff, Washington, D.C.

In November, 1990 he returned to Fort Huachuca to serve as commanding general, program manager, Army Information Systems, United States Army Information Systems Engineering Command, Arizona.

He was appointed brigadier general on February 1, 1991. His military awards and decorations include the Legion of Merit, Bronze Star Medal, Defense Meritorious Service Medal, Meritorious Service Medal (four oak leaf clusters), Army Commendation Medal, Parachutist Badge, Army Staff Identification Badge.

Raymond Watkins

★ ——————————————— ★

Brigadier General

Appointed to the one star rank in the Illinois Army National Guard. The source of this fact was *Black Americans in Defense of Our Nation* (1985) published by the Department of Defense, Office of Deputy Assistant Secretary of Defense for Equal Opportunity and Safety Policy. No other information could be obtained.

James T. Whitehead, Jr.

★★ ——————————————— ★★

Major General

Born on December 10, 1934, in Jersey City, New Jersey, he married the former Saunder L. Beard. They have six children: Janet, Sara, Rebecca, Marie, Joel, and Kenneth. He graduated from Dwight Morrow High School, Englewood, New Jersey, in 1952. He then received a bachelor of science degree in education from the University of Illinois in 1957, and he attended Monmouth College, Long Branch, New Jersey, completing 18 graduate credits in counseling.

He completed the Squadron Officers Course in 1961, the Air Command and Staff Course in 1978, and the Air War College Course in 1981. General Whitehead has attended many senior seminars and management courses, including the Reserve Component National Security Course. He began his military career by enlisting in the New Jersey Army National Guard in May 1952. He served until May 1955 when he was placed in the Army Standby Reserve with the rank of private.

He received his commission as a second lieutenant upon his graduation from Air Force ROTC in June 1957. In November 1957 he entered pilot training at Malden Air Base, Missouri, later at Vance AFB in Oklahoma. He was awarded his wings in November 1958 and completed combat crew training in the KC-135 at Castle AFB, California, and Barksdale AFB, Louisiana.

Upon completion, he was assigned as a KC-135 combat crew copilot in the 913th Air Refueling Squadron, Barksdale AFB, Louisiana, from May 1959 to April 1962. During this period he served as squadron assistant air operations officer, squadron ground training officer, and copilot on the Wing Standardization Evaluation Crew. In April 1962 General Whitehead received a regular officer appointment in the USAF, was transferred to the 68th Air Refueling Squadron at Bunker Hill AFB, Indiana, and was upgraded to aircraft commander. His crew flew special air missions from England, Turkey, Vietnam, and Laos.

In 1965 General Whitehead was selected to be the first black U-2 pilot. After completing his upgrade to a combat-ready U-2 pilot, he flew many JCS and higher HQ-directed missions. He separated from the Air Force in April 1967 with the rank of captain. He then completed short tours of duty as a guard member with the Nebraska and New Jersey Air National Guard, flying RF84s and C121s from October 1967 to September 1969.

General Whitehead joined the 103rd Tactical Air Support Squadron, Willow Grove NAS, Willow Grove, Pennsylvania, in September 1969. He served as flight commander and during this time was promoted to major. In March 1977 he was appointed as squadron commander of the 103rd and promoted to lieutenant colonel in April 1977. During his years of command, the unit transitioned from the O-2 to the OA-37 aircraft. In June 1983 General Whitehead was assigned to Headquarters, PaANG, as director of operations. During this period he was responsible for establishing a highly successful and now annual joint Army and Air Guard training exercise named Keystone Vigilant. He served in that capacity until April 15, 1987, when he was assigned duty as deputy commander. As deputy commander, General Whitehead was responsible to advise the commander, PaANG, on all matters relating to PaANG. General Whitehead served as

Maj. Gen. James T. Whitehead, Jr.

deputy commander from April 15, 1987, until his selection as ANG assistant to the director, Air National Guard.

As ANG assistant to the director, Air National Guard, Washington, D.C., General Whitehead's duties are to advise the director on all force management issues relating to Air National Guard units, including minority policy matters. This input will have a major impact on force preparedness and meeting the defense challenges of tomorrow.

In civilian life, he is an Accident Prevention Program manager with the FAA. He also performs duties as an air carrier operations specialist. Previously he was a pilot and flight engineer with Trans World Airlines at John F. Kennedy Airport, New York, from 1967 until his retirement in July 1986. During that period, he accumulated over 15,000 hours on the Boeing 727, 707, and 747. In addition to training TWA personnel, General Whitehead instructed and checked crew members from Olympic, Sandia, and Alia airlines and USAF E-4 crew members.

After his retirement from TWA in 1986, he was hired as manager and was later promoted to senior director, Flight Operations, for Orion Air, a major contractor of pilots for UPS, Emery, and Purolator Cargo.

His military awards and decorations include the Legion of Merit, Meritorious Service Medal, Air Force Commendation Medal (with oak leaf cluster), Air Force Outstanding Unit Award (with seven oak leaf clusters), Air Force Organizational Excellence Award, Combat Readiness Medal (with two oak leaf clusters), National Defense Service Medal, Vietnam Service Medal, Air Force Longevity Service Award Ribbon (with seven oak leaf clusters), Armed Forces Reserve Medal (with hourglass device), Pennsylvania Meritorious Service Medal, Pennsylvania Twenty-Year and

General Thomas J. Steward Award. A command pilot with over 5,000 hours of military flying time, General Whitehead has had experience flying numerous aircraft in a wide variety of scenarios. He was appointed major general on May 15, 1991.

Harvey Dean Williams

★★ ——————————————— ★★

Major General

Born July 30, 1930, Whiteville, North Carolina. He received a bachelor's in political science from West Virginia State College, a master's in international relations from George Washington University, Washington, D.C.

His military schooling includes the Armed Forces Staff College, the Naval War College, and Artillery School.

During his military career, his service included chief of staff for intelligence, Washington, D.C.; from 1971 through 1972, student at the Naval War College; from 1972 through 1973, military adviser, Control and Disarmament Agency, Washington, D.C.; from 1973 through 1974, commanding officer, 75th Field Artillery Group, III Corps Artillery, Fort Sill, Oklahoma.

In 1975 he was appointed to a special review board, Office of the Deputy Chief of Staff for Personnel, Washington, D.C. Later in 1975 he was assigned as commander of the United States Army Garrison, Fort Myer,

Maj. Gen. Harvey Dean Williams

Virginia. In 1977 he was assigned as chief of staff, United States Military District of Washington, Fort Lesley J. McNair, Washington, D.C., then commanding general, United States Military District, until 1978.

In 1978 he was assigned as commanding general, VII Corps Artillery, United States Army, Europe.

General Williams's decorations and awards include the Legion of Merit, Bronze Star Medal (one oak leaf cluster), Meritorious Service Medal (one oak leaf cluster), Air Medal, Army Commendation Medal (three oak leaf clusters).

He was appointed brigadier general on September 1, 1977. He retired on October 31, 1982.

Louis Alvin Williams

★★ ——————————————————— ★★

Rear Admiral

Born August 26, 1931, in Ypsilanti, Mississippi. He married the former Faye Ursula and they had two children, Ivan and Kirk. He attended Mississippi State Normal College in Ypsilanti from 1950 to 1951. He attended San Francisco City College from 1951 to 1952. He received a B.S. in business administration from the Naval Postgraduate School in 1975.

He has held a wide variety of important command and staff positions. He was a naval flight instructor (1958–1961). From 1962 to 1964, he served as the combat information officer on the USS *Hancock*. From 1964 to 1967, he served as a naval aviator. He served as the commander of the Carrier Airborne Early Warning Squadron from 1968 to 1970. From 1977 to 1978, he was the deputy director of the Aviation Programs Division (OPNAV). From 1978 to 1980, he served as the commander of the United States Atlantic Fleet. He retired a rear admiral.

Johnnie Edward Wilson

★★ ——————————————————— ★★

Major General

Born on February 4, 1944, Baton Rouge, Louisiana. He received a bachelor of science degree in business administration from the University of Nebraska at Omaha, a master of science degree in logistics management from Florida Institute of Technology.

He received an OCS commission to second lieutenant on May 31, 1967. From May 1967 to September 1969, he served as mechanical maintenance officer, later commander, Company A, 782nd Maintenance Battalion, 82nd Airborne Division, Fort Bragg, North Carolina.

On May 31, 1968, he was promoted to first lieutenant, and on May 31, 1969, he was promoted to captain. From October 1969 to November 1970, he was assistant brigade supply officer, later commander, Company C, 173rd Support Battalion (Airborne), 173rd Airborne Brigade, United States Army, Vietnam.

From January 1971 to September 1971, he was a student in the Ordnance Officer Advanced Course, United States Army Ordnance School, Aberdeen Proving Ground, Maryland. From December 1971 to December 1973, he was a student at the University of Nebraska, Omaha. From January 1974 to June 1976, he was the commander of Company B, later technical supply officer, 123rd Maintenance Battalion, 1st Armored Division, United States Army, Europe.

He was promoted to major on June 9, 1976. From August 1976 to June 1977, he was a student at the United States Army Command and General Staff College, Fort Leavenworth, Kansas. From June 1977 to November 1977, he was a student at Florida Institute of Technology, Melbourne, Florida.

From November 1977 to November 1980, he served as professional development officer, later personnel management officer, then chief, Ordnance Assignment Branch, Combat Service Support Division, United States Army Military Personnel Center, Alexandria, Virginia. From December 1980 to May 1983, he was commander, 709th Maintenance Battalion, 9th Infantry Division, Fort Lewis, Washington.

He was promoted to lieutenant colonel on July 13, 1980. From May 1983 to June 1984, he was a student at the Industrial College of the Armed Forces, Fort NcNair, Washington, D.C. From August 1984 to December 1986, was commander, Division Support Command, 1st Armored Division, United States Army, Europe.

After being promoted to colonel on November 1, 1984, from December 1986 to July 1988, he was commander, 13th Support Command, Fort Hood, Texas.

From July 1988 to July 1990, he was assigned as deputy commanding general, 21st Theater Army Area Command, United States Army, Europe, and Seventh Army.

On September 1, 1989, he was promoted to brigadier general. In July 1990 he was appointed commanding general, United States Ordnance Center, Aberdeen Proving Ground, Maryland.

Maj. Gen. Johnnie Edward Wilson

He has received numerous awards and decorations, including the Distinguished Service Medal, Legion of Merit, Bronze Star Medal (with two oak leaf clusters), Meritorious Service Medal (with two oak leaf clusters), Army Commendation Medal, Good Conduct Medal, Master Parachutist Badge.

Matthew Augustus Zimmerman

★★ ——————————————— ★★

Major General

Born December 9, 1941, in South Carolina. He received a bachelor of science degree in biology and chemistry from Benedict College in 1962, an M.D.V. in pastoral counseling from Duke University in 1965, a master's in education from Long Island University in 1975.

He received a commission by direct appointment to the rank of first lieutenant on March 21, 1967. From April 1967 to August 1967, he was a student at the Chaplain Officer Basic Course, United States Army Chaplain School, Fort Hamilton, New York. On April 3, 1967, he was promoted to captain.

From August 1967 to January 1968, he served as chaplain, Headquarters Detachment, 3rd Advanced Individual Training Bridge, United States Army Training Center (Infantry), Fort Gordon, Georgia. From January 1968 to February 1969, he served as assistant chaplain, IV Corps

Maj. Gen. Matthew Augustus Zimmerman

Tactical Zone, Advisory Team 51, United States Military Assistance Command, Vietnam.

From February 1969 to September 1970, he was an assistant chaplain, Headquarters and Headquarters Company and Band, Support Command, 1st Armored Division, Fort Hood, Texas. From March 1971 to August 1973, he served as staff chaplain, 3rd Armored Division, United States Army, Europe and Seventh Army. From August 1974 to June 1975, he was a student at the Chaplain Officer Advanced Course, United States Army Chaplain Center and School, Fort Wadsworth, New Jersey.

On October 3, 1974, he was promoted to major. From June 1975 to June 1976, he was the operations training staff officer in the Office of Chief of Chaplains, Washington, D.C. From June 1976 to June 1978, he served as staff parish development officer, Office of the Chief of Chaplains, Washington, D.C.

From June 1978 to June 1979, he was a student at the United States Army Command and General Staff College, Fort Leavenworth, Kansas. From June 1979 to July 1980, he was the deputy corps chaplain (administrative), VII Corps, United States Army, Europe, and Seventh Army. He was promoted to lieutenant colonel on August 6, 1979.

From July 1980 to June 1982, he served as the division staff chaplain, 3rd Infantry Division, United States Army, Europe, and Seventh Army. From June 1982 to June 1983, he was a student at the United States Army War College, Carlisle Barracks, Pennsylvania. From June 1983 to June 1984, he was assistant command chaplain, United States Army Training and Doctrine Command, Fort Monroe, Virginia.

He was promoted to colonel on July 1, 1984. From December 1985 to

August 1989, he served as a command staff chaplain at Forces Command, Fort McPherson, Atlanta, Georgia. From August 1989 to August 1990, he was deputy chief of chaplains, Office of the Chief of Chaplains, United States Army, Washington, D.C.

He was promoted to brigadier general, on October 1, 1989; on August 1, 1990, to major general. In August 1990, he was assigned as chief of chaplains, Office of the Chief of Chaplains, United States Army, Washington, D.C. His awards include the Legion of Merit, Bronze Star Medal, Meritorious Service Medal (with two oak leaf clusters).

Appendix

ARMY GENERALS

Four Stars (General)

Colin L. Powell
Roscoe Robinson, Jr.

Three Stars (Lieutenant General)

Julius W. Becton
Marvin D. Brailsford
Andrew P. Chambers, Jr.
Henry Doctor, Jr.
Samuel E. Ebbesen
Arthur J. Gregg

James R. Hall, Jr.
Edward Honor
James F. McCall
Emmett Paige, Jr.
Alonzo P. Short, Jr.
Calvin A. H. Waller

Two Stars (Major General)

Robert B. Adams
Wallace C. Arnold
Harry W. Brooks
John M. Brown
Charles D. Bussey
Eugene P. Cromartie
Jerry R. Curry
Frederic E. Davison
Oliver W. Dillard
Robert C. Gaskill
Fred A. Gorden
Robert F. Gray
Edward Greer
James F. Hamlet
Ernest J. Harrell
Charles A. Hines

Arthur Holmes, Jr.
Charles E. Honore
James R. Klugh
Frank L. Miller, Jr.
Julius Parker, Jr.
Hugh G. Robinson
Charles C. Rogers
Jackson E. Rozier
Fred G. Sheffey, Jr.
Issac D. Smith
John H. Stanford
Charles E. Williams
Harvey D. Williams
Johnnie E. Wilson
Matthew A. Zimmerman

One Star (Brigadier General)

Clara L. Adams-Ender
Joe N. Ballard
Dallas C. Brown, Jr.
Melvin L. Byrd
Alfred J. Cade
Sherian G. Cadoria
Roscoe C. Cartwright
John S. Cowings
Benjamin O. Davis, Sr.
Donald J. Delandro
Larry R. Ellis
Johnnie Forte, Jr.
Kenneth D. Gray
Robert A. Harleston
Hazel W. Johnson

Julius F. Johnson
Walter F. Johnson III
Larry R. Jordan
Fredric H. Leigh
Alphonso E. Lenhardt
James W. Monroe
Jude W. Patin
Thomas L. Prather
George B. Price
Donald L. Scott
George M. Shuffer, Jr.
Billy King Solomon
Robert L. Stephens, Jr.
Guthrie L. Turner, Jr.
John M. Watkins, Jr.

AIR FORCE GENERALS

Four Stars (General)

Daniel "Chappie" James
Bernard P. Randolph

Three Stars (Lieutenant General)

William E. Brown, Jr.
Benjamin O. Davis, Jr.

Winston D. Powers

Two Stars (Major General)

Rufus L. Billups
Thomas E. Clifford
Archer L. Durham
Albert Edmonds

Titus C. Hall
Lucius Theus
John H. Voorhees

One Star (Brigadier General)

James T. Boddie, Jr.
Elmer Brooks
Alonzo L. Ferguson
David M. Hall
Avon C. James
Charles B. Jiggets

Marcelite Jordan Harris
Lester L. Lyles
Raymond V. McMillan
Norris W. Overton
John F. Phillips
Horace L. Russell

NAVY ADMIRALS

Three Stars (Vice Admiral)

Samuel L. Gravely, Jr.

Two Stars (Rear Admiral)

Lawrence C. Chamber
Walter Jackson Davis, Jr.
Mack Charles Gaston
Benjamin T. Hacker

Wendell Johnson
William E. Powell
Gerald E. Thomas
Robert Lee Toney

MARINE CORPS GENERALS

Three Stars (Lieutenant General)

Frank E. Petersen, Jr.

Two Stars (Major General)

Jerome Gary Cooper

One Star (Brigadier General)

George H. Walls, Jr.

GENERALS OF THE ARMY AND AIR RESERVES AND NATIONAL GUARDS

Three Stars (Lieutenant General)

John Q. T. King

Two Stars (Major General)

Richard C. Alexander
Roger R. Blunt
Alvin Bryant
Cunningham Bryant
Allen E. Chandler

Russell C. Davis
Louis Duckett
Calvin G. Franklin
Joseph E. Turner

One Star (Brigadier General)

William C. Banton
Leroy C. Bell
Carl E. Brisco
George M. Brooks
Albert Bryant
Alonzo Dougherty
William S. Frye
Edward O. Gourdin
Johnny J. Hobbs
Chauncey Hooper

Benjamin Hunton
Talmadge Jacobs
Nathaniel James
Richard L. Jones
Kenneth U. Jordan
Marion Mann
Ernest R. Morgan
Guthrie L. Turner, Jr.
Raymond Watkins
James T. Whitehead, Jr.

THE FIRST BLACK GENERALS

The highest-ranking black officer served during the Civil War Reconstruction. However, ten men were appointed to general officer rank in various militia units:

1. Maj. Gen. Robert B. Elliott, Commanding General, National Guard, South Carolina (1870)
2. Maj. Gen. Prince R. Rivers, Commanding General, Third Division, National Guard, South Carolina (1873)
3. Maj. Gen. Robert Small, National Guard, South Carolina (1873)
4. Major General First Division, National Guard, South Carolina (1873)
5. Brig. Gen. Samuel J. Lee, Chief of Staff, National Guard, South Carolina (1872)
6. Brev. Brig. Gen. William Beverly Nash, National Guard, South Carolina (1873)
7. Brig. Gen. H. W. Purvis, Adjutant and Inspector General, National Guard, South Carolina (1873)
8. Brig. Gen. Joseph Hayne Rainey, Judge Advocate General, National Guard, South Carolina (1873)
9. Brig. Gen. William J. Whipper, Second Brigade, Second Brigade, Second Division, National Guard, South Carolina (1873)
10. Brig. Gen. T. Morris Chester, Fourth Brigade, National Guard, Louisiana (1873–1874)

SIGNIFICANT "FIRSTS"
IN THE MILITARY

Hon. Clifford Alexander, Jr.: first black Secretary of the Army.

Lt. Gen. Frank E. Petersen, Jr.: first black to attain the rank of general in the United States Marine Corps.

Maj. Gen. Jerome Gary Cooper, United States Marine Corps: first black officer to lead marines into battle in Vietnam.

Capt. Roscoe Brown: first American pilot to shoot down a German jet.

Merle J. Smith: first black to graduate from the Coast Guard Academy, 1962.

Maj. Gen. Cunningham C. Bryant: in 1968 became the first black National Guard general federally recognized in the history of the United States Army.

Cad. Edward A. Rice, of New Mexico: first black to be designated wing commander at the United States Air Force Academy.

Janie L. Mines, of Aiken, South Carolina: first black female to enter and graduate from the Naval Academy, 1980.

Capt. Bobby C. Wilks, USCG (Ret.): first black to attain the rank of captain in the Coast Guard, first black aviator, and first black to command a major unit, Coast Guard Air Station, Brooklyn, New York.

C.P.O. Alexander P. Haley: first chief journalist in the Coast Guard.

C.P.O. Pamela D. Autry: first black female chief petty officer in the Coast Guard.

C.W.O. Lavonia Bass: first black female warrant officer in the United States Coast Guard.

Clarence Samuels: first black chief photographer in the Coast Guard and first black to command a cutter during war.

Maj. Gen. Robert E. Gray: in August 1991, first black to assume command of the United States Army Signal Center and Fort Gordon; simultaneously "chief of signal."

Gen. Colin L. Powell: first black National Security Adviser, first black commander of FORSCOM, first black Chairman of the Joint Chiefs of Staff.

BIRTH STATES

Alabama

Roger Reckling Blunt
Russell C. Davis
Oliver W. Dillard
Fred Augustus Gorden
James R. Hall
Ernest James Harrell
Arthur Holmes, Jr.
Roscoe Robinson, Jr.
Preston M. Taylor, Jr.
John Marcella Watkins

Arkansas

Calvin G. Franklin

California

Archer L. Durham

District of Columbia

Wallace Cornelius Arnold
Julius W. Becton, Jr.
Harry William Brooks, Jr.
Thomas E. Clifford
Benjamin O. Davis, Jr.
Benjamin O. Davis, Sr.
Frederic Ellis Davison
Alonzo L. Ferguson
Benjamin Thurman Hacker
Charles Alfonso Hines
Lester L. Lyles

Thomas Levi Prather, Jr.
Joseph Paul Reason
Hugh G. Robinson

Florida

Leroy C. Bell
Alvin Bryant
Harold Eugene Burch
Eugene Rufus Cromartie
Edward O. Gourdin
Daniel James, Jr.
Emmett Paige, Jr.

Georgia

Albert J. Edmonds
Mack Charles Gaston
Richard L. Jones
Marion Mann

Indiana

Harry William Brooks, Jr.
David M. Hall
William E. Powell

Illinois

Louis Duckett

Kansas

Alonzo D. Dougherty, Jr.
Julius Frank Johnson
Larry Reginald Jordan
Frank Lee Miller, Jr.
Frank E. Petersen

Louisiana

William C. Banton, II
Dallas C. Brown, Jr.
Sherian Grace Cadoria
Jerome Gray Cooper
Donald J. Delandro
Edward Honor
Charles E. Honore
Jude Wilmot Paul Patin
Bernard P. Randolph
Isaac D. Smith
Robert L. Toney
Calvin A. H. Waller
Johnnie Edward Wilson

Maryland

Marvin Delano Brailsford
Allen E. Chandler
Benjamin L. Hunton

Massachusetts

Wendell Norman Johnson
Gerald E. Thomas

Mississippi

John M. Brown
Albert Bryant
George Baker Price

Missouri

Roscoe Conklin Cartwright
Donald Laverne Scott

New Jersey

Elmer T. Brooks
William S. Frye
Johnny J. Hobbs
Chauncey M. Hooper
John H. Voorhees
James T. Whitehead, Jr.

New York

Robert B. Adams
William E. Brown, Jr.
John Sherman Cowings
Robert Clarence Gaskill
Robert Harleston
Alfonso Emanual Lenhardt
Colin L. Powell
Winston D. Powers
Horace L. Russell

North Carolina

Clara L. Adams-Ender
Alfred Jackal Cade
Walter Jackson Davis
Arthur Truman Dean
Talmadge J. Jacobs
Charles B. Jiggetts
Raymond V. McMillan
James W. Monroe
Alonzo Earl Short, Jr.
Harvey Dean Williams

Ohio

Richard C. Alexander
James Frank Hamlet
Fredric Homer Leigh

Pennsylvania

Rufus L. Billups
Jerry Ralph Curry
Hazel W. Johnson-Brown
James Franklin McCall
Fred C. Sheffey

John Henry Stanford
George H. Walls, Jr.

Rhode Island

James T. Boddie, Jr.

South Carolina

Charles D. Bussey
Henry Doctor, Jr.
Arthur James Gregg
Nathaniel James
James R. Klugh
Matthew A. Zimmerman

Tennessee

Kenneth U. Jordan
John Q. Taylor King, Sr.
Norris W. Overton
Lucius Theus

Texas

Carl E. Briscoe
Johnnie Forte, Jr.

Titus C. Hall
Marcelite J. Harris
Emmett Parker, Jr.
John F. Phillips
George Macon Shuffer, Jr.

Virginia

Joe Nathan Ballard
Cunningham C. Bryant
Melvin Leon Byrd
Andrew P. Chambers
Lawrence C. Chambers
Samuel L. Gravely, Jr.
Avon C. James
Ernest R. Morgan

Virgin Islands

Samuel Emanuel Ebbesen

West Virginia

Kenneth D. Gray
Robert Earl Gray
Edward Greer
Charles C. Rogers
Robert Louis Stephens, Jr.
Joseph Ellis Turner

COLLEGES AND UNIVERSITIES ATTENDED

Alfred University
Robert L. Stephens

American University
Benjamin L. Hunton
Wendell N. Johnson

Arizona, University of
Ernest J. Harrell
Jude Wilmot Paul Patin

Arizona State University
Jude Wilmot Paul Patin

Atlanta University
Charles E. Williams

Auburn University
Samuel E. Ebbesen
Johnnie Forte, Jr.

Babson College
Melvin Leon Byrd

Benedict College
Matthew A. Zimmerman

Bradley University
Horace L. Russell

California State University
Robert L. Toney

Canisus College
Robert B. Adams

Central Michigan University
Albert Bryant
Arthur T. Dean
Alfonso E. Lenhardt
John H. Stanford
Preston M. Taylor, Jr.

Central State University
Fredric Homer Leigh
Fred C. Sheffey

Chicago, University of
Donald J. Delando

Cincinnati, University of
Richard L. Jones
James W. Monroe

Colorado, University of
Rufus L. Billups

Columbia College
Alonzo D. Dougherty, Jr.

Columbia University
Hazel W. Johnson-Brown

Dayton, University of
Eugene Rufus Cromartie

Fisk University
John Q. Taylor King

Florida A&M University
Leroy C. Bell
Alvin Bryant
Eugene Rufus Cromartie

Florida Institute of Technology
Billy King Solomon
Johnnie Edward Wilson

Franklin University
Richard A. Harleston

Georgetown University
Robert A. Harleston

George Washington University
Robert B. Adams
Wallace C. Arnold
Elmer T. Brooks
Fredric E. Davison
Oliver Williams Dillard
Archer L. Durham
Robert C. Gaskill
Edward Greer
Benjamin Thurman Hacker
Charles E. Honore
Colin E. Powell
Winston D. Powell
Fred C. Sheffey
Lucius Theus
Harvey D. Williams

Georgia State University
Henry Doctor, Jr.

Golden Gate University
John S. Cowings

Hampton Institute
Wallace Cornelius Arnold
Albert J. Edmonds
Arthur Holmes, Jr.

Harvard University
Edward O. Gourdin

Houston, University of
John M. Brown

Howard University
William C. Banton
James T. Boddie, Jr.
Alvin Bryant
Cunningham C. Bryant
Melvin Leon Byrd
Andrew P. Chambers
Thomas E. Clifford
Benjamin O. Davis, Sr.
Frederic Ellis Davison
Alonzo L. Ferguson
Robert C. Gaskill
Robert A. Harleston
Charles A. Hines
Benjamin L. Hunton
Charles B. Jiggetts
Lester L. Lyles
Marion Mann

Huston-Tillotson College
John Q. Taylor King

Illinois, University of
James T. Whitehead, Jr.

Indiana State University
Larry R. Jordan

252   *Appendix*

Indiana University
Dallas Coverdale Brown, Jr.
Charles D. Bussey
Larry Rudell Ellis
Norris W. Overton

Iowa State University
Marvin D. Brailsford

Jarvis Christian College
John F. Phillips

Johns Hopkins University
Charles Alfonso Hines

Kent State University
Arthur Holmes, Jr.

Lincoln University
Julius F. Johnson
Donald L. Scott

Long Island University
Matthew August Zimmerman

Loyola University
Johnny J. Hobbs

Maryland, University of
Julius W. Becton
Marcelite J. Harris
Ernest R. Morgan
Emmett Paige, Jr.

Marymount College of Virginia
Mack Charles Gaston

Massachusetts Institute of Technology
Roger Reckling Blunt
Hugh G. Robinson

McKendree College
Winston D. Powers

Miami (Ohio) University
Elmer T. Brooks

Michigan State University
Robert A. Harleston
Charles A. Hines

Middleburg College
Fred Augustus Gordon

Military Academy, United States
Roger Reckling Blunt
John M. Brown
Benjamin O. Davis, Jr.
Fred A. Gorden
Larry R. Jordan
Hugh Granville Robinson
Roscoe Robinson, Jr.

Minnesota, University of
Clara Leach Adams-Ender

Missouri, University of
Joe Ballard
Roscoe C. Cartwright

Morgan State University
Allen E. Chandler
Arthur T. Dean
Larry R. Ellis
Talmadge J. Jacobs
Avon C. James

Morehouse College
James R. Hall, Jr.

Morris Brown College
Albert J. Edmonds

National University in San Diego
Calvin G. Franklin

Naval Academy, United States
Lawrence C. Chambers
Frank E. Petersen
William E. Powell, Jr.
Joseph P. Reason

Nebraska, University of
Jerry Ralph Curry
Russell C. Davis
Alfonso E. Lenhardt
Johnnie E. Wilson

New Mexico State University
Lester L. Lyles

New York, City College of
Samuel Emanuel Ebbesen
Colin L. Powell

New York Institute of Technology
Alonzo Earl Short, Jr.
John M. Watkins, Jr.

New York University
John J. Cowings
Nathaniel James

North Carolina A&T State University
Clara Leach Adams-Ender
Charles D. Bussey
David M. Hall

North Carolina Central University
George H. Walls, Jr.

Notre Dame, University of
Jerome Gary Cooper

Ohio State University
Walter J. Davis
Robert Earl Gray
Fred Sheffey, Jr.

Oklahoma, University of
Sherian Grace Cadoria

Omaha, University of
Harry W. Brook, Jr.
Oliver Williams Dillard

Pennsylvania, University of
James Franklin McCall
John Henry Stanford

Pennsylvania State University
William E. Brown, Jr.
Emmett Paige, Jr.
John H. Stanford

Pepperdine University
Preston M. Taylor, Jr.

Philadelphia College
Talmadge J. Jacobs

Pittsburgh, University of
Roscoe Robinson, Jr.

Prairie View A&M
Julius W. Becton
Marvin D. Brailsford
Johnnie Forte, Jr.
Julius Parker, Jr.
Billy King Solomon
Calvin A. H. Waller
Harvey D. Williams

Purdue University
Alvin Bryant
Horace Russell

Rutgers University
William S. Frye
Johnny J. Hobbs
John H. Voorhees

St. Benedict's College
Arthur James Gregg
James F. Hamlet

San Francisco State College
Roscoe C. Cartwright

Shippensburg State College
Leroy C. Bell
Andrew P. Chambers
Robert C. Gaskill
James R. Hall
James R. Klugh
Julius Parker, Jr.
Charles C. Rogers
Isaac D. Smith
Calvin A. H. Waller

South Carolina State College
Henry Doctor, Jr.
George Baker Price

South Carolina State University
James R. Klugh

Southern University A&M
Joe N. Ballard
Sherian Grace Cadoria
Edward Honor
Isaac Smith

Southern University
Donald J. Delando

Southern California, University of
Titus C. Hall

Spelman College
Marcelite J. Harris

Syracuse University
Alfred Jackal Cade
Fredric Homer Leigh
James Franklin McCall

Tennessee, University of
Kenneth U. Jordan

Troy State
Frank Lee Miller
Donald L. Scott

Tuskegee Institute
Rufus L. Billups
Harold E. Burch
Benjamin O. Davis, Jr.
Russell C. Davis
Mack Charles Gaston
Titus C. Hall
Ernest J. Harrell
Marion Mann
John M. Watkins, Jr.
Charles E. Williams

Union University in Richmond
Samuel Lee Gravely, Jr.

Utah, University of
Joseph E. Turner

Utah State University
Archer L. Durham

Vanderbilt University
Kenneth U. Jordan

Villanova University
Hazel W. Johnson-Brown

Virginia State College
Alfred Jackal Cade
Ernest R. Morgan
Alonzo Earl Short, Jr.

Virginia State University
Leo Austin Brooks

Washington, University of
Frank Lee Miller

West Chester State College
George H. Walls, Jr.

West Virginia State College
Dallas C. Brown, Jr.

Kenneth D. Gray
Edward Greer
James W. Monroe
Charles C. Rogers
Robert Louis Stephens
Joseph E. Turner
Harvey D. Williams

Wichita State University
Alfonso E. Lenhardt

Wittenberg University
Benjamin Thurman Hacker

Wyoming
Raymond V. McMillan

INDEX